# Bookkeeping
## FOR
# DUMMIES®
### 3RD EDITION

# Bookkeeping

## FOR

# DUMMIES®

### 3RD EDITION

**by Jane Kelly, ACMA, Paul Barrow, MBA
and Lita Epstein, MBA**

**WILEY**

A John Wiley and Sons, Ltd, Publication

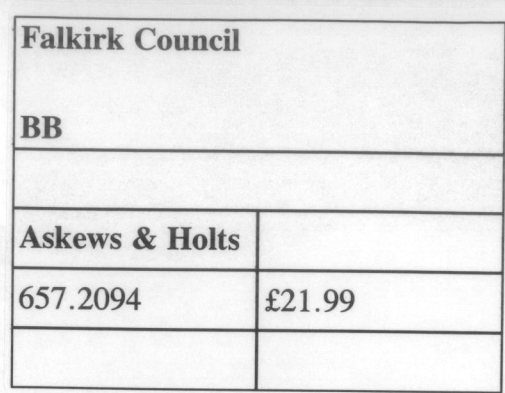
**Bookkeeping For Dummies®, 3rd Edition**

Published by: **John Wiley & Sons, Inc.,**
The Atrium,
Southern Gate,
Chichester, West Sussex, PO19 8SQ
www.wiley.com

This edition first published 2012

© 2012 John Wiley & Sons, Ltd, Chichester, West Sussex.

Registered office

John Wiley & Sons Ltd, The Atrium, Southern Gate, Chichester, West Sussex, PO19 8SQ, United Kingdom

For details of our global editorial offices, for customer services and for information about how to apply for permission to reuse the copyright material in this book please see our website at www.wiley.com.

Wiley publishes in a variety of print and electronic formats and by print-on-demand. Some material included with standard print versions of this book may not be included in e-books or in print-on-demand. If this book refers to media such as a CD or DVD that is not included in the version you purchased, you may download this material at http://booksupport.wiley.com. For more information about Wiley products, visit www.wiley.com. Screenshots from Sage UK remain copyright © Sage UK Ltd and are used with kind permission.

Designations used by companies to distinguish their products are often claimed as trademarks. All brand names and product names used in this book are trade names, service marks, trademarks or registered trademarks of their respective owners. The publisher is not associated with any product or vendor mentioned in this book.

LIMIT OF LIABILITY/DISCLAIMER OF WARRANTY: WHILE THE PUBLISHER AND AUTHOR HAVE USED THEIR BEST EFFORTS IN PREPARING THIS BOOK, THEY MAKE NO REPRESENTATIONS OR WAR-RANTIES WITH THE RESPECT TO THE ACCURACY OR COMPLETENESS OF THE CONTENTS OF THIS BOOK AND SPECIFICALLY DISCLAIM ANY IMPLIED WARRANTIES OF MERCHANTABILITY OR FIT-NESS FOR A PARTICULAR PURPOSE. IT IS SOLD ON THE UNDERSTANDING THAT THE PUBLISHER IS NOT ENGAGED IN RENDERING PROFESSIONAL SERVICES AND NEITHER THE PUBLISHER NOR THE AUTHOR SHALL BE LIABLE FOR DAMAGES ARISING HEREFROM. IF PROFESSIONAL ADVICE OR OTHER EXPERT ASSISTANCE IS REQUIRED, THE SERVICES OF A COMPETENT PROFESSIONAL SHOULD BE SOUGHT.

For general information on our other products and services, please contact our Customer Care Department within the U.S. at 877-762-2974, outside the U.S. at (001) 317-572-3993, or fax 317-572-4002. For technical support, please visit www.wiley.com/techsupport.

A catalogue record for this book is available from the British Library.

ISBN 978-1-118-34689-1 (pbk), ISBN 978-1-118-34683-9 (ebk), ISBN 978-1-118-34687-7 (ebk), ISBN 978-1-118-34688-4 (ebk)

Printed in Great Britain by TJ International Ltd, Padstow, Cornwall

10  9  8  7  6  5  4  3  2  1

# Contents at a Glance

# Table of Contents

# Introduction

● ● ● ● ● ● ● ● ● ● ● ● ● ● ● ● ● ● ● ● ● ● ● ● ● ● ● ● ● ● ● ● ● ● ● ● ● ● ● ● ● ● ● ● ● ● ●

*B*ookkeepers manage all the financial data for small businesses. If you subscribe to the idea that information is power (and we do), you can see that the bookkeeper has a tremendous amount of power within a business. Information recorded in the books helps business owners make key decisions involving sales planning and product offerings, as well as manage many other financial aspects of their businesses.

Without the hard work of bookkeepers, businesses wouldn't have a clue about what's happening with their financial transactions. Without accurate financial bookkeeping, a business owner can't know how many sales are being made, how much cash is being collected or how much cash was paid for the products sold to customers during the year. The owner also can't know how much cash was paid to employees or spent on other business needs throughout the year.

Accurate and complete financial bookkeeping is crucial to any business owner, and also important to those who work with the business, such as investors, financial institutions and employees. People inside (managers, owners and employees) and outside the business (investors, lenders and HM Revenue & Customs) depend on the bookkeeper's accurate recording of financial transactions.

Yes, the bookkeeper's job is crucial and requires certain skills and talents. Bookkeepers must be detail-oriented, enjoy working with numbers and be meticulous about accurately entering those numbers in the books. They must be vigilant about keeping a paper trail and filing all needed backup information about the financial transactions entered into the books.

Whether you're a business owner keeping the books yourself or an employee keeping the books for a small-business owner, your job is critical to the smooth financial operation of the business.

## About This Book

In this book, we introduce you to the key aspects of bookkeeping and how to set up and use your financial books. We walk you through the basics of bookkeeping, starting with the process of setting up your business's books and developing:

- A list of your business's accounts, called the Chart of Accounts.

- Your business's Nominal Ledger, which summarises all the activity in a business's accounts.

- We also discuss your Sales and Purchase ledgers, as well as the Cash Book where all your financial transactions are posted.

Then we take you through the process of recording those transactions – sales, purchases and other financial activity. We also talk about how to manage payroll, HM Revenue & Customs reporting and external financial reporting.

Finally, we discuss the procedures at year end and what bookkeeping tasks need to be done to prepare your year end accounts. Bookkeeping is a continuous cycle, starting with financial transactions, recording those transactions in ledgers, posting those transactions to the Nominal Ledger, testing your books to be sure that they're in balance, making any necessary adjustments or corrections to the books to keep them in balance, preparing financial reports to understand how well the business did during the year, and finally getting ready to start the process all over again for the next year.

# Conventions Used in This Book

We use the Sage 50 Accounts computerised accounting system throughout this book and show you some of its advanced features where appropriate. As in every *For Dummies* book, *italics* indicate a defined term or a point of emphasis, and **bold face** text shows off the key phrase in a bulleted or numbered list.

# Foolish Assumptions

While writing this book, we made some key assumptions about who you are and why you've picked up this book to get a better understanding of bookkeeping. We assume that you're one of the following:

- A business owner who wants to know how to do your own books. You have a good understanding of business and its terminology but have little or no knowledge of bookkeeping and accounting.

- A person who does, or plans to do, bookkeeping for a small business and needs to know more about how to set up and keep the books. You have some basic knowledge of business terminology but don't know much about bookkeeping or accounting.

✔ A staff person in a small business who's been asked to take over the bookkeeping duties. You need to know more about how transactions are entered into the books, how to check transactions to be sure that you're making entries correctly and accurately and how to prepare financial reports using the data you collect.

# What You're Not to Read

Throughout *Bookkeeping For Dummies*, we include a number of examples on how to apply the basics of bookkeeping to real-life situations. If you're primarily reading this book to gain a general knowledge of the subject and don't need to delve into all the nitty-gritty day-to-day aspects of bookkeeping, you may want to skip over the paragraphs marked with the Example icon (see the section 'Icons Used in This Book' later in this Introduction). Skipping the examples doesn't interfere with your grasp of the key aspects of how to keep the books.

# How This Book Is Organised

*Bookkeeping For Dummies* is divided into six parts, which we outline in the following sections. We also include a handy glossary at the end of the book where you can look up any of those terms you're not familiar with or have forgotten.

## Part 1: Basic Bookkeeping: Why You Need It

In Part I, we discuss the importance of bookkeeping, explain how it works and help you get started with setting up your business's books. We also touch on the terms that are unique to bookkeeping and tell you how to set up the roadmap for your books, the Chart of Accounts. We discuss the different ledgers that form the accounting system and show you how the transactions that you enter affect the nominal ledger. We also look at the different types of business structures that you can set up.

# Part II: Recording Day-to-Day Business Operations

In Part II, we talk about the importance of checklists and routines to help you complete your bookkeeping tasks. We give tips for developing a good internal control system for managing your books and your business's cash, and we also include a chapter that's all about planning your workload. You can find lots of useful hints and tips for running a well-organised bookkeeping system. We then look at entering your sales and purchases and discuss banking transactions.

In addition, we talk about the basics of setting up and managing employee payroll, as well as all the HM Revenue & Customs paperwork you need to complete as soon as you decide to hire employees.

# Part III: Preparing the Books for Year- (or Month-) End

In Part III, we introduce you to the process of preparing your books for closing the accounting period, whether you're closing the books at the end of a month or the end of a year. The closing down process involves making key adjustments such as recording depreciation, and posting accruals and prepayments. This part also covers various aspects of checking the accuracy of your books, including checking your Trial Balance, reviewing specific accounts and making any necessary adjustments or corrections. We also discuss preparing your VAT return which often forms part of a quarterly accounting process.

# Part IV: Reporting Results and Starting Over

In Part IV, we explain how to use the information in your books to prepare reports that show how well your business – or your not-for-profit organisation – did during the month, quarter or year. We also lay out all the paperwork you have to deal with, including year-end HM Revenue & Customs forms. Finally, you find out how to close the books at year-end and get ready for the next year.

## Part V: Payroll Preparation

In Part V, we talk about your payroll obligations on both a monthly basis and also at year end. We explain all the forms that you need to process throughout the year.

## Part VI: The Part of Tens

The Part of Tens is the hallmark of the *For Dummies* series. In this part, we highlight the top ten accounts that you need to know how to manage and ten ways that you can use your books to manage your business's cash efficiently. The cherry on the cake is the glossary in the Appendix to debunk all that bookkeeping jargon.

# Icons Used in This Book

*For Dummies* books use little pictures, called *icons*, to flag certain chunks of text. The icons in *Bookkeeping For Dummies* are:

Look to this icon for ideas on how to improve your bookkeeping processes and manage your business accounts.

This icon marks anything we really, really want you to recall about bookkeeping after you've finished reading this book.

This icon points out any aspect of bookkeeping that comes with pitfalls or hidden dangers. We also use this icon to mark anything that can get you into trouble with HM Revenue & Customs, your bank, your suppliers, your employees or your investors.

The Example icon gives real-life specifics on how to do a particular bookkeeping function.

This icon highlights paragraphs that are a bit more technical than the rest of the book. This information can be handy, but you can skip over it without missing anything essential.

# *Where to Go from Here*

You're now ready to enter the world of bookkeeping! Because of the way *Bookkeeping For Dummies* is set up, you can start anywhere you like.

If you need the basics or you're a little rusty and want to refresh your knowledge of bookkeeping, start with Part I. However, if you already know bookkeeping basics, are familiar with the key terminology and know how to set up a Chart of Accounts, consider diving in at Part II.

If you've set up your books already and feel comfortable with the basics of bookkeeping, you may want to start with Part III and how to enter various transactions. On the other hand, if your priority is using the financial information you've already collected, check out the financial reporting options in Part V. Have fun!

# Part I
# Basic Bookkeeping: Why You Need It

'So for all you eager investors, our latest financial report will be read to you by our new accountant, Mr Mesmero.'

# In this part . . .

**N**ot sure why bookkeeping is important? In this part, we explain the basics of how bookkeeping works and help you get started with the task of setting up your books.

This part also exposes you to terms that have a unique meaning in the world of bookkeeping, such as ledger, journal, posting, debit and credit. Finally, we start you on your bookkeeping journey by showing you how to set up the roadmap for your books, the Chart of Accounts.

# Chapter 1

# So You Want to Do the Books

## In This Chapter

▶ Introducing bookkeeping and its basic purpose

▶ Maintaining a paper trail

▶ Managing daily business finances

▶ Making sure that everything's accurate

For many small business owners, while they love working in their chosen field using the skills they know and love, they don't always like to perform 'bookkeeping' duties. Most company owners prefer to employ the skills of a qualified bookkeeper. Some may, perhaps, prefer to give their bag-full of receipts to their accountant and simply hope that a useful set of accounts comes out of the end of the accounting sausage machine!

In this chapter we help to demystify the role of a bookkeeper. It may be that you're just starting off in business and, as a result, can't afford the services of a bookkeeper just yet! Think of this chapter as a checklist of jobs that need to be done.

Throughout the book, we introduce Have a Go sections, which are practical exercises aimed at helping you understand the bookkeeping principles we discuss. Feel free to draw all over these sections of the book; we want it to be as useful for you as possible.

## Delving into Bookkeeping Basics

Like most businesspeople, you probably have great ideas for running your own business and just want to get started. You don't want to be distracted by the small stuff, like keeping detailed records of every penny you spend; you just want to build a business with which you can make lots of money.

Well slow down there – you're not in a race! If you don't carefully plan your bookkeeping system and figure out exactly how and what financial details you want to track, you've absolutely no way to measure the success (or failure, unfortunately) of your business efforts.

Bookkeeping, when done properly, gives you an excellent measure of how well you're doing and also provides lots of information throughout the year. This information allows you to test the financial success of your business strategies and make any necessary course corrections early in the year to ensure that you reach your year-end profit goals.

## *Looking at basic accounting methods*

You can't keep books unless you know how to go about doing so. The two basic accounting methods are *cash-based accounting* and *accrual accounting*. The key difference between the two methods is the point at which you record sales and purchases in your books. If you choose cash-based accounting, you only record transactions when cash changes hands. If you use accrual accounting, you record a transaction on its completion, even if cash doesn't change hands.

For example, suppose that your business buys products to sell from a supplier but doesn't actually pay for those products for 30 days. If you're using cash-based accounting, you don't record the purchase until you actually lay out the cash to the supplier. If you're using accrual accounting, you record the purchase when you receive the products, and you also record the future debt in an account called Trade Creditors.

HM Revenue & Customs, who have an interest in every business in the UK, accept only the accrual accounting method. So, in reality you can't use cash-based accounting. However, a special concession for smaller businesses allows them to use a form of cash-based accounting for VAT purposes (which is covered in Chapter 12). In essence, you can complete your VAT return on a cash-based accounting method, which HM Revenue & Customs refer to as cash accounting.

We talk about the pros and cons of each type of accounting method in Chapter 2.

# Understanding assets, capital and liabilities

Every business has three key financial parts that must be kept in balance: assets, capital and liabilities. Of course, for some of you these may be alien concepts, so maybe a quick accounting primer is in order.

We use buying a house with a mortgage as an example. The house you're buying is an asset, that is, something of value that you own. In the first year of the mortgage, you don't own all of it but by the end of the mortgage period (typically 25 years), you will. The mortgage is a liability, or a debt that you owe. As the years roll on and you reduce the mortgage (liability), your capital or ownership of the asset increases. That's it in a nutshell.

- ✔ **Assets** include everything the business owns, such as cash, stock, buildings, equipment and vehicles.

- ✔ **Capital** includes the claims that owners have on the assets based on their portion of ownership in the business.

- ✔ **Liabilities** include everything the business owes to others, such as supplier bills, credit card balances and bank loans.

The formula for keeping your books in balance involves these three elements:

Assets = Capital + Liabilities

Because this equation is so important, we talk a lot about how to keep your books in balance throughout this book. You can find an initial introduction to this concept in Chapter 2.

# Introducing debits and credits

To keep the books, you need to revise your thinking about two common financial terms: debits and credits. Most non-bookkeepers and non-accountants think of debits as subtractions from their bank accounts. The opposite is true with credits – people usually see credits as additions to their accounts, in most cases in the form of refunds or corrections in favour of the account holders.

Well, forget all you think that you know about debits and credits. Debits and credits are totally different animals in the world of bookkeeping. Because keeping the books involves a method called *double-entry bookkeeping,* you have to make at least two entries – a debit and a credit – into your bookkeeping system for every transaction. Whether that debit or credit adds or subtracts from an account depends solely upon the type of account.

We know all this debit, credit and double-entry stuff sounds confusing, but we promise that this system is going to become much clearer as you work through this book. We start explaining this important concept in Chapter 2.

## Charting your bookkeeping course

You can't just enter transactions in the books willy-nilly. You need to know exactly where those transactions fit into the larger bookkeeping system. To know where everything goes, you use your *Chart of Accounts*, which is essentially a list of all the accounts that your business has and the types of transactions that go into each one. (We talk more about the Chart of Accounts in Chapter 3.)

## Discovering different business types

Before you start up in business, you're wise to sit down and have a think about the structure of your business.

For example, if you're a window cleaner, and only ever see yourself doing your own rounds and not working with anyone else, then sole trader status would be more than adequate. However, if you're planning to be much bigger and take on staff, then you need to read Chapter 5 to see how you should structure your business and what sort of advice you may need.

## Planning and controlling your activities

Many businesses just start up and trade from day to day, without any real planning or control of the activities they undertake. Often, business people become so busy that they're fire-fighting continually and lack any real direction. We like using checklists, as they help to organise your bookkeeping activities in a methodical and orderly manner. This level of organisation means that you can pick up and put down the accounts from day to day or even week to week. You can always start from where you left off, quickly and easily, by simply adopting some of the hints and tips contained within Chapter 6.

## Keeping an accurate paper trail

Keeping the books is all about creating an accurate paper trail. A computerised accounting system would refer to this trail as the *Audit Trail*. You want to keep track of all your business's financial transactions so that if a question comes up at a later date, you can turn to the books to figure out what went wrong. We're big fans of using checklists, so you know exactly where you are in the monthly accounting cycle. While the first part of this book introduces the concept of bookkeeping, from Part 2 onwards we guide you through the accounting cycle in a systematic manner, in keeping with the order we'd approach our monthly accounts. See Chapter 6 for a monthly checklist.

All your business's financial transactions are summarised in the Nominal Ledger, and journals keep track of the tiniest details of each transaction. Information can be gathered quickly by using a computerised accounting system, which gives you access to your financial information in many different report formats. Controlling who enters this financial information into your books and who can access it afterwards is smart business practice, and involves critical planning on your part. We address all these concepts in the following sections.

## Instituting internal controls

Every business owner needs to be concerned with keeping tight controls on business cash and how that cash is used. One way to institute this control is by placing internal restrictions on who can enter information into your books and who has the necessary access to use that information.

You also need to control carefully who has the ability to accept cash receipts and spend your business's cash. Separating duties appropriately helps you to protect your business's assets from error, theft and fraud. We talk more about controlling your cash and protecting your financial records in Chapter 6.

# Defining and Maintaining a Ledger

You may get confused by terms such as *books*, *ledgers*, *journals* and *accounts*. Most of these words evolved from traditional bookkeeping methods, where accounts were handwritten in huge leather-bound ledgers. These looked like books, hence the name *bookkeeping* – simply, keeping financial records in the books!

The books are also known as *journals* or *ledgers* (we told you it was a bit confusing!). You'd normally have one book for your sales, one for purchases and then a general one used for everything (often known as the *General Ledger*). Sometimes, businesses would also keep a separate cash book, which would record cash received and cash paid.

Nowadays, most people use computers to do their accounts (anything to make our busy lives easier). The most simplistic set of accounts can be done on a spreadsheet, although we don't recommend it as mistakes can easily be made and you'll struggle to find an efficient way to make sure that the books balance.

In this book we demonstrate the use of ledgers using Sage 50 Accounts. However, it's worth pointing out at this stage, that if your budget is low and you're a micro business (for example, a one man band), you may find Sage One useful. Sage One is a new online accounting service developed by Sage, which is simple and easy to use. Refer to *Sage One For Dummies* by yours truly to find out more.

Most computerised accounting systems use the term *ledger*, so you usually find the following:

- ✔ **Sales Ledger:** A ledger that holds all the individual customer accounts and their balances. This ledger is sometimes known as the *Customer Ledger* or the *Debtors Ledger*.

- ✔ **Purchase Ledger:** A ledger that holds all the individual supplier accounts and their balances. This ledger is sometimes known as the *Supplier Ledger* or *Creditor Ledger*.

- ✔ **Nominal Ledger:** A ledger that includes balances and activities for all the Nominal accounts used to run the business. We discuss Nominal accounts in Chapter 4. This ledger is also known as the *General Ledger*.

- ✔ **Cashbook, or Bank:** In Sage, in particular, you can have numerous Bank current accounts and Petty Cash accounts all under the general 'Bank' heading. Any cash received or paid is recorded in this part of the accounting system.

- ✔ **Accounts:** Simply a collective term for all the ledgers.

The pinnacle of your bookkeeping system is the *Nominal Ledger*. In this ledger, you keep a summary of all your accounts and the financial activities that took place involving those accounts throughout the year.

The sum of each Nominal Ledger account can be used to develop your financial reports on a monthly, quarterly or annual basis. You can also use these account summaries to develop internal reports that help you to make key business decisions. We talk more about developing Profit and Loss Reports and Balance Sheets in Chapter 3, when we introduce the *Chart of Accounts*.

We explain more about developing and maintaining the Nominal Ledger in Chapter 4. We also discuss the importance of journals and talk about the accounts commonly journalised in Chapter 4.

# Using Bookkeeping Tools to Manage Daily Finances

After you set up your business's books and put in place your internal controls, you're ready to use the systems you've established to manage the day-to-day operations of your business. A well-designed bookkeeping system quickly makes the job of managing your business's finances much easier.

## Tracking sales

Everyone wants to know how well sales are doing. If you keep your books up-to-date and accurate, you can easily get those numbers on a daily basis. You can also watch sales trends as often as you think necessary: daily, weekly or monthly.

Use the information collected by your bookkeeping system to monitor sales, review discounts offered to customers and track the return of products. All three elements are critical to monitoring the success of the sales of your products.

 If you find that you need to offer discounts more frequently in order to increase sales, you may need to review your pricing, and you definitely need to do market research to determine the cause of this sales weakness. The cause may be the new activities of an aggressive competitor, or simply a slowdown in your particular market. Either way, you need to understand the problem and work out how to maintain your profit objectives in spite of any obstacles.

When sales tracking reveals an increase in the number of your products being returned, you need to find the reason for the increase. Perhaps the quality of the product you're selling is declining, and you need to find a new supplier. Whatever the reason, an increased number of product returns is usually a sign of a problem that needs to be researched and corrected.

We talk more about how to use the bookkeeping system for tracking sales, discounts and returns in Chapter 7.

### Keeping stock

If your business keeps stock on hand or in warehouses, tracking the costs of the products you plan to sell is critical for managing your profit potential. When you see stock costs escalating, you may need to adjust your own prices in order to maintain your profit margin. You certainly don't want to wait until the end of the year to find out how much your stock cost you.

You also must keep careful watch on how much stock you have on hand and how much was sold. Stock can get damaged, discarded or stolen, meaning that your physical stock counts may differ from the counts you have in your books. Do a physical count periodically – at least monthly for most businesses and possibly daily for active retail stores.

In addition to watching for signs of theft or poor handling of stock, make sure that you've enough stock on hand to satisfy your customers' needs. We explain how to use your bookkeeping system to manage stock in Chapter 8.

If you run a service-based business, you can count yourself lucky as stock isn't as significant a cost in your business. You're predominantly selling time and using stocks of materials as a part of your service. However, you can't ignore your material costs, so the same lessons on stock control apply to you.

# Running Tests for Accuracy

Tracking your transactions is a waste of time if you don't periodically test to be sure that you've entered those transactions accurately. The old adage, 'Garbage in, garbage out' is particularly true for bookkeeping: if the numbers you put into your bookkeeping system are garbage, the reports you develop from those numbers are also garbage.

## Checking the cash and bank

The first step in testing your books includes proving that your cash transactions are accurately recorded. This process involves checking a number of different transactions and elements, including the cash taken in on a daily basis by your staff and the accuracy of your bank account(s). We talk about all the necessary steps you can take to prove that your cash is correct in Chapter 9.

## Testing your balance

After you prove that your cash is right (see Chapter 9), you can check that you've recorded everything else in your books just as precisely. Review the accounts for any glaring errors and then test whether or not they're in balance by doing a Trial Balance. You can find out more about Trial Balances in Chapter 10.

## Doing bookkeeping corrections

You may find that when you first run your Trial Balance, you need to make adjustments. In Chapter 10, we explain common adjustments that may be needed as you close your books at the end of an accounting period, and we also explain how to make the necessary corrections.

You need to complete monthly journals on a regular basis. One of these is *depreciation*, which is where you aim to spread the cost of your assets over their useful economic life. We talk more about the different types of depreciation, and how you journal it, in Chapter 11.

## Understanding your VAT

For those of you who are VAT registered, you know that you need to submit a regular VAT Return, usually on a quarterly basis. In Chapter 12, we talk about how you can easily do this return using a computerised accounting system.

## Preparing financial reports

Most businesses prepare at least two key financial reports: the Balance Sheet and the Profit and Loss statement. These reports can be shown to business outsiders, including the financial institutions from which the business borrows money and the business's investors.

The *Balance Sheet* is a snapshot of your business's financial health as of a particular date, and ideally it shows that your business's assets are equal to the value of your liabilities and your capital. The Balance Sheet is so-called because of its balanced formula:

Assets = Capital + Liabilities

The *Profit and Loss statement* summarises your business's financial transactions for a particular time period, such as a month, quarter or year. This financial statement starts with your sales, subtracts the costs of goods sold and then subtracts any expenses incurred in operating the business. The bottom line of the Profit and Loss statement shows how much profit your business made during the accounting period. If you haven't done well, the Profit and Loss statement shows how much you've lost.

We explain how to prepare a Balance Sheet in Chapter 14, and we talk more about developing a Profit and Loss statement in Chapter 13.

Computers now play an important part in creating your reports. Provided that you've set up your nominal codes correctly, you can easily prepare reports at the click of a button! Having said all this, you need to understand the bookkeeping rules of *double entry*, which we explain in Chapter 2. So, when you need to make an adjustment to your accounts, you'll have the necessary confidence to complete journals by applying the rules of double-entry bookkeeping.

Throughout the book, we demonstrate using Sage software and you'll be pleased to know that the majority of double-entry bookkeeping is done automatically for you. For example, when you create a sales invoice on the system, Sage debits the Debtors Control account and credit the individual Sales account with the net value of the invoice. It also posts the VAT element (assuming that you're VAT registered) to the VAT Control account.

## *Handling payroll*

Payroll can be a huge nightmare for many businesses. It requires you to comply with loads of government and tax regulations and complete a lot of paperwork. You also have to worry about collecting and paying over such things as PAYE and National Insurance. And, if you pay employee benefits, you've yet another layer of record-keeping to deal with.

We talk more about managing payroll and government requirements in Chapter 17. We also walk through year-end payroll obligations in Chapter 18.

## A word about non-profit-making entities

Not everyone is in business to make money. Many clubs and societies are non-profit making organisations, and are happy to be so. However, these organisations do need to keep their books, and usually present their reports in a slightly different format, as we discuss in Chapter 15.

## *Out with the old, in with the new*

You draw a metaphorical line at the end of each accounting period (month, quarter, year) and close off entries for that period. Effectively, you say, 'That's it for now' and draw a line under it. In fact, in good old-fashioned manual bookkeeping, you do draw an actual line and total up entries for the period. Doing so is called *closing your books.* Nowadays, with the use of computers, this process is automated, and in Sage you would run what's known as a *period end* or *year-end*. The software effectively draws that line for you and prepares the opening balances for the next period.

In Chapter 16, we discuss the process of preparing your year-end accounts.

# Getting Down to Bookkeeping Basics

**A**ll businesses need to keep track of their financial transactions, which is why bookkeeping and bookkeepers are so important. Without accurate records, how can you tell if your business is making a profit or taking a loss?

In this chapter, we cover the key aspects of bookkeeping: we introduce you to the language of bookkeeping, familiarise you with how bookkeepers manage the accounting cycle and show you how to understand the more complex type of bookkeeping – double-entry bookkeeping.

## Bookkeeping: The Record-Keeping of the Business World

*Bookkeeping,* the methodical way in which businesses track their financial transactions, is rooted in accounting. *Accounting* is the total structure of records and procedures used to record, classify and report information about a business's financial transactions. Bookkeeping involves the recording of that financial information into the accounting system while maintaining adherence to solid accounting principles.

The bookkeeper's job is to work day in and day out to ensure that they record transactions accurately. Bookkeepers need to be detail-oriented and love working with numbers, because they deal with numbers and accounts all day long.

Bookkeepers don't need to belong to any recognised professional body, however, bookkeepers can join the Institute of Certified Bookkeepers as students and take the appropriate exams before achieving full membership status. To find out more visit www.bookkeepers.org.uk.

The Association of Accounting Technicians will offer a certificate in bookkeeping in early 2013, which will provide a good grounding in this subject. In reality, most bookkeepers tend to be qualified by experience.

If you're after an accountant to help your business, use the appropriate chartered accountants or a chartered certified accountant as they have the most relevant experience.

On starting up their businesses, many small-business people serve as their own bookkeepers until the business is large enough to hire a dedicated person to keep the books. Few small businesses have accountants on the payroll to check the books and prepare official financial reports; instead, they have bookkeepers (on the payroll or hired on a self-employed basis) who serve as the outside accountants' eyes and ears. Most businesses do seek out an accountant, usually a chartered accountant (ACA or FCA), but they do so typically to submit annual accounts to the Inland Revenue, which is now part of HM Revenue & Customs.

In many small businesses today, a bookkeeper enters the business transactions on a daily basis while working inside the business. Each month, the bookkeeper prepares financial statements such as the Profit and Loss (see Chapter 13) and the Balance Sheet (see Chapter 14). The bookkeeper sends copies of the accounts and data files to the accountant at the end of the financial year. From this information, the accountant can produce statutory accounts, and also calculate tax liabilities before submitting the details to both HMRC and/or Companies House.

In most cases, the accounting system is initially set up with the help of an accountant. The aim is to ensure that the system uses solid accounting principles and that the analysis it provides is in line with that required by the business, the accountant and HM Revenue & Customs. That accountant periodically reviews the system's use to make sure that staff are handling transactions properly.

 Accurate financial reports are the only way to ensure that you know how your business is doing. Your business develops these reports using the information that you, as the bookkeeper, enter into your accounting system. If that information isn't accurate, your financial reports are meaningless: remember, 'garbage in, garbage out'.

# Wading through Basic Bookkeeping Lingo

Before you can take on bookkeeping and start keeping the books, you first need to get a handle on the key accounting terms. This section describes the main terms that all bookkeepers use on a daily basis.

*Note:* This list isn't exhaustive and doesn't contain all the unique terms you have to know as a bookkeeper. For full coverage of bookkeeping terminology, turn to the Glossary at the back of the book.

## Accounts for the Balance Sheet

Here are a few terms that you need to know:

- **Balance Sheet:** The financial statement that presents a snapshot of the business's financial position (assets, liabilities and capital) as of a particular date in time. The Balance Sheet is so-called because the things owned by the business (assets) must equal the claims against those assets (liabilities and capital).

  On an ideal Balance Sheet, the total assets need to equal the total liabilities plus the total capital. If your numbers fit this formula, the business's books are in balance. (We discuss the Balance Sheet in greater detail in Chapter 14.)

- **Assets:** All the items a business owns in order to run successfully, such as cash, stock, buildings, land, tools, equipment, vehicles and furniture.

- **Liabilities:** All the debts the business owes, such as mortgages, loans and unpaid bills.

- **Capital:** All the money the business owners invest in the business. When one person (sole trader) or a group of people (partnership) own a small business, the owners' capital is shown in a Capital account. In an incorporated business (limited company), the owners' capital is shown as shares.

  Another key Capital account is *Retained Earnings,* which shows all business profits that have been reinvested in the business rather than paid out to the owners by way of dividends. Unincorporated businesses show money paid out to the owners in a Drawings account (or individual Drawings accounts in the case of a partnership), whereas incorporated businesses distribute money to the owners by paying *dividends* (a portion of the business's profits paid out to the ordinary shareholders, typically for the year).

## Accounts for the Profit and Loss statement

Following are a few terms related to the Profit and Loss statement that you need to know:

- **Profit and loss statement:** The financial statement that presents a summary of the business's financial activity over a certain period of time, such as a month, quarter or year. The statement starts with Sales made, subtracts out the Costs of Goods Sold and the Expenses, and ends with the bottom line – Net Profit or Loss. (We show you how to develop a Profit and Loss statement in Chapter 13.)

- **Income:** All sales made in the process of selling the business's goods and services. Some businesses also generate income through other means, such as selling assets that the business no longer needs or earning interest from investments. (We discuss how to track income in Chapter 7.)

- **Cost of Goods Sold:** All costs incurred in purchasing or making the products or services a business plans to sell to its customers. (We talk about purchasing goods for sale to customers in Chapter 8.)

- **Expenses:** All costs incurred to operate the business that aren't directly related to the sale of individual goods or services. (We review common types of expenses in Chapter 3.)

## Other common terms

Some other common terms include the following:

✔ **Accounting period:** The time for which financial information is being prepared. Most businesses monitor their financial results on a monthly basis, so each accounting period equals one month. Some businesses choose to do financial reports on a quarterly basis, so the accounting period is three months. Other businesses only look at their results on a yearly basis, so their accounting period is 12 months. Businesses that track their financial activities monthly usually also create quarterly and *annual reports* (a year-end summary of the business's activities and financial results) based on the information they gather.

✔ **Accounting year-end:** In most cases a business accounting year is 12 months long and ends 12 months on from when the business started or at some traditional point in the trading cycle for that business. Many businesses have year-ends of 31 March (to tie in with the tax year) and 31 December (to tie in with the calendar year). You're allowed to change your business year-end to suit your business.

For example, if you started your business on July 1, your year-end is 30 June (12 months later). If, however, your industry traditionally has 31 December as the year-end, you're quite in order to change to this date. For example, most retailers have 31 December as their year-end. You do, of course, have to let HM Revenue & Customs know and get their formal acceptance.

✔ **Trade Debtors (also known as Accounts Receivable):** The account used to track all customer sales made on credit. *Credit* refers not to credit-card sales, but to sales in which the business gives a customer credit directly, and which the business needs to collect from the customer at a later date. (We discuss how to monitor Trade Debtors in Chapter 7.)

✔ **Trade Creditors (also known as Accounts Payable):** The account used to track all outstanding bills from suppliers, contractors, consultants and any other businesses or individuals from whom the business buys goods or services. (We talk about managing Trade Creditors in Chapter 8.)

✔ **Depreciation:** An accounting method used to account for the ageing and use of assets. For example, if you own a car, you know that the value of the car decreases each year (unless you own one of those classic cars that goes up in value). Every major asset a business owns ages and eventually needs replacement, including buildings, factories, equipment and other key assets. (We discuss how you monitor depreciation in Chapter 11.)

✔ **Nominal (or General) Ledger:** A ledger that summarises all the business's accounts. The Nominal Ledger is the master summary of the bookkeeping system. (We discuss posting to the Nominal Ledger in Chapter 4.)

✔ **Stock (or Inventory):** The account that tracks all products sold to customers. (We review stock valuation and control in Chapter 8.)

✔ **Journals:** Where bookkeepers keep records (in chronological order) of daily business transactions. Each of the most active accounts, including cash, Trade Creditors and Trade Debtors, has its own journal. (We discuss entering information into journals in Chapter 4.)

✔ **Payroll:** The way a business pays its employees. Managing payroll is a key function of the bookkeeper and involves reporting many aspects of payroll to HM Revenue & Customs, including Pay As You Earn (PAYE) taxes to be paid on behalf of the employee and employer, and National Insurance Contributions (NICs). In addition, a range of other payments such as Statutory Sick Pay (SSP) and maternity/paternity pay may be part of the payroll function. (We discuss employee payroll in Chapter 17 and the government side of payroll reporting in Chapter 18.)

✔ **Trial Balance:** How you test to ensure that the books are in balance before pulling together information for the financial reports and closing the books for the accounting period. (We discuss the Trial Balance in Chapter 10.)

# Pedalling through the Accounting Cycle

As a bookkeeper, you complete your work by completing the tasks of the accounting cycle, so-called because the workflow is circular: entering transactions, manipulating the transactions through the accounting cycle, closing the books at the end of the accounting period and then starting the entire cycle again for the next accounting period.

The accounting cycle has six basic steps, shown in Figure 2-1.

1. **Transactions:** Financial transactions start the process. Transactions can include the sale or return of a product, the purchase of supplies for business activities or any other financial activity that involves the exchange of the business's assets, the establishment or payoff of a debt or the deposit from or pay out of money to the business's owners. All sales and expenses are transactions that must be recorded. We cover transactions in greater detail throughout the book as we discuss how to record the basics of business activities – recording sales, purchases, asset acquisition or disposal, taking on new debt or paying off debt.

   You post the transactions to the relevant account. These accounts are part of the *Nominal Ledger*, where you can find a summary of all the business's accounts. A computerised accounting system automatically journals the appropriate debits and credits to the correct accounts. For example, if a purchase invoice for British Telecom is entered as a transaction, the Creditors Ledger will be credited and the telephone Nominal account will be debited.

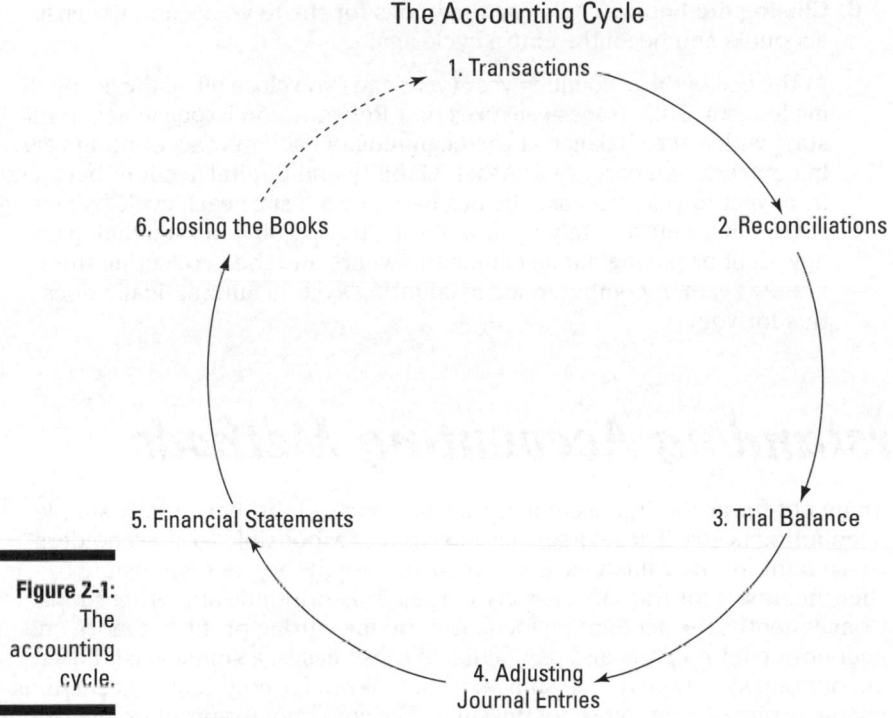

The Accounting Cycle

1. Transactions

6. Closing the Books

2. Reconciliations

5. Financial Statements

3. Trial Balance

4. Adjusting
Journal Entries

**Figure 2-1:**
The
accounting
cycle.

2. **Reconciliations**: Once you've entered all your transactions, you need to reconcile your bank account(s) to ensure that all your banking entries have been recorded correctly.

3. **Trial Balance:** At the end of the accounting period (which may be a month, quarter or year depending on your business's practices), you prepare a trial balance. You must then review each account on the Trial Balance to ensure accuracy.

4. **Adjusting journal entries:** Having reviewed the Trial Balance, you may need to make adjustments to some of the accounts in order to make corrections. You also need to account for the depreciation of assets and to adjust for one-time payments (such as insurance). These need to be allocated on a monthly basis, in order to match monthly expenses with monthly revenues more accurately. After you make the adjustments, run another Trial Balance to ensure that you're happy with the accounts.

5. **Financial statements:** You run the Balance Sheet and Profit and Loss statement using the corrected account balances.

6. **Closing the books:** You close the books for the Revenue and Expense accounts and begin the entire cycle again.

At the end of the accounting year (year-end) you close off all the accounting ledgers. This process ensures that Revenue and Expense accounts start with a zero balance at the beginning of each new accounting year. In contrast, you carry over Asset, Liability and Capital account balances from year to year, because the business doesn't start each cycle by getting rid of old assets and buying new assets, paying off and then taking on new debt or paying out all claims to owners and then collecting the money again. A computerised accounting system automatically does this for you.

# Understanding Accounting Methods

Many not-for-profit organisations, such as sports clubs, have really simple accounting needs. These organisations aren't responsible to shareholders to account for their financial performance, though they're responsible to their members for the safe custody of their subscriptions and other funds. Consequently, the accounting focus isn't on measuring profit but more on accounting for receipts and payments. In these cases, a simple cash-based accounting system may well suffice, which allows for only cash transactions – giving or receiving credit is not possible. (We cover not-for-profit organisations in more detail in Chapter 15.)

However, complications may arise when members don't pay their subscriptions during the current accounting year, and the organisation needs to reflect this situation in its accounts. In this case, the accrual accounting method is best (see the later section 'Recording right away with accrual accounting').

A few businesses operate on a cash basis, and their owners can put forward a good case for using this method. However, most accountants and HM Customs & Revenue don't accept this method as it doesn't give an accurate measure of profit (or loss) for accounting periods.

In the next sections, we briefly explain how cash-based accounting works before dismissing it in favour of the more accepted and acceptable accrual method.

## Realising the limitations of cash-based accounting

With *cash-based accounting,* you record all transactions in the books when cash actually changes hands, which means when the business receives cash payment from customers or pays out cash for purchases or other services.

Cash receipt or payment can be in the form of cash, cheque, credit card, electronic transfer or other means used to pay for an item.

Cash-based accounting can't be used when a business sells products on credit and collects the money from the customer at a later date. No provision exists in the cash-based accounting method to record and track money due from customers at some point in the future.

This situation also applies for purchases. With the cash-based accounting method, the business only records the purchase of supplies or goods that are to be sold later when it actually pays cash. When the business buys goods on credit to be paid later, it doesn't record the transaction until the cash is actually paid out.

Depending on the size of your business, you may want to start out with cash-based accounting. Many small businesses run by a sole proprietor or a small group of partners use the easier cash-based accounting system. When your business model is simple – you carry no stock, start and finish each job within a single accounting period, and pay and get paid within this period – the cash-based accounting method can work for you. But as your business grows, you may find it necessary to switch to accrual accounting in order to track revenues and expenses more accurately and to satisfy the requirements of the external accountant and HM Revenue & Customs. The same basic argument also applies to not-for-profit organisations.

Cash-based accounting does a good job of tracking cash flow, but the system does a poor job of matching revenues earned with money laid out for expenses. This deficiency is a problem particularly when, as often happens, a business buys products in one month and sells those products in the next month.

Say you buy products in June paying £1,000 cash, with the intent to sell them that same month. You don't sell the products until July, which is when you receive cash for the sales. When you close the books at the end of June, you have to show the £1,000 expense with no revenue to offset it, meaning that you have a loss that month. When you sell the products for £1,500 in July, you have a £1,500 profit. So, your monthly report for June shows a £1,000 loss, and your monthly report for July shows a £1,500 profit, when in reality you had revenues of £500 over the two months. Using cash-based accounting, you can never be sure that you have an accurate measure of profit or loss – but as cash-based accounting is for not-for-profit organisations, this isn't surprising.

Because accrual accounting is the only accounting method acceptable to accountants and HM Revenue & Customs, we concentrate on this method throughout the book. If you choose to use cash-based accounting because you have a cash-only business and a simple trading model, don't panic: most of the bookkeeping information here is still useful, but you don't need to maintain some of the accounts, such as Trade Debtors and Trade Creditors, because you aren't recording transactions until cash actually changes hands. When you're using a cash-based accounting system and you start to sell things on credit, though, you'd better have a way to track what people owe you!

Our advice is to use the accrual accounting method right from the beginning. When your business grows and your business model changes, you need the more sophisticated and legally required accrual accounting.

## Recording right away with accrual accounting

With *accrual accounting*, you record all transactions in the books when they occur, even when no cash changes hands. For example, when you sell on credit, you record the transaction immediately and enter it into a Trade Debtors account until you receive payment. When you buy goods on credit, you immediately enter the transaction into a Trade Creditors account until you pay out cash.

Like cash-based accounting, accrual accounting has drawbacks; it does a good job of matching revenues and expenses, but a poor job of tracking cash. Because you record income when the transaction occurs and not when you collect the cash, your Profit and Loss statement can look great even when you don't have cash in the bank. For example, suppose you're running a contracting business and completing jobs on a daily basis. You can record the revenue upon completion of the job even when you haven't yet collected the cash. When your customers are slow to pay, you may end up with lots of income but little cash. Remember – *never* confuse profit and cash. In the short term, cash flow is often more important than profit, but in the long term profit becomes more important. But don't worry just yet; in Chapter 7, we tell you how to manage your Trade Debtors so that you don't run out of cash because of slow-paying customers.

Many businesses that use the accrual accounting method monitor cash flow on a weekly basis to be sure that they've enough cash on hand to operate the business. If your business is seasonal, such as a landscaping business with little to do during the winter months, you can establish short-term lines of credit through your bank to maintain cash flow through the lean times.

## Seeing Double with Double-Entry Bookkeeping

All businesses use *double-entry bookkeeping* to keep their books, whether they use the cash-based accounting method or the accrual accounting method. Double-entry bookkeeping – so-called because you enter all transactions twice – helps to minimise errors and increase the chance that your books balance.

## Double-entry bookkeeping goes way back

No one's really sure who invented double-entry bookkeeping. The first person to put the practice on paper was Benedetto Cotrugli in 1458, but mathematician and Franciscan monk Luca Pacioli is most often credited with developing double-entry bookkeeping. Although Pacioli is called the Father of Accounting, accounting actually occupies only one of five sections of his book, *Everything About Arithmetic, Geometry and Proportions,* which was published in 1494.

Pacioli didn't actually *invent* double-entry bookkeeping; he just described the method used by merchants in Venice during the Italian Renaissance period. He's most famous for his warning to bookkeepers: 'A person should not go to sleep at night until the debits equal the credits!'

When it comes to double-entry bookkeeping, the key formula for the Balance Sheet (Assets = Liabilities + Capital) plays a major role.

## Golden rules of bookkeeping

You have some simple rules to remember when getting to grips with double-entry bookkeeping.

First of all, remember that a debit is on the left side of a transaction and a credit is on the right side of a transaction. Then apply the following rules:

- ✔ If you want to increase an asset, you must debit the Assets account.
- ✔ To decrease an asset, you must credit the Assets account.
- ✔ To increase a liability, you credit the Liabilities account.
- ✔ To decrease a liability, you debit the Liabilities account.
- ✔ If you want to record an expense, you debit the Expense account.
- ✔ If you need to reduce an expense, you credit the Expense account.
- ✔ If you want to record income, you credit the Income account.
- ✔ If you want to reduce income, you debit the Income account.

Copy Table 2-1 and have it on your desk when you start keeping your own books (a bit like the chief accountant in the 'Sharing a secret' sidebar). We guarantee that the table can help to keep your debits and credits straight.

Believe it or not, identifying the difference becomes second nature as you start making regular entries in your bookkeeping system. But, to make things easier for you, Table 2-1 is a chart that bookkeepers and accountants commonly use. Everyone needs help sometimes!

| Table 2-1 | How Credits and Debits Impact Your Accounts | |
|-----------|-----------|-----------|
| *Account Type* | *Debits* | *Credits* |
| Assets | Increase | Decrease |
| Liabilities | Decrease | Increase |
| Income | Decrease | Increase |
| Expenses | Increase | Decrease |

Here's an example of the practice in action. Suppose that you purchase a new desk for your office that costs £1,500. This transaction actually has two parts: you spend an asset – cash – to buy another asset, furniture. So, you must adjust two accounts in your business's books: the Cash account and the Furniture account. The transaction in a bookkeeping entry is as follows (we talk more about how to do initial bookkeeping entries in Chapter 4):

| Account | Debit | Credit |
|---------|-------|--------|
| Furniture | £1,500 | |
| Cash | | £1,500 |

*To purchase a new desk for the office.*

In this transaction, you record the accounts impacted by the transaction. The debit increases the value of the Furniture account, and the credit decreases the value of the Cash account. For this transaction, both accounts impacted are Asset accounts so, looking at how the Balance Sheet is affected, you can see that the only changes are to the asset side of the Balance Sheet equation:

| | | |
|---|---|---|
| Assets | = | Liabilities + Capital |
| Furniture increase | = | No change to this side of the equation |
| Cash decrease | | |

In this case, the books stay in balance because the exact pounds sterling amount that increases the value of your Furniture account decreases the value of your Cash account. At the bottom of any journal entry, include a brief explanation that explains the purpose of the entry. In the first example, we indicate that this entry was 'To purchase a new desk for the office'.

## Practising with an example

To show you how you record a transaction that impacts both sides of the Balance Sheet equation, here's an example that records the purchase of stock. Suppose that you purchase £5,000 worth of widgets on credit. (Have you always wondered what widgets were? Can't help you. They're just commonly used in accounting examples to represent something purchased where what's purchased is of no real significance.) These new widgets add value to your Stock Asset account and also add value to your Trade Creditors account. (Remember, the Trade Creditors account is a Liability account where you track bills that need to be paid at some point in the future.) The bookkeeping transaction for your widget purchase looks as follows:

| *Account* | *Debit* | *Credit* |
|---|---|---|
| Stock | £5,000 | |
| Trade Creditors | | £5,000 |

*To purchase widgets for sale to customers.*

This transaction affects the Balance Sheet equation as follows:

| Assets | = | Liabilities + Capital |
|---|---|---|
| Stock increases | = | Creditor increases + No change |

In this case, the books stay in balance because both sides of the equation increase by £5,000.

You can see from the two example transactions how double-entry bookkeeping helps to keep your books in balance – as long as you make sure that each entry into the books is balanced. Balancing your entries may look simple here, but sometimes bookkeeping entries can get complex when the transaction impacts more than two accounts.

---

# Sharing a secret

Don't feel embarrassed if you forget which side the debits go on and which side the credits go on. One often-told story is of a young clerk in an accounts office plucking up courage to ask the chief accountant, who was retiring that day, why for 30 years he had at the start of each day opened up his drawer and read the contents of a piece of paper before starting work. The chief accountant at first was reluctant to spill the beans, but ultimately decided he had to pass on his secret – and who better than an up-and-coming clerk? Swearing the young clerk to secrecy, he took out the piece of paper and showed it to him. The paper read: 'Debit on the left and credit on the right.'

# Have a Go

In this section you can have a practice with double-entry bookkeeping by having a go at the next few exercises. You can find the answers at the end of the chapter. Good Luck! By the way, if you get stuck, remember to look back at the section 'Golden rules of bookkeeping', earlier in this chapter.

1. **Have a look at the following list and decide whether the items described belong in the Profit and Loss account or the Balance Sheet:**

   | *Item* | *Profit and Loss or Balance Sheet?* |
   |---|---|
   | Telephone Bills | |
   | Purchase of Motor Vehicles | |
   | Bank Loan | |
   | Petty Cash | |
   | Sales | |
   | Materials Purchased for Resale | |

2. **Write the journal entry for the following, as shown in the furniture example in the previous section.**

   On 15 February, you buy new products (to be sold in your shop) on credit for £3,000. How would you enter this transaction in your books?

   | *Date* | *Account* | *Debit* | *Credit* |
   |---|---|---|---|

3. **Write down the journal entry for the following transaction:**

   On 31 March, you sold £5,000 worth of goods and received £5,000 in cash.

   | *Date* | *Account* | *Debit* | *Credit* |
   |---|---|---|---|

4. **Write down the journal entry for the following transaction:**

   On 30 June, you sold £3,000 worth of goods on credit. You didn't get cash. Customers will pay you after you bill them. How do you record the sales transaction?

   | *Date* | *Account* | *Debit* | *Credit* |
   |---|---|---|---|

5. **Write down the journal entry for the following transaction:**

   On 30 September, you buy office supplies for £500 using a cheque. How would you record the transaction?

   | *Date* | *Account* | *Debit* | *Credit* |
   |---|---|---|---|

6. In which two accounts would you record the cash purchase of goods to be sold?

7. In which two accounts would you record the purchase of furniture for your office using a credit card?

8. In which two accounts would you record the payment of rent to your landlord in cash?

9. If your accountant wants to know how many products are still on the shelves after you closed the books for an accounting period, which account would you show?

10. If a customer buys your product on credit, in which account would you record the transaction?

11. You receive an invoice for some goods received. Where do you record the invoice in the accounting system, so that you can pay it in the future?

12. Which report would you run to ensure that your accounts are in balance?

13. If you find a mistake, what type of entry would you make to get your books back in balance?

# Answering the Have a Go Questions

1. **Telephone Bill:** A telephone bill is usually considered to be an overhead of the business. As such, it would be included in the Profit and Loss account and classified as an expense.

   **Purchase of Motor Vehicle:** A motor vehicle is likely to be kept in the business for a long period of time, usually 3–4 years or more. This is categorised as a fixed asset and would be included in the Balance Sheet.

   **Bank Loan:** The owner or directors of the business may have taken out a bank loan to provide funds for a large purchase. A bank loan is something that the business owes to a third party, and it's considered to be a liability. As such, it'll be shown in the Balance Sheet.

   **Petty Cash:** Although it may be a small amount of money held in a petty cash tin, it's still considered to be an asset. It'll therefore be shown as an asset in the Balance Sheet.

   **Sales:** Once your business starts generating income through Sales, this must be entered into a Profit and Loss account. Sales is the first category of a Profit and Loss report; when you deduct costs from this, a profit or loss can be calculated.

   **Materials Purchased for Resale:** You may buy goods and sell them on in their present state, or you may buy materials, which can be used to manufacture a product. Either way, these costs are considered to be *direct costs* (they're directly attributed to making the products you sell) and as such they need to be shown as Cost of Goods Sold in the Profit and Loss account.

2. **In this transaction, you'd debit the Purchases account to show the additional purchases made during that period and credit the Creditors account.**

   Remember, if you're increasing a liability (such as Creditors) you must credit that account. When recording an expense such as Purchases, you should debit that account. Since you're buying the goods on credit, that means you have to pay the bill at some point in the future.

   | Date | Account | Debit | Credit |
   |------|---------|-------|--------|
   | 15 Feb | Purchases | £3,000 | |
   | 15 Feb | Creditors | | £3,000 |

3. **As you think about the journal entry, you may not know whether something is a credit or a debit.**

   As you know from our discussions earlier in the chapter, cash is an asset, and if you increase the value of an asset, you debit that account. In this question, because you received cash, you know that the Cash account needs to be a debit. So your only choice is to make the Sales account the account to be credited. This is correct as all Income accounts are increased by a credit. If you're having trouble figuring these entries out, look again at Table 2-1.

   | Date | Account | Debit | Credit |
   |------|---------|-------|--------|
   | 31 March | Cash | £5,000 | |
   | 31 March | Sales | | £5,000 |

4. **In this question, rather than taking in cash, the customers were allowed to pay on credit, so you need to debit the Asset account Debtors.**

   (Remember: When increasing an asset, you debit that account.) You'll credit the Sales account to track the additional revenue. (When recording income, you credit the Income account.)

   | Date | Account | Debit | Credit |
   |------|---------|-------|--------|
   | 30 June | Debtors | £3,000 | |
   | 30 June | Sales | | £3,000 |

5. **In this question, you're paying with a cheque, so the transaction is recorded in your Cash account.**

   The Cash account tracks the amount in your bank account. Any cash, cheques, debit cards or other types of transactions that are taken directly from your bank account are always entered as a credit. This is because you're decreasing an asset (say, cash), therefore, you must credit the Cash account. All money paid out for expenses is always a debit. When recording an expense, always post a debit to the Expense account.

| *Date* | *Account* | *Debit* | *Credit* |
|---|---|---|---|
| 30 Sept | Office Supplies | £500 | |
| 30 Sept | Cash | | £500 |

6. **Record the goods purchased in a Cost of Goods Sold account, called Purchases.**

   Record the cash spent in the Cash account. Don't record the goods purchased in the Stock account. Stock is adjusted at the end of an accounting period, after a physical count of the stock has been done. The one exception is a business that manages its stock system by computer. In most cases, when stock management is computerised, the system automatically adjusts stock with each purchase of goods. But even with this type of system, the initial entry would be to the Purchases account and the computer would then automatically update the Stock account.

7. **Record the furniture in an Asset account called Furniture, record the credit card transaction in a Liability account called Credit Card.**

   You'd record the charge on the credit card in a Liability account called Credit Card. Cash wouldn't be paid until the credit card bill is due to be paid. Furniture is always listed as an asset on your Balance Sheet. Anything you buy that you expect to use for more than one year is a fixed asset, rather than an expense.

8. **Record the rent payment in an Expense account called Rent.**

   Record the cash used in a Current Asset account called Cash. Cash is always a Current Asset account (unless your bank account is overdrawn and then it would be considered a liability and would be shown in Current Liabilities). Rent is always an expense.

9. **Stock account.**

   The Stock account is adjusted at the end of each accounting period to show the total number of products remaining to be sold at the end of the period.

10. **Debtors Ledger.**

    This is the account that is used to track all customer purchases bought on credit. In addition to this account, which summarises all products bought on credit, you'd also need to enter the purchases into the individual accounts of each of your customers so you can bill them and track their payments.

11. **Creditors Ledger.**

    You record all unpaid invoices in Trade Creditors.

12. **You would run a Trial Balance.**

    The Trial Balance is a working tool that helps you test whether your books are in balance before you prepare your financial statements.

13. **A journal.**

    At the end of an accounting period you correct any mistakes by entering journals. These entries also need to be in balance. You'll always have at least one account that's a debit and one that's a credit.

# Chapter 3

# Outlining Your Financial Roadmap with a Chart of Accounts

---

*In This Chapter*

▶ Introducing the Chart of Accounts

▶ Looking at Balance Sheet accounts

▶ Going over the Profit and Loss

▶ Creating your own Chart of Accounts

---

**C**an you imagine what a mess your cheque book would be if you didn't record each cheque you write? Like us, you've probably forgotten to record a cheque or two on occasion, but you certainly found out quickly enough when an important payment bounced as a result. Yikes!

Keeping the books of a business can be a lot more difficult than maintaining a personal cheque book. Each business transaction must be carefully recorded to make sure that it goes into the right account. This careful bookkeeping gives you an effective tool for working out how well the business is doing financially.

As a bookkeeper, you need a roadmap to help you determine where to record all those transactions. This roadmap is called the Chart of Accounts. In this chapter, we tell you how to set up the Chart of Accounts, which includes many different accounts. We also review the types of transactions you enter into each type of account in order to track the key parts of any business – assets, liabilities, capital, income and expenses.

# Getting to Know the Chart of Accounts

The *Chart of Accounts* is the roadmap that a business creates to organise its financial transactions. After all, you can't record a transaction until you know where to put it! Essentially, this chart is a list of all the accounts a business has, organised in a specific order; each account has a description that includes the type of account and the types of transactions to be entered into that account. Every business creates its own Chart of Accounts based on how the business is operated, so you're unlikely to find two businesses with the exact same Charts of Accounts.

However, you find some basic organisational and structural characteristics in all Charts of Accounts. The organisation and structure are designed around two key financial reports: the *Balance Sheet,* which shows what your business owns and what it owes, and the *Profit and Loss statement,* which shows how much money your business took in from sales and how much money it spent to generate those sales. (You can find out more about Profit and Loss statements in Chapter 13 and Balance Sheets statements in Chapter 14.)

The Chart of Accounts starts with the balance sheet accounts, which include the following:

- ✔ **Fixed assets:** Includes all accounts that show things the business owns that have a lifespan of more than 12 months, such as buildings, furniture, plant and equipment, motor vehicles and office equipment.

- ✔ **Current assets:** Includes all accounts that show things the business owns and expects to use in the next 12 months, such as cash, Trade Debtors (also known as Accounts Receivable, which is money due from customers), prepayments and stock.

- ✔ **Current liabilities:** Includes all accounts that show debts that the business must repay over the next 12 months, such as Trade Creditors (also known as Accounts Payable, which is bills from suppliers, contractors and consultants), hire purchase and other loans, VAT and income/corporation tax, accruals and credit cards payable.

- ✔ **Long-term liabilities:** Includes all accounts that show debts that the business must pay over a period of time longer than the next 12 months, such as mortgages repayable and longer-term loans that are repayable.

- ✔ **Capital:** Includes all accounts that show the owners of the business and their claims against the business's assets, including any money invested in the business, any money taken out of the business and any earnings that have been reinvested in the business.

The rest of the chart is filled with Profit and Loss statement accounts, which include the following:

- ✔ **Income:** Includes all accounts that track sales of goods and services as well as revenue generated for the business by other means.

- ✔ **Cost of Goods Sold:** Includes all accounts that track the direct costs involved in selling the business's goods or services.

- ✔ **Expenses:** Includes all accounts that track expenses related to running the businesses that aren't directly tied to the sale of individual products or services.

When developing the Chart of Accounts, start by listing all the Asset accounts, the Liability accounts, the Capital accounts, the Revenue accounts and, finally, the Expense accounts. All these accounts feed into two statements: the Balance Sheet and the Profit and Loss statement.

In this chapter, we review the key account types found in most businesses, but this list isn't cast in stone. You need to develop an account list that makes the most sense for how you're operating your business and the financial information you want to track. As we explore the various accounts that make up the Chart of Accounts, we point out how the structure may differ for different types of businesses.

The Chart of Accounts is a money-management tool that helps you follow your business transactions, so set it up in a way that provides you with the financial information you need to make smart business decisions. You're probably going to tweak the accounts in your chart annually and, if necessary, you may add accounts during the year if you find something for which you want more detailed tracking. You can add accounts during the year, but don't delete accounts until the end of a 12-month reporting period. We discuss adding and deleting accounts from your books in Chapter 10.

# *Starting with the Balance Sheet Accounts*

The first part of the Chart of Accounts is made up of balance sheet accounts, which break down into the following three categories:

- ✔ **Assets:** These accounts show what the business owns. Assets include cash on hand, furniture, buildings, vehicles and so on.

✔ **Liabilities:** These accounts show what the business owes, or more specifically, claims that lenders have against the business's assets. For example, mortgages on buildings and long-term loans are two common types of liabilities. Also, a mortgage (a legal charge) is a good example of a claim that the lender (bank or building society) has over a business asset (in this case, the premises being bought through the mortgage).

✔ **Capital:** These accounts show what the owners put into the business and the claims the owners have against the business's assets. For example, shareholders are business owners that have claims against the business's assets.

The balance sheet accounts, and the financial report they make up, are so-called because they have to *balance* out. The value of the assets must be equal to the claims made against those assets. (Remember, these claims are liabilities made by lenders and capital made by owners.)

We discuss the Balance Sheet in greater detail in Chapter 14, including how to prepare and use it. This section, however, examines the basic components of the Balance Sheet, as reflected in the Chart of Accounts.

## Tackling assets

The accounts that track what the business owns – its assets – are always the first category on the chart. The two types of asset accounts are fixed assets and current assets.

### Fixed assets

*Fixed assets* are assets that you anticipate your business is going to use for more than 12 months. This section lists some of the most common fixed assets, starting with the key accounts related to buildings and business premises that the business owns:

✔ **Land and Buildings:** This account shows the value of the land and buildings the business owns. The initial value is based on the cost at the time of purchase, but this asset can be (and often is) revalued as property prices increase over time. Because of the virtually indestructible nature of this asset, it doesn't depreciate at a fast rate. *Depreciation* is an accounting method that shows an asset is being used up. We talk more about depreciation in Chapter 11.

- **Accumulated Depreciation – Land and Buildings:** This account shows the cumulative amount this asset has depreciated over its useful lifespan.

- **Leasehold Improvements:** This account shows the value of improvements to buildings or other facilities that a business leases rather than purchases. Frequently when a business leases a property, it must pay for any improvements necessary in order to use that property as the business requires. For example, when a business leases a shop, the space leased is likely to be an empty shell or filled with shelving and other items that don't match the particular needs of the business. As with land and buildings, leasehold improvements depreciate as the value of the asset ages – usually over the remaining life of the lease.

- **Accumulated Depreciation – Leasehold Improvements:** This account tracks the cumulative amount depreciated for leasehold improvements.

The following are the types of accounts for smaller long-term assets, such as vehicles and furniture:

- **Vehicles:** This account shows any cars, lorries or other vehicles owned by the business. The initial value of any vehicle is listed in this account based on the total cost paid to put the vehicle into service. Sometimes this value is more than the purchase price if additions were needed to make the vehicle usable for the particular type of business. For example, when a business provides transportation for the handicapped and must add additional equipment to a vehicle in order to serve the needs of its customers, that additional equipment is added to the value of the vehicle. Vehicles also depreciate through their useful lifespan.

- **Accumulated Depreciation – Vehicles:** This account shows the depreciation of all vehicles owned by the business.

- **Furniture and Fixtures:** This account shows any furniture or fixtures purchased for use in the business. The account includes the value of all chairs, desks, store fixtures and shelving needed to operate the business. The value of the furniture and fixtures in this account is based on the cost of purchasing these items. Businesses depreciate these items during their useful lifespan.

- **Accumulated Depreciation – Furniture and Fixtures:** This account shows the accumulated depreciation of all furniture and fixtures.

- **Plant and Equipment:** This account shows equipment that was purchased for use for more than 12 months, such as process-related machinery, computers, copiers, tools and cash registers. The value of the equipment is based on the cost to purchase these items. Equipment is also depreciated to show that over time it gets used up and must be replaced.

- ✔ **Accumulated Depreciation – Plant and Equipment:** This account tracks the accumulated depreciation of all the equipment.

The following accounts show the fixed assets that you can't touch (accountants refer to these assets as *intangible assets*), but that still represent things of value owned by the business, such as start-up costs, patents and copyrights. The accounts that track them include:

- ✔ **Start-up Costs:** This account shows the initial start-up expenses to get the business off the ground. Many such expenses can't be set off against business profits in the first year. For example, special licences and legal fees must be written off over a number of years using a method similar to depreciation, called *amortisation*, which is also tracked.

- ✔ **Amortisation – Start-up Costs:** This account shows the accumulated amortisation of these costs during the period in which they're being written-off.

- ✔ **Patents:** This account shows the costs associated with *patents*, which are grants made by governments that guarantee to the inventor of a product or service the exclusive right to make, use and sell that product or service over a set period of time. Like start-up costs, patent costs are amortised. The value of this asset is based on the expenses the business incurs to get the right to patent its product.

- ✔ **Amortisation – Patents:** This account shows the accumulated amortisation of a business's patents.

- ✔ **Copyrights:** This account shows the costs incurred to establish copyrights, the legal rights given to an author, playwright, publisher or any other distributor of a publication or production for a unique work of literature, music, drama or art. This legal right expires after a set number of years, so its value is amortised as the copyright gets used up.

- ✔ **Goodwill:** This account is needed only if a business buys another business for more than the actual value of its tangible assets. Goodwill reflects the intangible value of this purchase for things like business reputation, store locations, customer base and other items that increase the value of the business bought. The value of goodwill isn't everlasting and so, like other intangible assets, must be amortised.

- ✔ **Research and Development:** This account shows the investment the business has made in future products and services, which may not see the light of day for several years. These costs are written off (amortised) over the life of the products and services as and when they reach the marketplace.

If you hold a lot of assets that aren't of great value, you can also set up an Other Assets account to show those assets that don't have significant business value. Any asset you show in the Other Assets account that you later want to show individually can be shifted to its own account. We discuss adjusting the Chart of Accounts in Chapter 10.

### Current assets

*Current assets* are the key assets that your business uses up within a 12-month period and are likely not to be there the next year. The accounts that reflect current assets on the Chart of Accounts are:

- **Current account:** This account is the business's primary bank account for operating activities, such as depositing receipts and paying expenses. Some businesses have more than one account in this category; for example, a business with many divisions may have an account for each division.

- **Deposit account:** This account is used for surplus cash. Any cash not earmarked for an immediate plan is deposited in an interest-earning savings account. In this way, the cash earns interest while the business decides what to do with it.

- **Cash on Hand:** This account is used to record any cash kept at retail stores or in the office. In retail stores, cash must be kept in registers in order to provide change to customers. In the office, petty cash is often kept for immediate cash needs that pop up from time to time. This account helps you keep track of the cash held outside the various bank and deposit accounts.

- **Trade Debtors:** This account shows the customers who still owe you money if you offer your products or services to customers on credit (by which we mean *your* own credit system).

    Trade Debtors isn't used to show purchases made on other types of credit cards, because your business gets paid directly by banks, not customers, when customers use credit cards. Check out Chapter 7 to read more about this scenario and the corresponding type of account.

- **Stock:** This account shows the value of the products you have on hand to sell to your customers. The value of the assets in this account varies depending upon the way you decide to track the flow of stock into and out of the business. We discuss stock valuation and recording in greater detail in Chapter 8.

- **Prepayments:** This account shows goods or services you pay for in advance: the payment is credited as it gets used up each month. For example, say that you prepay your property insurance on a building that you own one year in advance. Each month you reduce the amount that you prepaid by one-twelfth as the prepayment is used up.

Depending upon the type of business you're setting up, you may have other current Asset accounts to set up. For example, say that you're starting a service business in consulting. You're likely to have an account called Consulting Fees for tracking cash collected for those services.

## Laying out your liabilities

After you deal with assets, the next stop on the bookkeeping journey is the accounts that show what your business owes to others. These others can include suppliers from whom you buy products or supplies, financial institutions from which you borrow money and anyone else who lends money to your business. Like assets, you lump liabilities into current liabilities and long-term liabilities.

### Current liabilities

*Current liabilities* are debts due in the next 12 months. Some of the most common types of current liabilities accounts that appear on the Chart of Accounts are as follows:

- ✔ **Trade Creditors:** This account shows money that the business owes to suppliers, contractors and consultants that must be paid in less than 12 months. Most of these liabilities must be paid in 30 to 90 days from initial invoicing.

- ✔ **Value Added Tax (VAT):** This account shows your VAT liability. You may not think of VAT as a liability, but because the business collects the tax from the customer and doesn't pay it immediately to HM Customs & Revenue, the taxes collected become a liability. Of course you're entitled to offset the VAT that the business has been charged on its purchases before making a net payment. A business usually collects VAT throughout the month and then pays the net amount due on a quarterly basis. We discuss paying VAT in greater detail in Chapter 12.

- ✔ **Accrued Payroll Taxes:** This account shows payroll taxes, such as PAYE and National Insurance, collected from employees and the business itself, which have to be paid over to HM Revenue & Customs. Businesses don't have to pay these taxes over immediately and may pay payroll taxes on a monthly basis. We discuss how to handle payroll taxes in Chapter 17.

- ✔ **Credit Cards Payable:** This account shows all credit card accounts for which the business is liable. Most businesses use credit cards as short-term debt and pay them off completely at the end of each month, but some smaller businesses carry credit card balances over a longer period of time. In Chart of Accounts, you can set up one Credit Card Payable account, but you may want to set up a separate account for each card your business holds to improve your ability to track credit card usage.

The way you set up your current liabilities – and how many individual accounts you establish – depends upon the level of detail that you want to use to track each type of liability.

### Long-term liabilities

*Long-term liabilities* are debts due in more than 12 months. The number of long-term liability accounts you maintain on your Chart of Accounts depends on your debt structure. For example, if you've several different loans, then set up an account for each one. The most common type of long-term liability accounts is Loans Payable. This account tracks any long-term loans, such as a mortgage on your business building. Most businesses have separate Loans Payable accounts for each of their long-term loans. For example, you can have *Loans Payable – Mortgage Bank* for your building and *Loans Payable – Vehicles* for your vehicle loan.

In addition to any separate long-term debt that you may want to track in its own account, you may also want to set up an account called *Other Liabilities*. You can use this account to track types of debt that are so insignificant to the business that you don't think they need their own accounts.

# Controlling the capital

Every business is owned by somebody. *Capital accounts* track owners' contributions to the business as well as their share of ownership. For a limited company, ownership is tracked by the sale of individual shares because each stockholder owns a portion of the business. In smaller businesses owned by one person or a group of people, capital is tracked using capital and drawing accounts. Here are the basic capital accounts that appear in the Chart of Accounts:

✔ **Ordinary Share Capital:** This account reflects the value of outstanding ordinary shares sold to investors. A business calculates this value by multiplying the number of shares issued by the value of each share of stock. Only limited companies need to establish this account.

✓ **Retained Earnings:** This account tracks the profits or losses accumulated since a business opened. At the end of each year, the profit or loss calculated on the Profit and Loss statement is used to adjust the value of this account. For example, if a business made a £100,000 profit after tax in the past year, the Retained Earnings account is increased by that amount; if the business lost £100,000, that amount is subtracted from this account. Any dividends paid to shareholders reduce the profit figure transferred to Retained Earnings each year.

✓ **Capital:** This account is only necessary for small, unincorporated businesses, such as sole traders or partnerships. The Capital account reflects the amount of initial money the business owner contributed to the business as well as any additional contributions made after initial start-up. The value of this account is based on cash contributions and other assets contributed by the business owner, such as equipment, vehicles or buildings. When a small company has several different partners, each partner gets his own Capital account to track his contributions.

✓ **Drawing:** This account is only necessary for businesses that aren't incorporated. The Drawing account tracks any money that a business owner takes out of the business. If the business has several partners, each partner gets his own Drawing account to track what he takes out of the business.

# Keeping an Eye on the Profit and Loss Statement Accounts

The Profit and Loss statement is made up of two types of accounts:

✓ **Expenses:** These accounts track all costs that a business incurs in order to keep itself afloat.

✓ **Revenue:** These accounts track all income coming into the business, including sales, interest earned on savings and any other methods used to generate income.

The bottom line of the Profit and Loss statement shows whether your business made a profit or a loss for a specified period of time. We discuss how to prepare and use a Profit and Loss statement in greater detail in Chapter 13.

This section examines the various accounts that make up the Profit and Loss statement portion of the Chart of Accounts.

# Recording the profit you make

Accounts that show revenue coming into the business are first up in the Profit and Loss statement section of the Chart of Accounts. If you choose to offer discounts or accept returns, that activity also falls within the revenue grouping. The most common income accounts are:

- ✔ **Sales of Goods or Services:** This account, which appears at the top of every Profit and Loss statement, shows all the money that the business earns selling its products, services or both.

- ✔ **Sales Discounts:** This account shows any reductions to the full price of merchandise (necessary because most businesses offer discounts to encourage sales).

- ✔ **Sales Returns:** This account shows transactions related to returns, when a customer returns a product.

When you examine a Profit and Loss statement from a business other than the one you own or are working for, you usually see the following accounts summarised as one line item called *Revenue* or *Net Revenue*. Because not all income is generated by sales of products or services, other income accounts that may appear on a Chart of Accounts include the following:

- ✔ **Interest Income:** This account shows any income earned by collecting interest on a business's savings accounts. If the business lends money to employees or to another business and earns interest on that money, that interest is recorded in this account as well.

- ✔ **Other Income:** This account shows income that a business generates from a source other than its primary business activity. For example, a business that encourages recycling and earns income from the items recycled records that income in this account.

# Recording the cost of goods sold

Of course, before you can sell a product, you must spend money to buy or make that product. The type of account used to track the money spent is called a Cost of Goods Sold account. The most common cost of goods sold accounts are:

- ✔ **Purchases:** This account shows the purchases of all items you plan to sell.

- ✔ **Purchase Discount:** This account shows the discounts you may receive from suppliers when you pay for your purchase quickly. For example, a business may give you a 2 per cent discount on your purchase when you pay the bill in ten days rather than wait until the end of the 30-day payment period.

- ✔ **Purchase Returns:** This account shows the value of any returns when you're unhappy with a product you bought.

- ✔ **Freight Charges:** This account shows any charges related to shipping items that you purchase for later sale. You may or may not want to keep this detail.

- ✔ **Other Sales Costs:** This account is a catch-all account for anything that doesn't fit into one of the other cost of goods sold accounts.

## *Acknowledging the other costs*

Expense accounts take the cake for the longest list of individual accounts. Anything you spend on the business that can't be tied directly to the sale of an individual product falls under the Expense account category. For example, advertising a sale isn't directly tied to the sale of any one product, so the costs associated with advertising fall under the Expense account category.

The Chart of Accounts mirrors your business operations, so you decide how much detail you want to keep in your expense accounts. Most businesses have expenses that are unique to their operations, so your list is likely to be longer than the one we present here. However, you also may find that you don't need some of these accounts. Small businesses typically have expense headings that mirror those required by HM Revenue & Customs on their self-assessment returns.

On your Chart of Accounts, the expense accounts don't have to appear in any specific order, so we list them alphabetically. The most common expense accounts are:

- ✔ **Advertising:** This account shows all expenses involved in promoting a business or its products. Expenditure on newspaper, television, magazine and radio advertising is recorded here, as well as any costs incurred to print flyers and mailings to customers. Also, when a business participates in community events such as cancer walks or craft fairs, associated costs appear in this account.

- ✔ **Amortisation:** This account is similar to the Depreciation account (see later in this list) and shows the ongoing monthly charge for the current financial year for all your intangible assets.

✔ **Bank Service Charges:** This account shows any charges made by a bank to service a business's bank accounts.

✔ **Depreciation:** This account shows the ongoing monthly depreciation charge for the current financial year for all your fixed assets – buildings, cars, vans, furniture and so on. Of course, when the individual depreciation values are large for each fixed asset category, you may open up individual depreciation accounts.

✔ **Dues and Subscriptions:** This account shows expenses related to business-club membership or subscriptions to magazines for the business.

✔ **Equipment Rental:** This account records expenses related to renting equipment for a short-term project; for example, a business that needs to rent a van to pick up new fixtures for its shop records that van rental in this account.

✔ **Insurance:** This account shows insurance costs. Many businesses break this account down into several accounts such as Building Insurance, Public Liability Insurance and Car Insurance.

✔ **Legal and Accounting:** This account shows the cost of legal or accounting advice.

✔ **Miscellaneous Expenses:** This account is a catch-all account for expenses that don't fit into one of a business's established accounts. If certain miscellaneous expenses occur frequently, a business may choose to add an account to the Chart of Accounts and move related expenses into that new account by subtracting all related transactions from the Miscellaneous Expenses account and adding them to the new account. With this shuffle, you need to carefully balance out the adjusting transaction to avoid any errors or double counting.

✔ **Office Expenses:** This account shows any items purchased in order to run an office. For example, office supplies such as paper and pens or business cards fit in this account. As with miscellaneous expenses, a business may choose to track certain office expense items in their own accounts. For example, when you find that your office is using a lot of copy paper and you want to track that separately, set up a Copy Paper Expense account. Just be sure that you really need the detail because a large number of accounts can get unwieldy and hard to manage.

✔ **Payroll Taxes:** This account records any taxes paid related to employee payroll, such as Pay As You Earn (PAYE), Statutory Sick Pay (SSP) and maternity/paternity pay.

✔ **Postage:** This account shows any expenditure on stamps, express package shipping and other shipping. If your business does a large amount of shipping through suppliers such as UPS or Federal Express, you may want to track that spending in separate accounts for each supplier. This option is particularly helpful for small businesses that sell over the Internet or through mail-order sales.

✔ **Profit (or Loss) on Disposal of Fixed Assets:** This account records any profit when a business sells a fixed asset, such as a car or furniture. Make sure that you only record revenue remaining after subtracting the accumulated depreciation from the original cost of the asset.

✔ **Rent:** This account records rental costs for a business's office or retail space.

✔ **Salaries and Wages:** This account shows any money paid to employees as salary or wages.

✔ **Telephone:** This account shows all business expenses related to the telephone and telephone calls.

✔ **Travel and Entertainment:** This account records any expenditure on travel or entertainment for business purposes. Some businesses separate these expenses into several accounts, such as Travel and Entertainment – Meals, Travel and Entertainment – Travel and Travel and Entertainment – Entertainment, to keep a close watch.

✔ **Utilities:** This account shows utility costs, such as electricity, gas and water.

✔ **Vehicles:** This account shows expenses related to the operation of business vehicles.

# Setting Up Your Chart of Accounts

You can use all the lists of accounts provided in this chapter to set up your business's own Chart of Accounts. No secret method exists for creating your own chart – just make a list of the accounts that apply to your business.

When first setting up your Chart of Accounts, don't panic if you can't think of every type of account you may need for your business. You can easily add to the Chart of Accounts at any time. Just add the account to the list and distribute the revised list to any employees who use the Chart of Accounts for recording transactions into the bookkeeping system. (Employees who code invoices or other transactions and indicate the account to which those transactions are to be recorded need a copy of your Chart of Accounts as well, even if they aren't involved in actual bookkeeping.)

The Chart of Accounts usually includes at least three columns:

- **Account:** Lists the account names.
- **Type:** Lists the type of account – Asset, Liability, Capital, Income, Cost of Goods Sold or Expense.
- **Description:** Contains a description of the type of transaction that is to be recorded in the account.

Many businesses also assign numbers to the accounts, to be used for coding charges. If your company uses a computerised system, the computer automatically assigns the account number. For example, Sage 50 Accounts provides you with a standard Chart of Accounts that you can adapt to suit your business. Sage also allows you to completely customise your Chart of Accounts to codes that suit your business; however, most businesses find that the standard Chart of Accounts is sufficient. A typical numbering system is as follows:

- Asset accounts: 0010 to 1999
- Liability accounts: 2000 to 2999
- Capital accounts: 3000 to 3999
- Sales and cost of goods sold accounts: 4000 to 6999
- Expense accounts: 7000 to 9999

This numbering system matches the one used by some computerised accounting systems, so you can easily make the transition if you decide to automate your books using a computerised accounting system in the future.

One major advantage of a computerised accounting system is the number of different Charts of Accounts that have been developed based on the type of business you plan to run. When you get your computerised system, whichever accounting software you decide to use, you can review the list of chart options included with that software for the type of business you run, delete any accounts you don't want and add any new accounts that fit your business plan.

If you're setting up your Chart of Accounts manually, be sure to leave a lot of room between accounts to add new accounts. For example, number your Trade Debtors account 1100 and then start your bank accounts from 1200. If you've a number of bank accounts, you can number them 1210, 1220, 1230 and so on. That leaves you plenty of room to add new bank accounts as well as petty cash. The same applies to your revenue accounts: you need to allow plenty of room in your codes for your business to grow. For example, 4000 may be Retail Sales from your shop, but you may start to develop an online presence and need a code to track online sales, perhaps 4050. You can add further codes for foreign online sales as opposed to UK online sales. Don't be too rigid in your choice of codes – leave as large a gap as possible between codes to give you maximum flexibility.

Figure 3-1 is a sample Chart of Accounts developed using Sage 50 Accounts, the accounts package we use throughout this book. This sample chart highlights the standard overhead accounts that Sage has already set up for you.

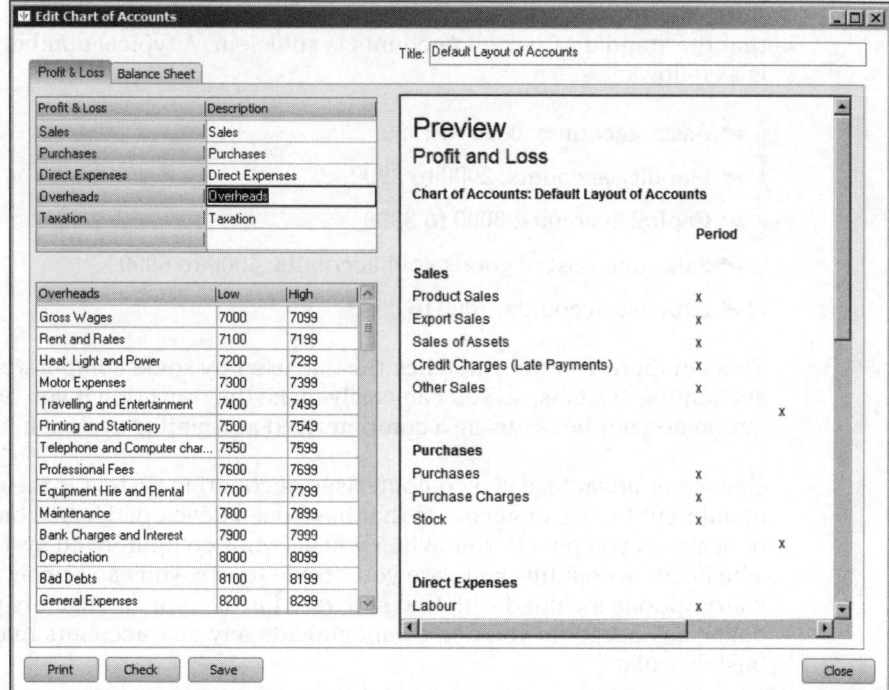

**Figure 3-1:** The top portion of a sample Chart of Accounts showing overheads.

# *Have a Go*

1. Describe three types of current assets and state in which financial statement you'd find them.

2. In which financial statement would you expect to see expenses?

   List 5 different types of expenses.

3. In which financial statement would you find current liabilities, and describe some of the entries you might find there.

4. In which financial statement would you expect to find capital?

   As well as capital introduced by the owner, what else would you expect to see there?

5. Think about the current assets you need to track for your business, and write down the accounts in this section.

6. Think about the Fixed Asset accounts you need to track for your business, and write down the accounts for those assets in this section.

7. Think about the Current Liabilities accounts you need to track for your business, and write down the accounts for those liabilities in this section.

8. Think about the Long-term Liabilities accounts you need to track for your business, and write down the accounts for those liabilities in this section.

9. Think about the Capital accounts you need to track for your business, and write down the accounts you need in this section.

10. Think about the Revenue accounts you need to track for your business, and write down those accounts in this section.

11. Think about the Cost of Goods Sold accounts you need to track for your business, and write down those accounts in this section.

12. Think about the Expense accounts you need to track for your business, and write down those accounts in this section.

# Answering the Have a Go Questions

1. **You can find current assets in the Balance Sheet.**

   The usual types of current assets are:

   - Stock
   - Debtors
   - Cash at bank
   - Cash in hand
   - Prepayments

   See the previous section 'Current Assets' for descriptions.

2. **You can find expenses in the Profit and Loss statement.**

   Typical expenses can be:

   - Wages
   - Office stationery
   - Telephone costs
   - Rent & Rates
   - Heat, light & power
   - Fuel expenses

   Find more examples in 'Acknowledging the other costs'.

3. **You can find current liabilities in the Balance Sheet.**

   Typical items include:

   - Trade Creditors (suppliers you owe money to)
   - Accrued expenses (costs you've incurred but you may not have an invoice for)
   - HMRC payments due such as PAYE/NI and VAT
   - Overdrafts

   We go into more detail in the section 'Laying out your Liabilities'.

4. **You find capital in the Balance Sheet.**

   As well as capital introduced, you also find drawings (cash taken out of the business for personal use) and dividends, as well as *retained profits* (profits made from previous periods, but retained in the business). If your business is structured as a company, then you also have ordinary share capital, which reflects each individual's share of the company.

5-12. **The remaining exercises in this chapter don't have right or wrong answers.**

   You need to set up your Chart of Accounts with accounts that match how your business operates.

# Chapter 4

# Looking at Ledgers

. . . . . . . . . . . . . . . . . . . . . . . . . . . . . . . . . . . . . . . . . . .

*In This Chapter*

▶ Understanding the value of the Nominal Ledger

▶ Developing ledger entries

▶ Posting entries to the ledger accounts

▶ Adjusting ledger entries

. . . . . . . . . . . . . . . . . . . . . . . . . . . . . . . . . . . . . . . . . . .

In this chapter, we discuss the accounting ledgers. You meet the Sales Ledger, Purchase Ledger and Cashbook and discover how they interact with the Nominal Ledger. We tell you how to develop entries for the ledger and also how to enter (or post) them from the original sources. In addition, we explain how you can change already posted information or correct entries in the Nominal Ledger.

The most common ledgers include:

✔ **Sales Ledger:** This tracks day to day sales, and contains the accounts of debtors (customers).

✔ **Purchases Ledger:** This tracks day to day purchases, and contains the accounts of creditors (suppliers).

✔ **Nominal Ledger:** Sometimes called the General Ledger, this ledger is used for all the remaining accounts, such as income and expense accounts as well as including the Purchase Ledger account balance and the Sales Ledger account balance. There are also accounts for items such as stock, VAT, loans and so on. The Nominal Ledger basically contains all the transactions that a business has ever made.

✔ **Cashbook:** This tracks the daily use of cash.

If you're using a computerised accounting system, your ledgers are integrated (see Figure 4-1). This means that as you enter transactions into, say, your Sales Ledger, the Nominal Ledger is automatically updated. The same applies to entries that are made via your Cashbook or Purchase Ledger.

---

## Keeping watch: The eyes and ears of a business

The Nominal Ledger serves as the figurative eyes and ears of bookkeepers and accountants who want to know what financial transactions have taken place historically in a business. By reading the Nominal Ledger – not exactly interesting reading unless you love numbers – you can see, account by account, every transaction that has taken place in the business.

The Nominal Ledger is the master summary of your business. You can find all the transactions

that ever occurred in the history of the business in the Nominal Ledger account. In just one place you can find transactions that impact Cash, Stock, Trade Debtors (Accounts Receivable), Trade Creditors (Accounts Payable) and any other account included in your business's Chart of Accounts. (See Chapter 3 for more information about setting up the Chart of Accounts and the kinds of transactions you can find in each account.)

---

Your computerised system follows the principles of double-entry bookkeeping; so, for every debit, you have a corresponding credit.

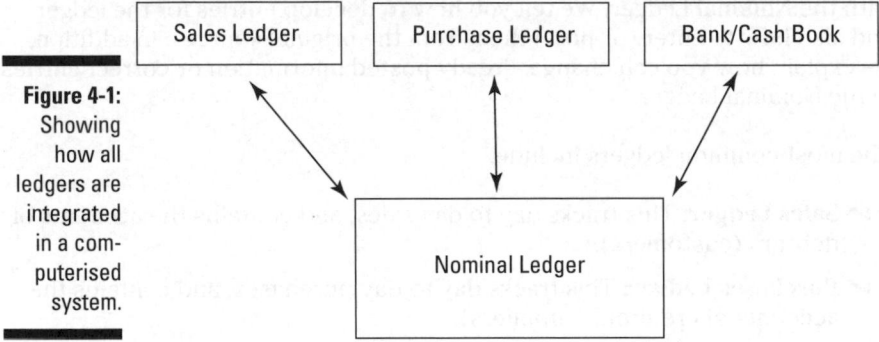

**Figure 4-1:**
Showing how all ledgers are integrated in a computerised system.

# *Developing Entries for the Ledger*

In the next section, we take you through the process of entering transactions on each of the ledgers, and we look at the bookkeeping entries for all transactions. You can practise your double-entry bookkeeping at the end of this chapter, in the 'Have a Go' section. Because most people now use computerised accounting systems, we demonstrate the types of reports and documents that you can run off to prove your transactions. We use Sage 50 to demonstrate these reports.

You enter your transactions using source documents or other data. Source documents tend to be the following:

✔ Sales invoices (unless automatically generated from your accounts program)

✔ Sales credit notes

✔ Purchase invoices from your suppliers

✔ Purchase credit notes

✔ Cheque payments

✔ Cash receipts (from your paying-in book)

✔ Remittance advice slips received from customers, which usually accompany the cheque or BACs receipt confirmation

✔ Bank statements (to pick up other bank payments and receipts)

# Posting Sales Invoices

Have a look at the bookkeeping that occurs when you post some sales invoices. Assume that the invoices aren't paid straight away; they're credit sales.

Using the double-entry bookkeeping rules from Chapter 2, you know the following:

***If you want to record income, you credit the Income account.***

***If you want to increase an asset, you debit the Asset account.***

So, if you raise an invoice for £200 (ignoring VAT for the moment), then the following bookkeeping takes place:

|         | *Debit* | *Credit* |
|---------|---------|----------|
| Debtors | £200    |          |
| Sales   |         | £200     |

Every time you post a sales invoice, this same double entry takes place.

A computerised accounting system does the double entry for you, but you still need to understand the bookkeeping rules, so that you can create journals if corrections are necessary at any point in the future. See the section 'Adjusting for Nominal Ledger Errors', later in this chapter.

In Figure 4-2, we show you the Customer Invoices Daybook for Sweet Dreams (a fictitious company). This daybook simply provides a list of sales invoices that have been entered in Sage. If you were still operating a manual system, the same information would be reflected in the Sales journal.

Make sure that you understand the bookkeeping here: you make the following double entry based on the information shown in the Customer Invoice Daybook as shown in Figure 4-2:

| Account | Debit | Credit |
|---------|-------|--------|
| Trade Debtors | £960 | |
| Sales | | £800 |
| VAT | | £160 |

| Date: | 07/02/2012 | | | | | **Sweet Dreams** | | | | Page: | 1 |
|---|---|---|---|---|---|---|---|---|---|---|---|
| Time: | 13:46:33 | | | | **Day Books: Customer Invoices (Detailed)** | | | | | | |

| Date From: | 01/06/2011 | | | | | Customer From: | |
|---|---|---|---|---|---|---|---|
| Date To: | 30/06/2011 | | | | | Customer To: | ZZZZZZZZ |

| Transaction From: | 1 | N/C From: | |
|---|---|---|---|
| Transaction To: | 99,999,999 | N/C To: | 99999999 |

| Dept From: | 0 |
|---|---|
| Dept To: | 999 |

| Tran No. | Type | Date | A/C Ref | N/C | Inv Ref | Dept. | Details | Net Amount | Tax Amount | T/C | Gross Amount | V | B |
|---|---|---|---|---|---|---|---|---|---|---|---|---|---|
| 1 | SI | 01/06/2011 | SMITHS | 4000 | 243 | 0 | Sweet sales | 200.00 | 40.00 | T1 | 240.00 | N | - |
| 2 | SI | 01/06/2011 | CHARLIES | 4000 | 244 | 0 | Machine refilled | 300.00 | 60.00 | T1 | 360.00 | N | - |
| 3 | SI | 03/06/2011 | PERRYP | 4000 | 245 | 0 | Tuck shop stock | 100.00 | 20.00 | T1 | 120.00 | N | - |
| 4 | SI | 05/06/2011 | JONESJ | 4000 | 246 | 0 | Machine refilled | 200.00 | 40.00 | T1 | 240.00 | N | - |
| | | | | | | | **Totals:** | 800.00 | 160.00 | | 960.00 | | |

| | Page 1 of 1 | 100% |
|---|---|---|

**Figure 4-2:**
Showing the Customer Invoices Daybook.

Note that this entry is balanced. You increase the Trade Debtors account to show that customers owe the business money because they bought items on credit. You increase the Sales account to show that even though no cash changed hands, the business in Figure 4-2 took in revenue. You collect cash when the customers pay their bills.

You give each transaction a reference to its original source point. For example, the first invoice listed for Smith's account has the invoice reference 243. If you went to the sales invoice file and found invoice no. 243, you'd have the original source of the transaction in your hands. This is very useful when it comes to customer queries, as you can immediately locate the invoice and check the details.

As an aside, Sage 50 also gives each transaction a unique transaction number. It's the first number in the first column of each report. If you need to make a correction to a transaction, this number is the way you'd identify that specific transaction and be able to amend it.

# Posting Purchase Invoices

Your business needs to account for the invoices received from its suppliers. Often, you won't pay these invoices straight away, so you post them into the Creditors Ledger (sometimes known as the Suppliers Ledger).

Using the double-entry rules as discussed in Chapter 2, you then get the following double entry:

***To increase a liability, you credit the Liabilities account.***

***If you want to increase an asset, you debit the Asset account.***

Because you're recording a liability when you post invoices that you owe money for, you credit the Creditors Ledger. Hence, you must make the opposite debit entry to the Nominal account to which the invoice has been coded. For example, Materials Purchased.

Have a look at some purchase invoices that have been entered for Sweet Dreams. See Figure 4-3.

Date: 14/02/2012 **Sweet Dreams** Page: 1
Time: 14:00:03

**Day Books: Supplier Invoices (Detailed)**

Date From: 01/06/2011
Date To: 30/06/2011
Supplier From:
Supplier To: ZZZZZZZZ

Transaction From: 1
Transaction To: 99,999,999
N/C From:
N/C To: 99999999

Dept From: 0
Dept To: 999

| Tran No. | Type | Date | A/C Ref | N/C | Inv Ref | Dept | Details | Net Amount | Tax Amount | T/C | Gross Amount | V | B |
|---|---|---|---|---|---|---|---|---|---|---|---|---|---|
| 14 | PI | 01/06/2011 | HENRYS | 5000 | 1575 | 0 | Sweets | 625.00 | 125.00 | T1 | 750.00 | N | - |
| 15 | PI | 05/06/2011 | BARRYS | 5000 | 1285 | 0 | Boxes | 83.33 | 16.67 | T1 | 100.00 | N | - |
| 16 | PI | 08/06/2011 | HELENS | 5000 | 1745 | 0 | Paper | 62.50 | 12.50 | T1 | 75.00 | N | - |
| | | | | | | | Totals | 770.83 | 154.17 | | 925.00 | | |

**Figure 4-3:** Supplier Invoices Daybook for Sweet Dreams.

In Figure 4-3 Sweet Dreams have posted three purchase invoices for the gross value of £925.

Because this report is a Sage daybook report, you can see the nominal code that Sweet Dreams's bookkeeper, Kate, used when she entered the invoices. In this case, 5000 is the nominal code used for all invoices, which happens to be the nominal code for the Materials Purchased account.

So, the double entry that Kate made for these combined transactions is as follows:

| *Account* | *Debit* | *Credit* |
|---|---|---|
| Materials Purchased | £770.83 | |
| VAT | £154.17 | |
| Creditors Ledger | | £925.00 |

Like the entry for the Sales account, this entry is balanced. The Trade Creditors account is increased to show that money is due to suppliers, and the Materials Purchased account is also increased to show that more supplies were purchased.

Note: An invoice reference number is shown on the daybook report. This relates to the sequential invoice number given to each purchase invoice. For example, the invoice posted for Henry's has a reference of 1575. If you were to select the purchase invoice file and locate invoice number 1575, you'd find the original purchase invoice for Henry's. This is especially important in the event of a supplier query. It provides an easy method of locating the exact invoice.

# Entering Items into the Nominal Ledger

Many transactions don't impact the Sales Ledger or the Purchase Ledger, but they still have to be accounted for. The Nominal Ledger, as stated before, is the master ledger and is a place where all transactions can be found.

Figure 4-4 shows an example of a Nominal Ledger Daybook from Sage. You can see two separate transactions noted here, each with a debit entry and a credit entry.

Neither of these transactions has impacted the Purchase Ledger or the Sales Ledger, which is why they show up here.

The first two lines show a transfer between two different bank accounts. Basically, a payment has been made from account 1200, which happens to be the Current account, and the payment has been made to 1240, which is a Credit Card account.

| Date: | 08/02/2012 | | Sweet Dreams | | | | | | Page: | 1 | |
|---|---|---|---|---|---|---|---|---|---|---|---|
| Time: | 15:37:57 | | Day Books: Nominal Ledger | | | | | | | | |
| Date From: | | 01/06/2011 | | | | | | N/C From: | | | |
| Date To: | | 30/06/2011 | | | | | | N/C To: | | 99999999 | |
| Transaction From: | | 1 | | | | | | Dept From: | | 0 | |
| Transaction To: | | 99,999,999 | | | | | | Dept To: | | 999 | |
| No | Type | N/C | Date | Ref | Ex.Ref | Details | Dept | T/C | Debit | Credit | V B |
| 11 | JC | 1200 | 10/06/2011 | CC | | Credit Card Payment to | 0 | T9 | | 150.00 | - N |
| 12 | JD | 1240 | 10/06/2011 | CC | | Credit Card Payment to | 0 | T9 | 150.00 | | - N |
| 19 | JD | 0050 | 08/06/2011 | Vehicles | | Van purchased | 0 | T9 | 10,000.00 | | - - |
| 20 | JC | 3010 | 08/06/2011 | Vehicles | | Capital Introduced | 0 | T9 | | 10,000.00 | - - |
| | | | | | | | | Totals: | 10,150.00 | 10,150.00 | |

**Figure 4-4:**
Showing the Nominal Daybook report for Sweet Dreams

The second two entries show a journal that was carried out by Kate, the bookkeeper for Sweet Dreams. They show a van, which was purchased for the business, using capital introduced by the owner of the company.

# Cashbook Transactions

Everyone likes to be paid, and that includes suppliers. You use the Cashbook to post all transactions that relate to payments or receipts to the business.

Sage uses separate daybooks for Customer Receipts and Other Income Received, as well as Supplier Payments and Other Payments Made.

This section shows you copies of all the relevant daybooks and the bookkeeping entries that are associated with each daybook.

## Bank payments

Businesses always make payments to people other than suppliers. For example, they might have salaries, loans, interest and other types of charges to pay. These payments are made from the Bank account or Cashbook, but impact the Nominal Ledger, as part of the double-entry process.

We demonstrate some bank payments that have been made by Sweet Dreams, using Figure 4-5. You'll notice that we've printed the Bank Payments Daybook report. If you'd made any payments using cash, you'd also have to print out the Cash Payments Daybook report.

| Date: | 10/02/2012 | | Sweet Dreams | | | | | | | | Page: | 1 | |
|---|---|---|---|---|---|---|---|---|---|---|---|---|---|
| Time: | 10:51:15 | | Day Books: Bank Payments (Detailed) | | | | | | | | | | |

| Date From: | 01/06/2011 | | | | | | | | | Bank From: | 1200 | |
|---|---|---|---|---|---|---|---|---|---|---|---|---|
| Date To: | 30/06/2011 | | | | | | | | | Bank To: | 1200 | |

| Transaction From: | 1 | | | | | | | | N/C From: | | |
|---|---|---|---|---|---|---|---|---|---|---|---|
| Transaction To: | 99,999,999 | | | | | | | | N/C To: | 99999999 | |

| Dept From: | 0 |
|---|---|
| Dept To: | 999 |

| Bank: | 1200 | | Currency: | Pound Sterling | | | | | | | | | | Bank Rec. |
|---|---|---|---|---|---|---|---|---|---|---|---|---|---|---|
| No | Type | N/C | Date | Ref | Details | Dept | Net £ | Tax | £ T/C | Gross £ | V | B | Date |
| 8 | BP | 7100 | 01/06/2011 | 1065 | Rent | 0 | 800.00 | 0.00 | T9 | 800.00 - | N | | |
| 10 | BP | 7003 | 04/06/2011 | 1068 | Salaries | 0 | 350.00 | 0.00 | T9 | 350.00 - | N | | |
| | | | | | | Totals £ | 1,150.00 | 0.00 | | 1,150.00 | | | |

**Figure 4-5:**
Bank Payments Daybook report.

You can see that Sweet Dreams have paid rent and some salaries. These payments have been made from the Bank account. You can see from the report, that the Bank account nominal code used is 1200 (which is the default Bank account for Sage). You can also see that the nominal codes used for Rent and Salaries are 7100 and 7003 respectively.

The double-entry bookkeeping that has taken place is shown below:

| Nominal Code | Account | Debit | Credit |
| --- | --- | --- | --- |
| 7100 | Rent | £800 | |
| 7003 | Salaries | £350 | |
| 1200 | Bank | | £1,150 |

This Nominal Ledger summary balances out at £1,150 each for the debits and credits. The Bank account is decreased to show the cash outlay; the Rent and Salaries Expense accounts are increased to show the additional expenses.

Looking at the Bank Payments Daybook, you can also see a reference column. The numbers in the reference column refer to the cheque number used to make that payment. For example, cheque number 1065 was used to pay the rent.

Whether you use a computerised or a manual system, always use references to point towards the original source of the data. In this example, a cheque stub reference has been used.

## Supplier payments

When businesses pay their suppliers, unless they've paid cash immediately, the two accounts that are affected are the Supplier (Creditors) Ledger and the Bank account.

Figure 4-6 shows an example of the Supplier Payments Daybook for Sweet Dreams.

You can see from the daybook report that Sweet Dreams have paid two suppliers in June 2011. They've paid Helen's £250 and Henry's £500. Therefore, Sweet Dreams have taken a total of £750 out of the bank to pay suppliers. The double entry for these two transactions can be summarised as shown below:

| Nominal Code | Account | Debit | Credit |
| --- | --- | --- | --- |
| 2100 | Creditors | £750 | |
| 1200 | Bank | | £750 |

You can see that the bank has been credited, because you're reducing an asset (that is, cash), and the Creditors Account has been debited, because you're reducing a liability. Think back to your double-entry rules if you're not sure.

| | | | | | | | | | | | | | |
|---|---|---|---|---|---|---|---|---|---|---|---|---|---|

Date: 10/02/2012      **Sweet Dreams**      Page: 1
Time: 11:06:24      **Day Books: Supplier Payments (Detailed)**

| Date From: | 01/06/2011 | | | | | | Bank From: | 1200 |
| Date To: | 30/06/2011 | | | | | | Bank To: | 1200 |

| Transaction From: | 1 | | | | | | Supplier From: | |
| Transaction To: | 99,999,999 | | | | | | Supplier To: | ZZZZZZZZ |

| Bank | 1200 | | Currency | Pound Sterling | | | | | | | | | |
|---|---|---|---|---|---|---|---|---|---|---|---|---|---|
| No | Type | A/C | | Date | Ref | Details | Net £ | Tax | £ T/C | Gross | £ V | B | Bank Rec. Date |
| 9 | PP | HELENS | | 03/06/2011 | 1067 | Purchase Payment | 250.00 | | 0.00 T9 | 250.00 | - | N | |
| | | | - | 03/06/2011 | 1493 | £ 250.00 (£ 250.00) to PI 6 | | | | | | | |
| 13 | PP | HENRYS | | 03/06/2011 | 1066 | Purchase Payment | 500.00 | | 0.00 T9 | 500.00 | - | N | |
| | | | - | 03/06/2011 | 1462 | £ 500.00 (£ 500.00) to PI 5 | | | | | | | |
| | | | | | | Totals £ | 750.00 | | 0.00 | 750.00 | | | |

**Figure 4-6:**
Supplier
Payment
Daybook.

# Bank receipts

A business receives money from a variety of sources, not just from its customers. For example, in a new business, the owners of the business may decide to introduce capital into the business to help pay the bills for the first few months until sales pick up. Perhaps they receive start up grants, or receive interest from savings accounts. Figure 4-7 shows the daybook report for Bank Received for Sweet Dreams.

Sweet Dreams

Day Books: Bank Receipts (Detailed)

Date: 10/02/2012
Time: 11:28:43
Page: 1

Date From: 01/06/2011
DateTo: 30/06/2011
Bank From: 1200
Bank To: 1200

Transaction From: 1
Transaction To: 99,999,999
N/C From:
N/C To: 99999999

Dept From: 0
Dept To: 999

Bank: 1200 Currency: Pound Sterling

| No | Type | N/C | Date | Ref | Details | Dept | Net £ | Tax £ | T/C | Gross £ | V | B | Bank Rec. Date |
|---|---|---|---|---|---|---|---|---|---|---|---|---|---|
| 21 | BR | 4000 | 01/06/2011 | Cash Sales | Cash Sales | 0 | 300.00 | 60.00 | T1 | 360.00 | N | N | |
| 22 | BR | 4000 | 02/06/2011 | Cash Sales | Cash Sales | 0 | 250.00 | 50.00 | T1 | 300.00 | N | N | |
| 23 | BR | 4000 | 03/06/2011 | Cash Sales | Cash Sales | 0 | 150.00 | 30.00 | T1 | 180.00 | N | N | |
| 24 | BR | 4000 | 05/06/2011 | Cash Sales | Cash Sales | 0 | 200.00 | 40.00 | T1 | 240.00 | N | N | |
| 28 | BR | 3010 | 04/06/2011 | HG Capital | HG Capital | 0 | 1,500.00 | 0.00 | T9 | 1,500.00 | - | N | |
| | | | | | | Totals £ | 2,400.00 | 180.00 | | 2,580.00 | | | |

**Figure 4-7:** Bank Receipt Daybook Report for Sweet Dreams.

You may have noticed that some cash sales are listed here. This is money taken at the tills and paid directly into the bank account for Sweet Dreams. The owner has also introduced £1,500 of capital.

The transactions that are posted to the Nominal Ledger can be summarised as follows:

| *Nominal Code* | *Account* | *Debit* | *Credit* |
|---|---|---|---|
| 1200 | Bank | £2580 | |
| 4000 | Sales | | £900 |
| 3050 | Capital Introduced | | £1500 |
| 2201 | VAT | | £180 |

Both sides total £2,580, so the books are in balance.

Once again, you can apply double-entry rules. You debit the bank, because an asset (the bank) is being increased, due to the money being paid in. You credit the Sales account as it's an Income account, and you also credit the Capital Introduced account, as the amount is a liability for the business. The reason is that the business technically owes the owner this money. You also credit VAT, because VAT is a liability and is money owed to HM Revenue & Customs.

## Customer receipts

Obviously, you hope to be paid quite often! If you're doing a good job as a bookkeeper, you know how much money is owed to the business at any one time. You also know who's behind with their payments. We discuss how you can find out who owes you money in Chapter 7.

Receipts from customers can come in several formats. They're cash received, cheques received or a BACs payment received directly into your Bank account. Either way, the money has to be accounted for.

Figure 4-8 shows an example of a Customer Receipts Daybook for Sweet Dreams.

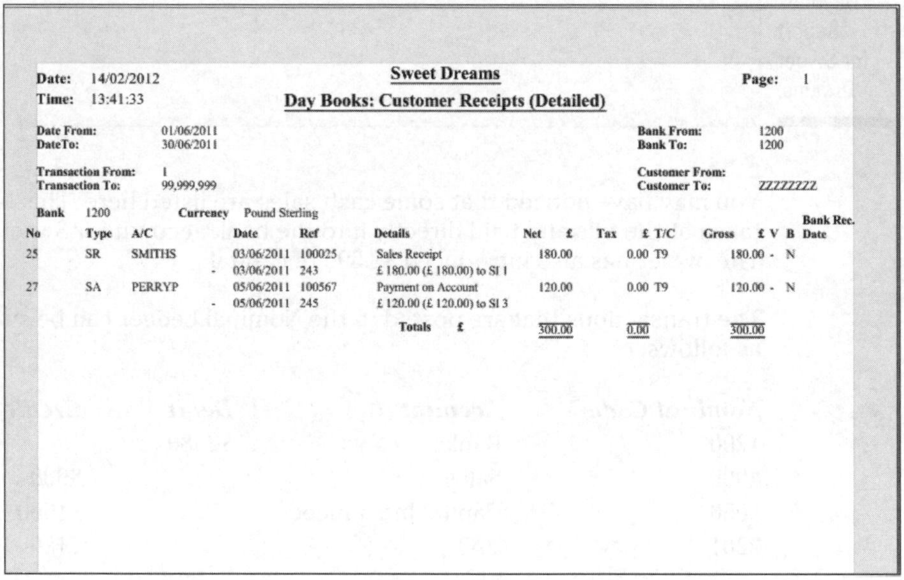
Date: 14/02/2012 | Sweet Dreams | Page: 1
Time: 13:41:33 | Day Books: Customer Receipts (Detailed)

Date From: 01/06/2011 | Bank From: 1200
DateTo: 30/06/2011 | Bank To: 1200

Transaction From: 1 | Customer From:
Transaction To: 99,999,999 | Customer To: ZZZZZZZZ

Bank 1200 Currency Pound Sterling

| No | Type | A/C | | Date | Ref | Details | Net £ | Tax £ | T/C | Gross £ | V | B | Bank Rec. Date |
|---|---|---|---|---|---|---|---|---|---|---|---|---|---|
| 25 | SR | SMITHS | | 03/06/2011 | 100025 | Sales Receipt | 180.00 | 0.00 | T9 | 180.00 | - | N | |
| | | | - | 03/06/2011 | 243 | £ 180.00 (£ 180.00) to SI 1 | | | | | | | |
| 27 | SA | PERRYP | | 05/06/2011 | 100567 | Payment on Account | 120.00 | 0.00 | T9 | 120.00 | - | N | |
| | | | - | 05/06/2011 | 245 | £ 120.00 (£ 120.00) to SI 3 | | | | | | | |
| | | | | | | Totals £ | 300.00 | 0.00 | | 300.00 | | | |

**Figure 4-8:** Customer Receipts Daybook for Sweet Dreams.

You can see that Sweet Dreams has a couple of cheques received from customers. S Smith paid £180 and has the reference 100025 against the sales receipt. This refers to the paying-in slip number used when paying the cheque into the bank. This is especially useful when you come to reconcile your bank account later in the accounting process. Underneath, the reference 243 is the invoice number that's being paid.

You can also see that P Perry sent a cheque for £120. The paying-in slip reference was 100567 and the invoice being paid was 245.

This transaction can be summarised as follows:

| Nominal Code | Account | Debit | Credit |
|---|---|---|---|
| 1200 | Bank account | £300 | |
| 1100 | Debtors Ledger | | £300 |

Following your double-entry rules, you can see that the Bank account has been debited, because you're increasing an asset, namely the Bank account balance. The Debtors Ledger has been credited, as you're also reducing an asset, namely Debtors. The books still balance, as an equal and opposite entry has been made in the accounts.

# Introducing Control Accounts

So far we've discussed how you enter transactions into your bookkeeping system, and we've demonstrated the double-entry bookkeeping associated with each of the transactions.

At the end of the month, check that the Sales Ledger, the Purchase Ledger and the Nominal Ledger are in agreement. The easiest way to do this check is to perform Control Account Reconciliations.

'What on earth are these?' we hear you say!

Well, don't panic, they're quite straightforward, particularly in a computerised accounting system, where the double entry is all done for you!

In performing a Control account reconciliation, all you're doing is checking that the Nominal Ledger agrees with both the Debtors (Customers) and Creditors (Suppliers) Ledgers.

## Debtors Control account

This account totals all the Sales Invoices, Sales Credit Notes and Customer receipts for the month and is held in the Nominal Ledger.

The Debtors Control account shows you how much is owing to your business by your customers. It can be reconciled against the Aged Debtors report for the same period to ensure accuracy of your information. This would be known as a *Debtors Control account reconciliation*.

Figure 4-9 shows you an example of Sweet Dreams Debtors Control account for the month of June 2011.

You can access the account via the Nominal Ledger and print off a nominal activity report for the month of June. See Figure 4-9.

| Date: | 10/02/2012 | | | Sweet Dreams | | | | Page: | 1 | |
|-------|-----------|---|---|--------------|---|---|---|-------|---|---|
| Time: | 12:13:34 | | | Nominal Activity | | | | | | |

| Date From: | 01/06/2011 | | | | | | N/C From: | 1100 |
|------------|-----------|---|---|---|---|---|-----------|------|
| Date To: | 30/06/2011 | | | | | | N/C To: | 1100 |

| Transaction From: | 1 |
|-------------------|---|
| Transaction To: | 99,999,999 |

| N/C: | 1100 | | Name: | Debtors Control Account | | | | | Account Balance: | | 500.00 DR |
|------|------|---|-------|--------------------------|---|---|---|---|------------------|---|-----------|

| No | Type | Date | Account | Ref | Details | Dept | T/C | Value | Debit | Credit | V | B |
|----|------|------|---------|-----|---------|------|-----|-------|-------|--------|---|---|
| 1 | SI | 01/06/2011 | SMITHS | 243 | Sweet sales | 0 | T1 | 240.00 | 240.00 | | N | - |
| 2 | SI | 01/06/2011 | CHARLIE | 244 | Machine refilled | 0 | T1 | 360.00 | 360.00 | | N | - |
| 3 | SI | 03/06/2011 | PERRYP | 245 | Tuck shop stock | 0 | T1 | 120.00 | 120.00 | | N | - |
| 4 | SI | 05/06/2011 | JONESJ | 246 | Machine refilled | 0 | T1 | 240.00 | 240.00 | | N | - |
| 17 | SC | 03/06/2011 | SMITHS | 124 | Credit for faulty goods | 0 | T1 | 60.00 | | 60.00 | N | - |
| 25 | SR | 03/06/2011 | SMITHS | | Sales Receipt | 0 | T9 | 180.00 | | 180.00 | - | N |
| 26 | SA | 05/06/2011 | JONESJ | | Payment on Account | 0 | T9 | 100.00 | | 100.00 | - | N |
| 27 | SA | 05/06/2011 | PERRYP | 567 | Payment on Account | 0 | T9 | 120.00 | | 120.00 | - | N |
| | | | | | | | Totals: | | 960.00 | 460.00 | | |
| | | | | | | | History Balance: | | 500.00 | | | |

**Figure 4-9:**
Debtors
Control
account
for Sweet
Dreams

You can see that the account balance is £500 – this sum is the total amount owed by debtors at 30 June 2011. The Debtors Control account details all the transactions that have taken place in the month of June. You can see that Kate, the Sweet Dreams bookkeeper, has raised sales invoices, created a credit note and made a couple of payments on account (which means that she hasn't allocated the cash amount directly against an invoice). There's also a sales receipt of £180, which is the sales receipt for S. Smith that we identified in the Customer Receipts Daybook earlier in this chapter.

If you want to verify the amount in the Sales Ledger, you can run an Aged Debtor report which shows all outstanding invoices for the month (see Figure 4-10). We've run the report for Sweet Dreams for June 2011 (the same period as the nominal activity report shown above).

Here, you can see that the total amount outstanding at 30 June 2011 was £500, as agreed with the Debtors Control account balance of the same period.

This proves that the Nominal Ledger and the Sales Ledger are in agreement. This is an important reconciliation you need to do at the end of each month, and should always form part of your bookkeeping routine.

**Figure 4-10:** An Aged Debtor report for Sweet Dreams for June 2011.

# Creditors Control account

Similarly, the Creditors Control account shows you how much you owe your suppliers. This can be reconciled against the Aged Creditors report, to verify the accuracy of your information.

Figure 4-11 shows an example of Sweet Dreams's Creditors Control account for the month of June 2011. You can see that the balance is £725, made up of a number of purchase invoices, a credit note and a couple of payments.

You can check that the information contained in the Nominal Ledger (Creditors Control account) is accurate by running an Aged Creditors report from the Creditors Ledger.

See Figure 4-12 for an example of an Aged Creditors report for Sweet Dreams, for the month of June 2011.

**Figure 4-11:** Creditors Control account for Sweet Dreams for June 2011

| Date: | 13/02/2012 | | | | | Sweet Dreams | | | | Page: | 1 |
| Time: | 11:40:33 | | | | | Nominal Activity | | | | | |

| Date From: | 01/06/2011 | | | N/C From: | 2100 |
| Date To: | 30/06/2011 | | | N/C To: | 2100 |

| Transaction From: | 1 |
| Transaction To: | 99,999,999 |

N/C: 2100   Name: Creditors Control Account   Account Balance: 725.00 CR

| No | Type | Date | Account | Ref | Details | Dept | T/C | Value | Debit | Credit | V | B |
|----|------|------|---------|-----|---------|------|-----|-------|-------|--------|---|---|
| 9 | PP | 03/06/2011 | HELENS | 1067 | Purchase Payment | 0 | T9 | 250.00 | 250.00 | - | | N |
| 13 | PP | 03/06/2011 | HENRYS | 1066 | Purchase Payment | 0 | T9 | 500.00 | 500.00 | - | | N |
| 14 | PI | 01/06/2011 | HENRYS | 1575 | Sweets | 0 | T1 | 750.00 | | 750.00 | N | - |
| 15 | PI | 05/06/2011 | BARRYS | 1285 | Boxes | 0 | T1 | 100.00 | | 100.00 | N | - |
| 16 | PI | 08/06/2011 | HELENS | 1745 | Paper | 0 | T1 | 75.00 | | 75.00 | N | - |
| 18 | PC | 05/06/2011 | HENRYS | 346 | Returning goods | 0 | T1 | 200.00 | 200.00 | | N | - |

Totals: 950.00 925.00
History Balance: 25.00

**Figure 4-12:** Aged Creditor Report for Sweet Dreams for June 2011.

| Date: | 13/02/2012 | | | | Sweet Dreams | | | | | Page: | 1 |
| Time: | 11:38:09 | | | | Aged Creditors Analysis (Detailed) | | | | | | |

| Date From: | 01/06/2011 | | | Supplier From: | |
| Date To: | 30/06/2011 | | | Supplier To: | ZZZZZZZZ |

| Include future transactions: | No |
| Exclude later payments: | No |

** NOTE: All report values are shown in Base Currency, unless otherwise indicated **

A/C: BARRYS   Name: Barry's Packaging   Contact:   Tel:

| No: | Type | Date | Ref | Details | Balance | Future | Current | Period 1 | Period 2 | Period 3 | Older |
|-----|------|------|-----|---------|---------|--------|---------|----------|----------|----------|-------|
| 15 | PI | 05/06/2011 | 1285 | Boxes | 100.00 | 0.00 | 100.00 | 0.00 | 0.00 | 0.00 | 0.00 |
| | | | | Totals: | 100.00 | 0.00 | 100.00 | 0.00 | 0.00 | 0.00 | 0.00 |

Turnover: 83.33
Credit Limit £ 0.00

A/C: HELENS   Name: Helens   Contact:   Tel:

| No: | Type | Date | Ref | Details | Balance | Future | Current | Period 1 | Period 2 | Period 3 | Older |
|-----|------|------|-----|---------|---------|--------|---------|----------|----------|----------|-------|
| 16 | PI | 08/06/2011 | 1745 | Paper | 75.00 | 0.00 | 75.00 | 0.00 | 0.00 | 0.00 | 0.00 |
| | | | | Totals: | 75.00 | 0.00 | 75.00 | 0.00 | 0.00 | 0.00 | 0.00 |

Turnover: 270.83
Credit Limit £ 0.00

A/C: HENRYS   Name: Henrys   Contact:   Tel:

| No: | Type | Date | Ref | Details | Balance | Future | Current | Period 1 | Period 2 | Period 3 | Older |
|-----|------|------|-----|---------|---------|--------|---------|----------|----------|----------|-------|
| 14 | PI | 01/06/2011 | 1575 | Sweets | 750.00 | 0.00 | 750.00 | 0.00 | 0.00 | 0.00 | 0.00 |
| 18 | PC | 05/06/2011 | 346 | Returning goods | -200.00 | 0.00 | -200.00 | 0.00 | 0.00 | 0.00 | 0.00 |
| | | | | Totals: | 550.00 | 0.00 | 550.00 | 0.00 | 0.00 | 0.00 | 0.00 |

Turnover: 875.00
Credit Limit £ 0.00

Grand Totals: 725.00 0.00 725.00 0.00 0.00 0.00 0.00

You can see that the balance on the Aged Creditors report is also £725, so the two reports reconcile.

In performing both of the above reconciliations, you're checking that the Nominal Ledger agrees with both the Debtors (customers) and Creditors (suppliers) Ledgers.

# Understanding How the Ledgers Impact the Accounts

The three accounts – Cash, Trade Debtors and Trade Creditors – are part of the Balance Sheet, which we explain fully in Chapter 14. Asset accounts on the Balance Sheet usually carry debit balances because they reflect assets (in this case, cash) that the business owns. Cash and Trade Debtors are Asset accounts. Liability and Capital accounts usually carry credit balances because Liability accounts show claims made by creditors (in other words, money the business owes to financial institutions, suppliers or others), and Capital accounts show claims made by owners (in other words, how much money the owners have put into the business). Trade Creditors is a Liability account.

Here's how these accounts impact the balance of the business:

| _Assets_ | = | _Liabilities_ | + | _Capital_ |
|----------|---|---------------|---|-----------|
| Cash | | | | |
| Trade Debtors | | Trade Creditors | | |
| (Usually debit balance) | | (Usually credit balance) | | |

Here's how these accounts affect the balances of the business.

The Sales account (see Figure 4-13) isn't a balance sheet account. Instead, the Sales account is used to develop the Profit and Loss statement, which shows whether or not a business made a profit in the period being examined. A profit means that you earned more through sales than you paid out in costs or expenses. Expense and cost accounts usually carry a debit balance.

| | | | | | | | | | | | | |
|---|---|---|---|---|---|---|---|---|---|---|---|---|

Date: 07/03/2012 **Sweet Dreams** Page: 1
Time: 15:52:57 **Nominal Activity**

Date From: 01/06/2011 N/C From: 4000
Date To: 30/06/2011 N/C To: 4000

Transaction From: 1
Transaction To: 99,999,999

N/C: 4000 Name: Sweet Sales Account Balance: 1,650.00 CR

| No | Type | Date | Account | Ref | Details | Dept | T/C | Value | Debit | Credit | V | B |
|---|---|---|---|---|---|---|---|---|---|---|---|---|
| 1 | SI | 01/06/2011 | SMITHS | 243 | Sweet sales | 0 | T1 | 200.00 | | 200.00 | N | - |
| 2 | SI | 01/06/2011 | CHARLIE | 244 | Machine refilled | 0 | T1 | 300.00 | | 300.00 | N | - |
| 3 | SI | 03/06/2011 | PERRYP | 245 | Tuck shop stock | 0 | T1 | 100.00 | | 100.00 | N | - |
| 4 | SI | 05/06/2011 | JONESJ | 246 | Machine refilled | 0 | T1 | 200.00 | | 200.00 | N | - |
| 17 | SC | 03/06/2011 | SMITHS | 124 | Credit for faulty goods | 0 | T1 | 50.00 | 50.00 | | N | - |
| 21 | BR | 01/06/2011 | 1200 | Cash Sales | Cash Sales | 0 | T1 | 300.00 | | 300.00 | N | R |
| 22 | BR | 02/06/2011 | 1200 | Cash Sales | Cash Sales | 0 | T1 | 250.00 | | 250.00 | N | R |
| 23 | BR | 03/06/2011 | 1200 | Cash Sales | Cash Sales | 0 | T1 | 150.00 | | 150.00 | N | R |
| 24 | BR | 05/06/2011 | 1200 | Cash Sales | Cash Sales | 0 | T1 | 200.00 | | 200.00 | N | R |
| | | | | | | | Totals: | | 50.00 | 1,700.00 | | |
| | | | | | | | History Balance: | | | 1,650.00 | | |

**Figure 4-13:**
The Sales account for Sweet Dreams as shown in the Nominal Ledger.

(For the low-down on Profit and Loss statements, see Chapter 13.) Credits and debits are pretty straightforward in the Sales account: credits increase the account and debits decrease it. Fortunately, the Sales account usually carries a credit balance, which means that the business has income.

The Profit and Loss statement's bottom line figure shows whether or not the business made a profit. When the business makes a profit, the Sales account credits exceed Expense and Cost account debits. The profit is in the form of a credit, which gets added to the Capital account called Retained Earnings, which tracks how much of your business's profits are reinvested to grow the business. When the business loses money and the bottom line of the Profit and Loss statement shows that costs and expenses exceeded sales, the number is a debit. That debit is subtracted from the balance in Retained Earnings, to show the reduction to profits reinvested in the business.

When your business earns a profit at the end of the accounting period, the Retained Earnings account increases thanks to a credit from the Sales account. When you lose money, your Retained Earnings account decreases.

Because the Retained Earnings account is a Capital account and Capital accounts usually carry credit balances, Retained Earnings usually carries a credit balance as well.

# *Adjusting for Nominal Ledger Errors*

Your entries in the Nominal Ledger aren't cast in stone. If necessary, you can always change or correct an entry with an *adjusting entry*. Four of the most common reasons for Nominal Ledger adjustments are:

- ✔ **Depreciation:** A business shows the ageing of its assets through depreciation. Each year, you write off a portion of the original cost of an asset as an expense, and you note that change as an adjusting entry. Determining how much to write off is a complicated process that we explain in greater detail in Chapter 11.

- ✔ **Prepaid expenses:** You allocate expenses that are paid up front, such as a year's worth of insurance, by the month using an adjusting entry. You usually make this type of adjusting entry as part of the closing process at the end of an accounting period. We show you how to develop entries related to prepaid expenses in Chapter 10.

- ✔ **Adding an account:** You can add accounts by way of adjusting entries at any time during the year. If you're creating the new account to track transactions separately that at one time appeared in another account, you must move all transactions already in the books to the new account. You do this transfer with an adjusting entry to reflect the change.

- ✔ **Deleting an account:** Only delete an account at the end of an accounting period.

We talk more about adjusting entries and how you can use them in Chapter 10.

Sometimes, you may simply make a mistake and need to journal a balance from one account to another. For example, you may have coded paper that you bought into the postage account in error. In order to correct this mistake, you need to carry out the following correction:

|  | *Debit* | *Credit* |
|---|---|---|
| Office Stationery | £30 | |
| Postage | | £30 |

*To correct the postage account*

The double entry above has now corrected both accounts, but you need to have knowledge of the bookkeeping rules set out in Chapter 2 to feel confident to be able to carry out this nominal adjustment. In Sage 50, you would use a nominal journal to complete this transaction, as shown in Figure 4-14.

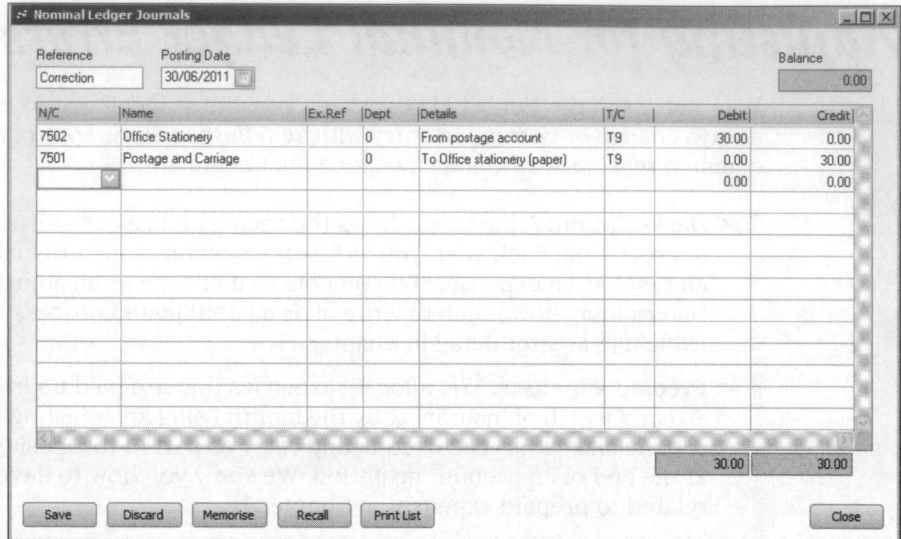

**Figure 4-14:**
Showing a
correcting
journal
entry.

# Have a Go

Grab a piece of paper and have a go at practising how to create your own
entries and how to post them to the Nominal Ledger.

1. **In which ledger would you record the purchase of new furniture for a
   business on credit?**

2. **In which ledger would you record the payment of invoices with cash?**

3. **In which ledger would you record the sale of goods to a customer on
   credit?**

4. **Using the information in Figure 4-15, how would you develop an entry
   for the Nominal Ledger to record transactions from the Sales Ledger
   for the month of July?**

**Sweet Dreams**

**Day Books: Customer Invoices (Detailed)**

Date: 07/03/2012
Time: 16:23:51
Page: 1

Date From: 01/07/2011
Date To: 31/07/2011
Customer From:
Customer To: ZZZZZZZZ

Transaction From: 1
Transaction To: 99,999,999
N/C From:
N/C To: 99999999

Dept From: 0
Dept To: 999

| Tran No. | Type | Date | A/C Ref | N/C | Inv Ref | Dept. | Details | Net Amount | Tax Amount | T/C | Gross Amount | V | B |
|---|---|---|---|---|---|---|---|---|---|---|---|---|---|
| 32 | SI | 01/07/2011 | SMITHS | 4000 | 247 | 0 | Boxes of sweets | 75.00 | 15.00 | T1 | 90.00 | N | - |
| 33 | SI | 07/07/2011 | JOHN | 4000 | 248 | 0 | Peppermint display | 250.00 | 50.00 | T1 | 300.00 | N | - |
| 34 | SI | 15/07/2011 | PAMS | 4000 | 249 | 0 | Lolly stands | 175.00 | 35.00 | T1 | 210.00 | N | - |
| 35 | SI | 20/07/2011 | HARRYS | 4000 | 250 | 0 | Misc sweets for hotel gift shop | 1,550.00 | 310.00 | T1 | 1,860.00 | N | - |
| 36 | SI | 25/07/2011 | LENS | 4000 | 251 | 0 | Desserts | 1,325.00 | 265.00 | T1 | 1,590.00 | N | - |
| | | | | | | | Totals: | 3,375.00 | 675.00 | | 4,050.00 | | |

**Figure 4-15:** Customer Invoice Daybook for Sweet Dreams for July 2011.

5. **Using the information from Figure 4-16, how would you develop an entry for the Nominal Ledger to record purchase invoices posted for the month of July?** Assume that the invoices aren't going to be paid straight away.

**Sweet Dreams**

**Day Books: Supplier Invoices (Detailed)**

Date: 07/03/2012
Time: 16:47:29
Page: 1

Date From: 01/07/2011
Date To: 31/07/2011
Supplier From:
Supplier To: ZZZZZZZZ

Transaction From: 1
Transaction To: 99,999,999
N/C From:
N/C To: 99999999

Dept From: 0
Dept To: 999

| Tran No. | Type | Date | A/C Ref | N/C | Inv Ref | Dept | Details | Net Amount | Tax Amount | T/C | Gross Amount | V | B |
|---|---|---|---|---|---|---|---|---|---|---|---|---|---|
| 37 | PI | 01/07/2011 | RUTHS | 5000 | 1801 | 0 | Multi pack sweets | 2,000.00 | 400.00 | T1 | 2,400.00 | N | - |
| 38 | PI | 10/07/2011 | HENRYS | 5000 | 1802 | 0 | Crates for transporting | 1,500.00 | 300.00 | T1 | 1,800.00 | N | - |
| 39 | PI | 15/07/2011 | DEBS | 5000 | 1803 | 0 | Paper bags for shops | 575.00 | 115.00 | T1 | 690.00 | N | - |
| 40 | PI | 25/07/2011 | KARENS | 5000 | 1804 | 0 | Multi pack sweets | 175.00 | 35.00 | T1 | 210.00 | N | - |
| | | | | | | | Totals | 4,250.00 | 850.00 | | 5,100.00 | | |

**Figure 4-16:** The Supplier Invoices Day Book for Sweet Dreams for July 2011.

6. **On 1 July, Kate the bookkeeper transfers £150 from the business Current Bank account to the Petty Cash account.** Can you confirm the double entry that takes place in the accounts system? Which accounts are debited and which are credited and why?

7. **Kate writes some cheques out as follows (see Figure 4-17):**

| Chq No | Details | Amount |
|--------|---------|--------|
| 1069 | Rent | £800 |
| 1070 | Salaries | £500 |

Can you confirm the double entry that takes place for these two transactions?

| Date: | 09/03/2012 | | Sweet Dreams | | | | | | | Page: | 1 | |
|-------|-----------|---|-----|---|---|---|---|---|---|------|---|---|
| Time: | 12:31:09 | | **Day Books: Bank Payments (Detailed)** | | | | | | | | | |

| Date From: | 01/07/2011 | | | | | | | | Bank From: | 1200 |
| DateTo: | 31/07/2011 | | | | | | | | Bank To: | 1200 |

| Transaction From: | 1 | | | | | | | | N/C From: | |
| Transaction To: | 99,999,999 | | | | | | | | N/C To: | 99999999 |

| Dept From: | 0 |
| Dept To: | 999 |

| Bank: | 1200 | | Currency: | Pound Sterling | | | | | | | | | Bank Rec. |
|-------|------|-----|-----------|----------------|-----|---------|------|--------|-------|-----------|-------|-----|------|
| No | Type | N/C | Date | Ref | Details | Dept | Net £ | Tax | £ T/C | Gross | £ V | B | Date |
| 46 | BP | 7100 | 01/07/2011 | 1069 | Rent for July | 0 | 800.00 | 0.00 | T9 | 800.00 - | N | | |
| 47 | BP | 7004 | 15/07/2011 | 1070 | Wages for shop staff | 0 | 500.00 | 0.00 | T9 | 500.00 - | N | | |
| | | | | | | Totals £ | 1,300.00 | | 0.00 | 1,300.00 | | | |

**Figure 4-17:** The Bank Payment Day Book for Sweet Dreams for July 2011.

Notice that the cheque numbers have been used in the reference field, thus allowing the transaction to be traced back to the original source document.

8. **On 31 July, Kate decided to pay the following suppliers (see Figure 4-18):**

| Supplier | Chq No | Amount |
|----------|--------|--------|
| Barry's Packaging | 1071 | £100 |
| Helen's | 1072 | £75 |
| Henry's | 1073 | £550 |

Can you confirm the double entry that takes place in the accounting system?

**Figure 4-18:**
Supplier
Payments
Day Book
for Sweet
Dreams for
July 2011.

9. **Kate receives a grant on 1 July for £200.** She pays this grant into the business current account. Can you confirm the double entry that takes place and say why?

10. **On 15 July, Kate receives a cheque from her customer J Jones for £140.** Can you confirm the double entry that takes place In the accounts system and explain why?

11. **At the end of the month, Kate runs a copy of her Trial Balance and sees that a large balance has been coded to Materials Purchased.** Using her Sage reports, she can see a couple of items that have been coded to Materials Purchased incorrectly.

The following individual items need to be taken out of materials purchased and coded to the following accounts:

Office Stationery £62.50

Distribution Costs £1500

Can you confirm the double entry that needs to take place to correct the accounts?

# Answering the Have a Go Questions

1. **The purchase of new furniture for the business would actually be an asset and not a cost, for the purpose of purchasing or manufacturing items for sale.**

   Therefore, the following double entry would take place:

   | Account | Debit | Credit |
   |---|---|---|
   | Office Furniture | £xx | |
   | Creditors Ledger | | £xx |

   The rules of double entry applied are:

   *To increase an asset (Office Furniture), you debit the Asset account.*

   *To increase a liability (Creditors Ledger), you credit the Liability account.*

2. **Cashbook.**

   All cash payments are entered into the Cashbook as a cash payment.

3. **Sales Ledger: All sales are tracked in the Sales Ledger.**

4. **The double entry would be as follows:**

   | Account | Debit | Credit |
   |---|---|---|
   | Trade Debtors | £4,050 | |
   | Sales | | £3,375 |
   | VAT | | £675 |

5. **The double entry would be as follows:**

   | Account | Debit | Credit |
   |---|---|---|
   | Materials Purchased | £4,250 | |
   | VAT | £850 | |
   | Trade Creditors | | £5,100 |

6. **The double entry that takes place is as follows:**

   | Account | Debit | Credit |
   |---|---|---|
   | Petty Cash account | £150 | |
   | Bank Current account | | £150 |

   The double entry rules that have been applied are:

   *If you want to increase an Asset account (for example, Petty Cash) you debit that account.*

   *To decrease an Asset account (for example, Bank Current account) you credit that account.*

See Figure 4-19 for the Nominal Daybook report to see confirmation of the double entry that has taken place.

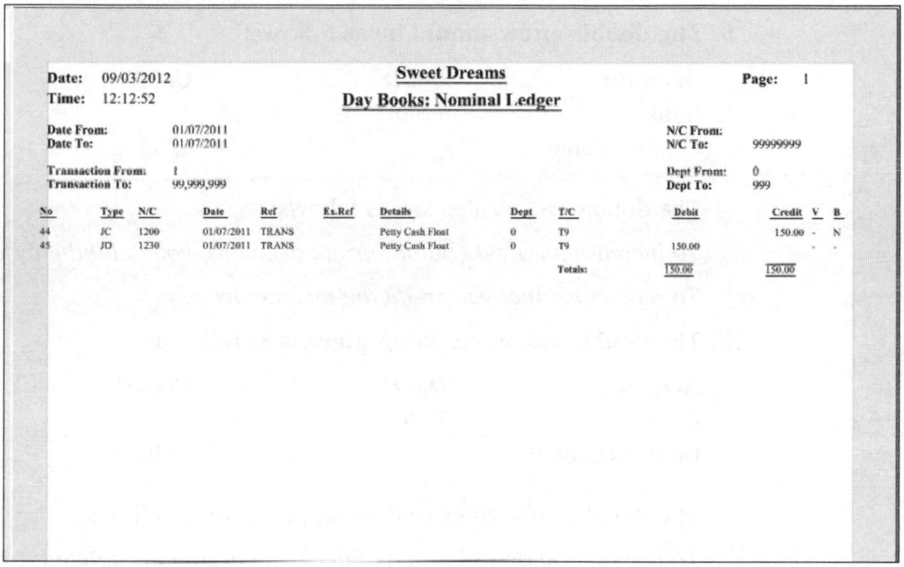

Date: 09/03/2012
Time: 12:12:52

**Sweet Dreams**

**Day Books: Nominal Ledger**

Page: 1

Date From: 01/07/2011
Date To: 01/07/2011

N/C From:
N/C To: 99999999

Transaction From: 1
Transaction To: 99,999,999

Dept From: 0
Dept To: 999

| No | Type | N/C | Date | Ref | Ex.Ref | Details | Dept | T/C | Debit | Credit | V | B |
|---|---|---|---|---|---|---|---|---|---|---|---|---|
| 44 | JC | 1200 | 01/07/2011 | TRANS | | Petty Cash Float | 0 | T9 | | 150.00 | - | N |
| 45 | JD | 1230 | 01/07/2011 | TRANS | | Petty Cash Float | 0 | T9 | 150.00 | | - | - |
| | | | | | | | | Totals: | 150.00 | 150.00 | | |

**Figure 4-19:** The Nominal Daybook for Sweet Dreams for July 2011.

You can see that Sage 50 has debited nominal code 1230 (Petty Cash) and credited nominal code 1200 (Bank Current Account).

7. **The double entry that should take place when the bank payments are made is as follows:**

| ***Account*** | ***Debit*** | ***Credit*** |
|---|---|---|
| Rent | £800 | |
| Wages | £500 | |
| Bank | | £1300 |

The double entry rules that have been adhered to are as follows:

*To record an expense (such as Rent or Wages), you debit the Expense account.*

*To decrease an asset (in this case the Bank account), you credit the Asset account.*

8. **The double entry that takes place is as follows:**

| ***Account*** | ***Debit*** | ***Credit*** |
|---|---|---|
| Creditors Ledger | £725 | |
| Bank | | £725 |

The double entry rules used are as follows:

*To decrease a liability (Trade Creditors), you must debit the account.*

*To decrease an asset (Bank Current account), you must credit the account.*

9. **The double entry should be as follows:**

| Account | Debit | Credit |
|---|---|---|
| Bank | £200 | |
| Other Income | | £200 |

The double entry rules are as follows:

*To increase an asset (Bank Current account), you debit the asset account.*

*To record income, you credit the income account.*

10. **The double entry that takes place is as follows:**

| Account | Debit | Credit |
|---|---|---|
| Bank | £140 | |
| Debtors Ledger | | £140 |

The double entry rules that are applied are as follows:

*To increase an asset (such as Bank), the account is debited.*

*To decrease an asset (such as Debtors), the account is credited.*

11. **The double entry that needs to take place to correct the materials purchased code is as follows;**

| Account | Debit | Credit |
|---|---|---|
| Office Stationery | £62.50 | |
| Distribution costs | £1500 | |
| Materials Purchased | | £1562.50 |

This now corrects the appropriate codes.

# Chapter 5

# Discoverics Different Business Types

. . . . . . . . . . . . . . . . . . . . . . . . . . . . . . . . . . . . . . .

. . . . . . . . . . . . . . . . . . . . . . . . . . . . . . . . . . . . . . .

*B*efore you begin your business, think ahead and determine what you think your business is going to look like over the next few years. For example, do you see yourself heading up a multinational corporation with lots of people working for you? Or, do you perhaps see yourself on your own, working the hours that suit you, picking the jobs that you want to do? Make sure that you take a few minutes to consider this, as your answers to these questions have an impact on which structure is most suitable for your business.

Whichever structure that you decide to start with determines how much administration needs to be done and who you need to inform that you've started a business. For example, paying taxes and reporting income for your business are very important jobs, and the way in which you complete these tasks properly depends on your business's legal structure. From sole traders (self-employment) to limited companies and everything in between, this chapter briefly reviews business types and explains how taxes are handled for each type.

## Finding the Right Business Type

Business type and tax preparation and reporting go hand in hand. If you work as a bookkeeper for a small business, you need to know the business's legal structure before you can proceed with reporting and paying tax on the business income. Not all businesses have the same legal structure, so they don't all pay tax on the profits they make in the same way.

But before you get into the subject of tax procedures, you need to understand the various business structures you may encounter as a bookkeeper. This section outlines each type of business. You can find out how these structures pay taxes in the separate sections that follow.

## Sole trader

The simplest legal structure for a business is the *sole trader,* a business owned by one individual. Most new businesses with only one owner start out as sole traders, and some never change this status. Others, however, grow by adding partners and become *partnerships.* Some businesses add lots of staff and want to protect themselves from lawsuits, so they become *Limited Liability Partnerships (LLPs).* Those seeking the greatest protection from individual lawsuits, whether they have employees or are simply single-owner companies without employees, become limited companies. We cover these other structures later in this chapter.

## Partnership

HM Revenue & Customs considers any unincorporated business owned by more than one person to be a *partnership.* The partnership is the most flexible type of business structure involving more than one owner. Each partner in the business is equally liable for the activities of the business. This structure is slightly more complicated than a sole trader (see the preceding 'Sole trader' section), and partners need to work out certain key issues before the business opens its doors. These issues include:

✔ How are the partners going to divide the profits?

✔ How does each partner sell their share of the business, if they so choose?

✔ What happens to each partner's share if a partner becomes sick or dies?

✔ How is the partnership going to be dissolved if one of the partners wants out?

Partners in a partnership don't always have to share equal risks. A partnership may have two different types of partners: general and limited. The general partner runs the day-to-day business and is held personally responsible for all activities of the business, no matter how much he or she has personally invested. Limited partners, on the other hand, are passive owners of the business and not involved in day-to-day operations. If someone files a claim against the business, the limited partners can be held personally liable only for the amount of money they individually invested in the business.

## Growth of the LLP

Limited Liability Partnerships are the latest business vehicle and were introduced on 6 April 2001 after the Limited Liability Partnerships Act 2000 received royal assent on 20 July 2000. Many law firms and accounting firms are set up as LLPs. More and more small-business owners are choosing this structure rather than a limited company because the LLP is easier and cheaper to maintain (it involves a lot less paperwork, plus fewer legal and accounting fees), and yet still provides personal protection from legal entanglements.

# *Limited Liability Partnerships (LLPs)*

The *Limited Liability Partnership,* or LLP, is a structure that provides the owners of partnerships with some protection from being held personally liable for their business activities. This business structure is somewhere between a partnership and a limited company: the business ownership and tax rules are similar to those of a partnership, but like a limited company, if the business is sued, the owners aren't held personally liable.

Rather like forming a limited company, an LLP is formed by filing the appropriate forms with Companies House. On receipt of these forms, the Registrar of Companies issues a Certificate of Incorporation.

Both for business and practical reasons, we recommend drawing up an agreement to establish the rights, responsibilities and duties of the partners to each other, and to outline how they're going to run the business, because few provisions are contained within the act governing these relationships.

# *Limited companies*

If your business faces a great risk of being sued, the safest business structure for you is the *limited company.* Courts in the UK have clearly determined that a limited company is a separate legal entity (Saloman v Saloman 1897) and that its owners' personal assets are protected from claims against the company. Essentially, an owner or shareholder in a company can't be sued or face collections because of actions taken by the company. This veil of protection is the reason why many small-business owners choose to incorporate even though it involves a lot of expense (to pay for both lawyers and accountants) and paperwork.

## Roles and responsibilities of the limited company board

Limited companies provide a veil of protection for company owners, but in order to maintain that protection, the owners must comply with many rules unique to corporations. The *board of directors* takes on the key role of complying with these rules, and it must maintain a record of meeting minutes that prove the board is following key operating procedures, such as:

- Establishment of records of banking associations and any changes to those arrangements
- Tracking of loans from shareholders or third parties
- Selling or redeeming shares
- Payment of dividends
- Authorisation of salaries or bonuses for officers and key executives

- Undertaking of any purchases, sales or leases of corporate assets
- Buying another company
- Merging with another company
- Making changes to the Articles of Incorporation
- Election of corporate officers and directors

Corporate board minutes are considered official and must be available for review by HM Revenue & Customs and the courts. If a company's owners want to invoke the veil of protection that corporate status provides, they must prove that the board has met its obligations and that the company operated as a limited company. In other words, you can't form a board and have no proof that it ever met and managed these key functions.

In a limited company, each share represents a portion of ownership, and profits must be split based on share ownership. You don't have to sell shares on the public stock markets in order to be a limited company, though. In fact, most limited companies are private entities that sell their shares privately among friends and investors.

If you're a small-business owner who wants to incorporate, first you must form a *board of directors* (see the sidebar 'Roles and responsibilities of the limited company board'). Boards can be made up of owners of the company as well as non-owners. You can even have your spouse and children on the board – bet those board meetings are interesting.

## *Tax Reporting for Sole Traders*

HM Revenue & Customs doesn't consider sole traders and partnerships to be individual legal entities, so they're not taxed as such. Instead, sole proprietors report any business earnings on their annual tax returns – that's the only financial reporting they must do. In effect, sole traders and partnerships pay income tax on their business profits. To be technical, they pay their income tax on their business profit under what is called *trading income.* A sole trader may well have another job as well, on which he or she pays tax under the normal PAYE system. All these sources (and other sources of income) are pulled together on the tax return to assess the overall income tax liability.

The basic tax return covers everything that a person in paid employment needs to tell HM Revenue & Customs to get his or her tax assessed correctly. The numerous pages of questions cover every aspect of tax related to normal tax life – working, receiving dividends, earning interest, paying and receiving pensions, making small capital gains – as we said, everything.

As the bookkeeper for a sole trader, you're probably responsible for pulling together the sales, cost of goods sold and expense information needed for the forms. In most cases, you send off this information to the business's accountant to fill out all the required forms.

Ultimately, because sole traders pay income tax on all their earnings, you need to note the current rates of tax for sole traders (and other unincorporated bodies) based on their taxable profits. Table 5-1 gives this information.

| Table 5-1 | 2012/13 Taxable Profits |
|---|---|
| *Tax Rate* | *2012/13 Taxable Profits* |
| Basic rate: 20% | £0–£34,370 |
| Higher rate: 40% | £34,370–£150,000 |
| Additional rate: 50% | Over £150,000 |

Fortunately most people have simple tax affairs. Because employment is usually taxed under the PAYE system (the employer acts as the unpaid tax collector) and most other sources of income have basic rate of tax deducted at source, you don't need to complete a tax return each year. The tax return is needed to pull all the earnings together only where an individual may have a liability to higher rate tax, for example other earnings that have not had tax deducted at source that pushes their taxable earnings above the basic tax rate.

## *Expanding to the supplementary pages*

To deal with liability at a higher tax rate or areas too complex for the standard annual tax return, you need supplementary pages. The supplementary pages cover:

- ✓ **Employment:** To cover more complicated employment situations, for example, an employee who has more than one job.

- ✓ **Share schemes:** To cover an employee who receives shares under an employee share ownership scheme.

- ✓ **Self-employment:** These pages cover business profits for the sole trader. We look at this subject more closely in the next section.

- ✓ **Partnerships:** To declare your share of any partnership profits.

- ✓ **Land and property**: For example, where any rental income is received from any property.

- ✓ **Foreign:** To cover any overseas sources of income.

- ✓ **Trusts:** To cover any income received by means of a distribution from any trust set up for you.

- ✓ **Capital gains:** To cover any gains made from the disposal of assets rather than trading income.

- ✓ **Non-residence:** To cover any income received by non-residents in the UK and thus liable to UK tax.

HM Revenue & Customs sends supplementary pages only if you ask for them or have received them before. As a taxpayer, you're responsible for asking for a tax return and completing one every year.

## Filling out the self-employment supplementary pages

This section concentrates on the supplementary pages that relate to running a business. Depending on your turnover, you use one of two different self-employment supplementary pages. If your turnover is less than £70,000, you can complete the shortened version, which is only two pages long. Double-check that you're eligible to use the shortened form by referring to the guide to completing the self-employment supplementary pages. You can find it on the HMRC website, www.hmrc.gov.uk.

On the first page, SES1, you put down details of the business name and address and when it began or ceased trading. You also use this page to enter your business income and allowable business expenses. (Refer to Chapter 13 for a refresher.) You put your total business expenses in box 19 if your turnover is less than £70,000. On the second page, SES 2, you summarise the capital allowances that the business is claiming for any of its assets (capital allowances are covered in Chapter 11). You then calculate your taxable profits and read page SESN9 of the notes to see whether you need to make any adjustments.

Losses, Class 4 NICs and CIS deductions are entered in the final section. (Make sure that you read page SESN10 of the notes to help you complete this section correctly.)

# Filing Tax Forms for Partnerships

If your business is structured as a partnership (meaning that it has more than one owner) and isn't a limited liability company, your business doesn't pay taxes. Instead, all money earned by the business is split up among the partners and they pay the tax due between them very much as if they were sole traders. However, a partnership is required to complete a partnership tax return to aid the assessment of the members of the partnership. Essentially, the partnership tax return is sent out to the nominated partner and he or she completes the partnership tax return in a manner similar to the sole trader tax return explained in the preceding sections. That partner states what profit share is attributable to each partner, and each partner is responsible for showing this profit figure in his or her own personal tax return.

Don't be tempted to forget to include partnership profits (or any other source of income for that matter), because HM Revenue & Customs knows from the partnership tax return what you earned in that tax year.

# Paying Taxes for Limited Companies

Limited companies are more complex than sole traders and partnerships. Although many aspects of their accounting and taxation are similar, their accounts are open to public scrutiny because each year a limited company must file its accounts at Companies House, the UK government organisation responsible for tracking information about all UK limited companies. This requirement means that although only HM Revenue & Customs knows the full details of a sole trader or partnership, the whole world has access (for a fee) to a limited company's accounts.

Companies make a separate tax return, known as a CT600, to HM Revenue & Customs, in which they detail their financial affairs. As a result, the limited company pays corporation tax on its earnings (profit) as well as tax on any dividends paid out to its shareholders. This arrangement means that its shareholders receive dividends net of basic rate of income tax because the company has already paid it for them. Two forms of CT600 exist: a short version, only four pages, is sufficient for companies with straightforward tax affairs, but more complicated companies, as designated by HM Revenue & Customs, must complete the eight-page return. Check with your accountant, whether you need to complete the eight-page return.

From April 2011, companies must file their corporation tax online for accounting periods ending after 31 March 2010, and pay electronically, too. The HMRC website provides a lot of help and advice, so don't panic – just click on Corporation Tax on the Businesses and Corporations menu from the home page.

Corporation tax rates vary according to how much taxable profit the company makes. Although starting rates are low for a limited company, they soon escalate to the higher (main) rate. Current corporation tax rates on profits are shown in Table 5-2.

| Table 5-2 | Corporation Tax Rates | |
|---|---|---|
| *Rates for financial years starting on 1 April* | | |
| *Tax Rate* | *2011 Taxable Profits* | *2012 Taxable Profits* |
| Small profits rate: | 20% | 20% |
| Small profits rate can be claimed by qualifying companies with profits not exceeding: | £300,000 | £300,000 |
| Marginal relief: lower limit | £300, 000 | £300,000 |
| Marginal relief: upper limit | £1,500,000 | £1,500,000 |
| Main rate: | 26% | 25% |

Check with your accountant to determine whether incorporating your business makes sense for you. A strong argument exists in favour of some smaller businesses incorporating, because they pay less corporation tax than income tax at certain levels. But tax savings isn't the only issue you have to think about; operating a limited company also increases administrative, legal and accounting costs. Make sure that you understand all the costs before incorporating.

# *Have a Go*

Try these questions to work out which type of business structure is suited to each occasion:

1. **You decide to start your own home business, but want protection from being held personally liable for your business's activity. Which type of business structure would you be likely to pick?**

2. **You and two of your friends decide to start a band and you need to pick a business structure. Which type of business structure would you pick if you want to keep things as simple as possible?**

3. **You decide to start your own home business. Which type of business structure would be easiest for you to use in order to get started?**

# *Answering the Have a Go Questions*

1. **You'd be likely to choose a Limited Company.** You can be sued personally if you structure your business as a sole proprietorship, but you've additional protection with a Limited Company; your personal assets are protected.

2. **The simplest structure is likely to be a Partnership.** However, you'd need to agree how to share profits and what would happen if a member decided to leave the band. You should set up a simple partnership agreement up to avoid complications in the future.

3. **Choosing to be a Sole Trader is the easiest way to start up in business.** You can start trading immediately, using your own name or a trading name.

# Part II
# Recording Day-to-Day Business Operations

'This is _real_ hell – The books
down here _never_ balance!'

## In this part . . .

This part introduces you to the basics of entering financial transactions, posting transactions to your Nominal Ledger (the pinnacle of your bookkeeping system), and recording all the transaction details in your sales and purchase ledgers.

Good internal controls are a must-have for any bookkeeping system, and so we tell you how to put them in place to be sure that all your financial transactions are not only entered into the books but also entered correctly. In addition, you want to be sure that cash coming in and going out of the business is properly handled, and so we provide recommendations about how to separate various money-related duties.

Finally, we discuss doing your banking and consider the importance of reconciling your cash and bank accounts.

# Chapter 6

# Planning and Controlling Your Workload

. . . . . . . . . . . . . . . . . . . . . . . . . . . . . . . . . . . . . . . . . . . . . .

## In This Chapter

▶ Using checklists

▶ Filing and processing your sales and purchases invoices

▶ Entering your banking transactions

▶ Reconciling your bank account

▶ Tackling month-end journals

▶ Setting up systems and controls for your business

▶ Separating duties

. . . . . . . . . . . . . . . . . . . . . . . . . . . . . . . . . . . . . . . . . . . . . .

A s a bookkeeper, you need to work in an orderly manner and be aware of which jobs need doing on a daily, weekly and monthly basis, which is why checklists are so useful. You need to do certain jobs on a daily basis, depending on the size of your business, for example entering invoices, while other jobs are done on a monthly basis, such as reconciling your bank account. Most businesses only receive one statement once a month and wait until they've received it before they reconcile their bank account.

As the company bookkeeper, you should analyse all the jobs that require completing and decide on an appropriate order in which to conduct those tasks. You then need to allocate the work to the appropriate person or department, so that everyone in the office is aware of what responsibilities they have. If your business is so small that you're the only person in it, you have to do everything. Nothing like hands-on experience!

This chapter offers hints and tips to help you process your transactions in an efficient manner.

# Introducing Checklists

Having a list of all the jobs that need to be carried out in a month is always a good idea. That way, you know what you're working towards. In bookkeeping, the number of transactions that you deal with varies massively from company to company. You're reacting both to the number of invoices that a business generates itself for customers and also the invoices that it receives from its suppliers. Every business differs in the number of invoices that it handles.

Some businesses have entire departments that process just invoices. For example, you may have a department that processes just purchase invoices. The business may receive so many that you have purchase journal clerks who only process and write up purchase invoices. The bigger your company, the more likely you are to use a computerised accounting system. However, whether you use computers or not, you still benefit from using checklists to guide you through the monthly bookkeeping routine.

Figure 6-1 is an example of a checklist that we use on a monthly basis.

| Bookkeeping Checklist | Apr | May | Jun | Jul | Aug | Sep | Oct | Nov | Dec | Jan | Feb | Mar |
|---|---|---|---|---|---|---|---|---|---|---|---|---|
| **Monthly** | | | | | | | | | | | | |
| Enter Sales Invoices | | | | | | | | | | | | |
| Enter Purchase Invoices | | | | | | | | | | | | |
| Enter Cheque Payments | | | | | | | | | | | | |
| Enter Receipts from paying in book | | | | | | | | | | | | |
| Enter prepayment journals | | | | | | | | | | | | |
| Enter accruals journals | | | | | | | | | | | | |
| Enter wages journals | | | | | | | | | | | | |
| Enter stock journal | | | | | | | | | | | | |
| Enter depreciation | | | | | | | | | | | | |
| Pay Inland Revenue | | | | | | | | | | | | |
| Bank Reconciliation | | | | | | | | | | | | |
| **Quarterly** | | | | | | | | | | | | |
| VAT Return | | | | | | | | | | | | |

**Figure 6-1:**
An example of a monthly book-keeping checklist.

# Sorting Out Your Sales Invoices

If your business produces sales invoices for customers who are buying on credit, read on! Your business may produce these invoices by hand, a word processor or a computerised system. We talk about cash sales and computer-generated invoices in Chapter 7. Here we discuss the filing and management of those invoices after they've been produced.

Referring to the checklist shown in Figure 6-1, you can see that the first job on the list is entering sales invoices. Make sure that the person who produces the sales invoices puts them somewhere you can easily find them, for example, an in-tray simply for sales invoices or a concertina-style file that invoices are kept in prior to you entering them into your bookkeeping system.

If you have a computerised system that produces sales invoices automatically, you can skip this step, as the computer produces those invoices automatically and the Sales journal updated accordingly, as detailed in Chapter 7.

You should find that each sales invoice has already been given an invoice number. Adopt a sequential numbering system that allows you to notice whether invoices have been missed or not. The invoice numbers can be alpha-numeric if it helps with your business, but the invoices should be filed in numerical order, so that you file and enter them into your bookkeeping system in roughly chronological order.

As you enter each invoice into your Sales Ledger, tick or mark the invoice in some way to indicate that you've posted it into your bookkeeping system so you avoid entering the same invoice twice.

File your invoices neatly in a lever arch file.

# Entering Your Purchases Invoices

You receive purchase invoices in the post on an almost daily basis. Whoever opens the post needs to know where to put those invoices until it is time to enter them into the bookkeeping system. Again, as with the sales invoices, keep the purchase invoices in one dedicated place until you're ready to enter them into your Purchase Ledger.

## Sequential numbering and coding

Some companies like to keep a separate lever arch file for each supplier, or at least file the invoices in supplier order. Others simply number the purchase invoices sequentially with a stamping machine and use this number within the bookkeeping system. Using this method, you can file all your purchase invoices in one file and just keep them in numerical order.

When you enter the invoice into the bookkeeping system, you need to know which nominal code to apply in order to enter the invoice. It may not be immediately obvious what the invoice is for. For example, as a bookkeeper, you need to know whether the invoice relates to a direct cost of the business or whether it is simply an overhead of the business.

Some companies use a data-entry stamp, which has spaces to enter vital information such as the date the invoice was posted, nominal code and maybe a space for the data-entry clerk to initial, to confirm that the transaction has been entered.

You may find that you're entering invoices on a daily basis. When you begin to enter invoices at the start of each day, check your bookkeeping system to see what the last invoice entered was. You can check the last invoice number used and then you know which invoice number to start with when you enter your next invoice.

If you're using a computerised system such as Sage 50 Accounts, you can check the Purchase Daybook. See Figure 6-2 for an example of the report you can run to check the last purchase invoice entered.

| Date: 09/03/2012 | | | | | | **Sweet Dreams** | | | Page: 1 | |
|---|---|---|---|---|---|---|---|---|---|---|
| Time: 14:22:37 | | | | | | **Day Books: Supplier Invoices (Detailed)** | | | | |

| Date From: | 01/07/2011 | | | | | | Supplier From: | | |
|---|---|---|---|---|---|---|---|---|---|
| Date To: | 31/12/2019 | | | | | | Supplier To: | ZZZZZZZZ | |
| Transaction From: | 1 | | | | | | N/C From: | | |
| Transaction To: | 99,999,999 | | | | | | N/C To: | 99999999 | |
| Dept From: | 0 | | | | | | | | |
| Dept To: | 999 | | | | | | | | |

| Tran No. | Type | Date | A/C Ref | N/C | Inv Ref | Dept | Details | Net Amount | Tax Amount | T/C | Gross Amount | V | B |
|---|---|---|---|---|---|---|---|---|---|---|---|---|---|
| 37 | PI | 01/07/2011 | RUTHS | 5000 | 1801 | 0 | Multi pack sweets | 2,000.00 | 400.00 | T1 | 2,400.00 | N | - |
| 38 | PI | 10/07/2011 | HENRYS | 5000 | 1802 | 0 | Crates for transporting | 1,500.00 | 300.00 | T1 | 1,800.00 | N | - |
| 39 | PI | 15/07/2011 | DEBS | 5000 | 1803 | 0 | Paper bags for shops | 575.00 | 115.00 | T1 | 690.00 | N | - |
| 40 | PI | 25/07/2011 | KARENS | 5000 | 1804 | 0 | Multi pack sweets | 175.00 | 35.00 | T1 | 210.00 | N | - |
| | | | | | | | **Totals** | 4,250.00 | 850.00 | | 5,100.00 | | |

**Figure 6-2:** Check your Purchase Daybook to see the last invoice entered.

Notice the 'Invoice Reference' column. This column is where the sequential purchases invoice number appears.

## Paying your suppliers

Although we don't include this task on the checklist, paying your suppliers on time is vital to any business. Flip to Chapter 8 to see just why!

You may decide to pay your suppliers at specific times in the month, so add this task to your monthly bookkeeping routine.

# Checking Cash Payments and Receipts

In Chapter 9, we discuss the importance of ensuring that all banking entries are included in your bookkeeping system, particularly when you need to reconcile your bank account. In this chapter, we discuss the practical ways to ensure that you include all your data in your system.

## Cash payments

Most businesses make payments in several ways. Cash payments include:

- ✔ Cash (naturally!) – usually from the petty cash tin
- ✔ Cheque
- ✔ Bank transfer, CHAPS or BACS, or another form of electronic payment

As a bookkeeper, make sure that you collect all the payment information from all the relevant sources. The bank reconciliation process highlighted in Chapter 9 ensures that you do this; however, here are a few more practical tips so that the reconciliation process is made as simple as possible.

An easy way to ensure that you've entered all your petty cash payments is to physically tick or initial the petty cash voucher or cash receipt after entering it into your bookkeeping system. You then avoid entering items twice. You can batch up your petty cash payments and give them a batch reference so that they can be easily retrieved from your filing system.

Look at Figure 6-3 to see an example of a batch entry of petty cash receipts being posted onto Sage 50 Accounts. The batch of receipts has been given the reference PC01. A separate bank account has been set up called Petty Cash.

To make life as easy as possible, when you write out cheques, ensure that you include clear information about who you're paying on the cheque stub. Don't attempt to write *War and Peace* here, but include the date, the payee and the amount. Write this information clearly, especially if it may not be you that ultimately writes up the Cash Payments book or enters the amount into your computerised accounting system. If you've spidery handwriting, spare a thought for the person who needs to read this information! Entering wrong amounts or the wrong account leads to problems when trying to reconcile the bank account.

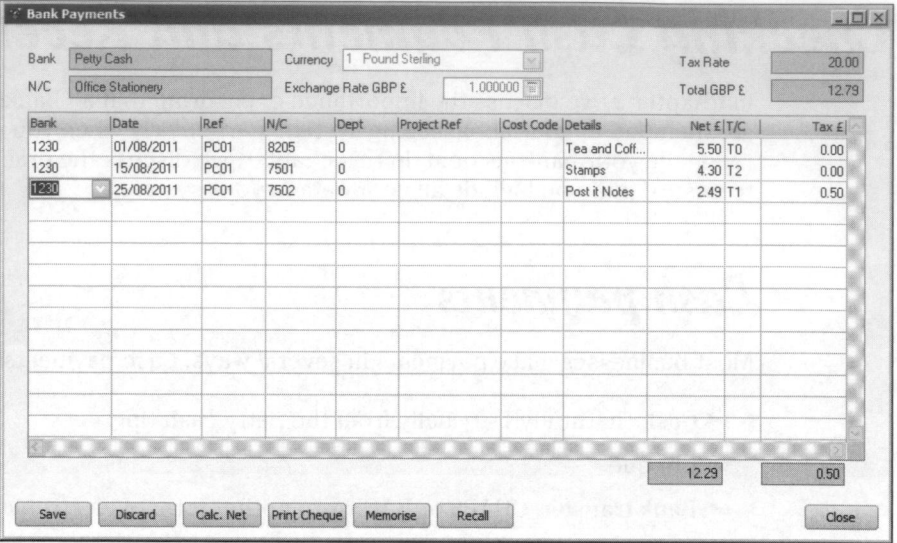

**Figure 6-3:**
Petty cash payment showing PC01 as a batch reference.

At some point, you enter the information written on the cheque stub into the bookkeeping system. After you write the information up in your Cash Payments book or enter it onto your computing system, make sure that you physically tick the cheque stub. This way, you know that you've entered that information, and can easily flick through the cheque stubs at a later date and find where you last entered information.

You won't be aware of what electronic payments have been made until you see the bank statements for the month. Most businesses don't receive the previous month's statements until the end of the first week of the following month. For most businesses, this timing is impractical, so with the advent of Internet banking, most businesses can print out copies of their bank statements on a daily basis if necessary. Therefore you can reconcile your bank account on a much more regular basis than simply once a month, which was the traditional way. You can also identify your electronic payments sooner and enter them accordingly.

Again, an easy way to ensure that you're entering the information correctly is to physically tick the transaction on your copy of the bank statement.

Avoid printing too many copies of your bank statements, as doing so can lead to mistakes happening, with the same information entered twice.

## *Cash receipts*

These transactions include:

- ✔ Items physically paid in at the bank via the paying-in book.
- ✔ Electronic receipts via BACS and other electronic methods, including interest earned on the Bank account.

For items paid in using the paying-in book, make sure that you include as much detail as possible. If you can, include the invoice numbers that the customer is paying, so that you can easily allocate the receipt to the correct invoices. Knowing which invoices the customer is paying is crucial so that the Aged Debtor report is correct. (See Chapter 7 for more on Aged Debtor reports.)

After you've entered the information from your bank pay-in slips to your bookkeeping system, tick the stub to show that the information's been entered so you can see at a glance where you're up to.

# *Reconciling Your Bank Account*

Reconciling your bank account to check that your manual or computerised Cashbook matches your bank statement is usually part of your monthly accounting process. Chapter 9 shows you how to carry out the reconciliation process both manually and using computer software. Make sure that you reconcile your bank accounts, as this reconciliation ensures the accuracy of the information that has been posted to your accounting system. You should also reconcile any credit card statements that you've received; by doing this, you accurately record credit card liabilities that the business may have incurred.

# *Entering Your Journals*

Monthly journals always need to be completed. If you refer back to the checklist shown in Figure 6-1, we refer to prepayments, accruals, wages, stock and depreciation. Your business may have some or all these journals, but you may also have additional ones that are specific to your business. Ensure that all the journals that you need to process are on your checklist so that they aren't missed out.

For more information on Accruals, Prepayments, Depreciation and Stock journals, see Chapter 10.

# Controlling Your Books, Records and Money

Cash is an extremely important part of any business and you need to accurately record and monitor it. Before you take in any money, you must be sure that systems are in place to control the flow of cash in and out of the business.

Here are some tips:

✔ Initially, when your business is small, you can sign each cheque and keep control of the outflow of money. But as the business grows, you may find that you need to delegate cheque-signing responsibilities to someone else, especially if you travel frequently.

Many small business owners set up cheque-signing procedures that allow one or two of their staff to sign cheques up to a designated amount, such as £5,000. Any cheques above that designated amount require the owner's signature, or the signature of an employee and a second designated person, such as an officer of the business.

✔ A good practice is to record cheques received immediately as part of a daily morning routine. Enter the details onto the paying-in slip and update your computerised or manual accounting system at the same time. Make sure that you pay in any money received before 3:30 p.m. on the same day, to ensure that your bank account gets credit that day rather than the next.

✔ No matter how much you keep in petty cash, make sure that you set up a good control system that requires anyone who uses the cash to write a petty cash voucher specifying how much was used and why. Also ask that a cash receipt, for example from the shop or post office, is attached to the voucher in order to justify the cash withdrawal whenever possible.

In most cases, a member of staff buys something for the business and then gets reimbursed for that expense. If the expense is small enough, you can reimburse through the petty cash fund. If the expense is more than a few pounds, ask the person to fill out an expense account form and get reimbursed by cheque. Petty cash is usually used for minor expenses of £10 or less.

✔ The best way to control petty cash is to pick one person in the office to manage the use of all petty cash. Before giving that person more cash, he or she should be able to prove the absence of cash used and why it was used.

# *Dividing staff responsibilities*

Your primary protection against financial crime is properly separating staff responsibilities when the flow of business cash is involved. In a nutshell, never have one person handling more than one of the following tasks:

- **Bookkeeping:** Involves reviewing and entering all transactions into the business's books. The bookkeeper makes sure that transactions are accurate, valid, appropriate and have the proper authorisation. For example, if a transaction requires paying a supplier, the bookkeeper makes sure that the charges are accurate and someone with proper authority has approved the payment. The bookkeeper can review documentation of cash receipts and the overnight deposits taken to the bank, but shouldn't actually make the deposit.

  Also, if the bookkeeper is responsible for handling payments from external parties, such as customers or suppliers, he or she shouldn't enter those transactions in the books.

- **Authorisation:** Involves being the manager or managers delegated to authorise expenditures for their departments. You may decide that transactions over a certain amount must have two or more authorisations before cheques can be sent to pay a bill. Spell out authorisation levels clearly and make sure that everyone follows them, even the owner or managing director of the business. (Remember, if you're the owner, you set the tone for how the rest of the office operates; when you take shortcuts, you set a bad example and undermine the system you put in place.)

- **Money-handling:** Involves direct contact with incoming cash or revenue, whether cheque, credit card or credit transactions, as well as outgoing cash flow. People who handle money directly, such as cashiers, shouldn't also prepare and make bank deposits. Likewise, the person writing cheques to pay business bills shouldn't be authorised to sign those cheques; to be safe, have one person prepare the cheques based on authorised documentation and a second person sign those cheques, after reviewing the authorised documentation.

  When setting up your cash-handling systems, try to think like an embezzler to figure out how someone can take advantage of a system.

- **Financial report preparation and analysis:** Involves the actual preparation of the financial reports and any analysis of those reports. Someone who's not involved in the day-to-day entering of transactions in the books needs to prepare the financial reports. For most small businesses, the bookkeeper turns over the raw reports from the computerised accounting system to an outside accountant who reviews the materials and prepares the financial reports. In addition, the accountant does a financial analysis of the business activity results for the previous accounting period.

We realise that you may be just starting up a small business and therefore not have enough staff to separate all these duties. Until you do have that capability, make sure that you stay heavily involved in the inflow and outflow of cash in your business. At least once a month:

- **Open your business's bank statements and review the transactions.** Someone else can be given the responsibility of reconciling the statement, but you still need to keep an eye on the transactions listed.

- **Look at your business cheque book counterfoils to ensure that no cheques are missing.** A bookkeeper who knows that you periodically check the books is less likely to find an opportunity for theft or embezzlement. If you find that a cheque or page of cheques is missing, act quickly to find out whether the cheques were used legitimately. If you can't find the answer, call your bank and put a stop on the missing cheque numbers.

- **Observe your cashiers and managers handling cash to make sure that they're following the rules you've established.** This practice is known as *management by walking around* – the more often you're out there, the less likely you are to be a victim of employee theft and fraud.

## Balancing control costs

As a small-business person, you're always trying to balance the cost of protecting your cash and assets with the cost of adequately separating those duties. Putting in place too many controls, which end up costing you money, can be a big mistake.

For example, you may create stock controls that require salespeople to contact one particular person who has the key to your product warehouse. This kind of control may prevent employee theft, but can also result in lost sales, because salespeople can't find the key-holder while dealing with an interested customer. In the end, the customer gets mad, and you lose the sale.

When you put controls in place, talk to your staff both before and after instituting the controls to see how they're working and to check for any unforeseen problems. Be willing and able to adjust your controls to balance the business needs of selling your products, managing the cash flow and keeping your eye on making a profit. Talk to other businesspeople to see what they do and pick up tips from established best practice. Your external accountant can be a good source of valuable information.

# Have a Go

Grab a pencil and some paper and test your knowledge on the best way of working as a bookkeeper.

1. **You work in the accounts department for a small business. Write a procedure for a new member of staff to follow, which shows them what to do when a cheque arrives by post into the business.**

   Consider who opens the post, who writes up the paying-in book and who ultimately takes the cheques to the bank. Try to remember that these responsibilities should be split up as much as possible to minimise any possibility of fraud.

2. **Review your petty cash procedure.**

   Decide who is responsible for maintaining the petty cash tin, and how much the petty cash float is going to be. Make sure that all staff are aware of the petty cash procedure.

3. **Imagine that you're setting up the accounting department. Jot down the types of tasks that require separation of duties?**

# Answering the Have a Go Questions

1. **The following is an example of what you may have written.**

   Procedure for banking cheques:

   - The person responsible for opening the post should ensure that all cheques and notifications of payments from customers (for example a remittance advice) are passed to the accounts department on the day that they're received.

   - One person in the accounts department should be responsible for writing up the bank paying-in book and recording all the money received, along with details of the customer and which invoice they're paying. As much detail as possible should be written on the paying-in slip stub.

   - If possible, a different individual should ensure that the paying-in book is taken to the bank and the money deposited, the same day it is received.

- When the bank paying-in book has been returned to the accounts department, the customer receipts should be entered into your bookkeeping system. If you have a computerised system, you should enter the customer receipts against the appropriate account, using the bank paying-in reference and details shown on the paying-in book to identify which invoices the payment should be allocated to. Tick the paying-in slip, when you've entered the information into your bookkeeping system.

2. **Here are the main elements of a petty cash procedure:**

   - Designate a member of staff to be responsible for petty cash. Ensure that all members of staff know who this person is.

   - Complete petty cash vouchers for all petty cash payments detailing the type of expenditure and noting VAT if applicable. Attach the receipts to the vouchers, so that VAT may be claimed at a later date.

   - Ensure that the individual claiming money from petty cash signs the petty cash voucher to acknowledge receipt of the money and also ensure that the petty cashier authorises the payment by signing the voucher accordingly.

   - Number each petty cash voucher so that it can be filed and easily located later if necessary.

   - Write up the petty cash book, or enter the petty cash vouchers onto your computerised system, using the number mentioned in the last step as a reference.

   - Petty cash should be counted and balanced on a regular basis. This task is usually done when the float needs topping up.

3. **The following are the types of duties that you should consider separating among different members of staff.**

   Obviously in a very small company this separation may not be possible, so let common sense prevail!

   - The person who opens the post and accepts the cash should not enter the transaction in the books.

   - The person who enters the data in the books on a daily basis should not prepare the financial statements.

   - The person who prepares the cheques should not have the authority to sign the cheques.

   - The person who pays the money into the bank should not be the person who completes the paying in slips.

# Chapter 7

# Counting Your Sales

. . . . . . . . . . . . . . . . . . . . . . . . . . . . . . . . . . . . . . . . . .

## In This Chapter

▶ Taking in cash

▶ Discovering the ins and outs of credit

▶ Managing discounts for best results

▶ Staying on top of returns and allowances

▶ Monitoring payments due

▶ Dealing with bad debt

. . . . . . . . . . . . . . . . . . . . . . . . . . . . . . . . . . . . . . . . . .

*E*very business loves to take in money, and this means that you, the bookkeeper, have lots to do to ensure that sales are properly recorded in the books. In addition to recording the sales themselves, you must monitor customer accounts, discounts offered to customers and customer returns and allowances.

If the business sells products on credit, you have to monitor customer accounts carefully in Trade Debtors (Accounts Receivable), including monitoring whether customers pay on time and alerting the sales team when customers are behind on their bills and future purchases on credit need to be declined. Some customers never pay, and in that case, you must adjust the books to reflect non-payment as a bad debt.

This chapter reviews the basic responsibilities of a business's bookkeeping and accounting staff for tracking sales, making adjustments to those sales, monitoring customer accounts and alerting management to slow-paying customers.

# Collecting on Cash Sales

Most businesses collect some form of cash as payment for the goods or services they sell. Cash receipts include more than just notes and coins; you can consider cheques and credit and debit card payments as cash sales for book-keeping purposes. In fact, with electronic transaction processing (when a customer's credit or debit card is swiped through a machine), a deposit is usually made to the business's bank account the same day (sometimes within seconds of the transaction, depending on the type of system the business sets up with the bank).

The only type of payment that doesn't fall under the umbrella of a cash payment is purchases made on credit. And by *credit,* we mean the credit your business offers to customers directly rather than through a third party, such as a bank credit card or loan. We talk more about this type of sale in the section 'Selling on Credit', later in this chapter.

## Discovering the value of sales receipts

Modern businesses generate sales receipts in one of three ways: by the cash register, by the credit or debit card machine or by hand (written out by the salesperson). Whichever of these three methods you choose to handle your sales transactions, the sales receipt serves two purposes:

- ✔ Gives the customer proof that the item was purchased on a particular day at a particular price in your shop in case he needs to exchange or return the merchandise.

- ✔ Gives the shop a receipt that can be used at a later time to enter the transaction into the business's books. At the end of the day, the receipts are also used to cash up the cash register and ensure that the cashier has taken in the right amount of cash based on the sales made.

You're familiar with cash receipts, no doubt, but just to show you how much useable information can be generated for the bookkeeper on a sales receipt, Figure 7-1 shows a sample receipt from a hardware shop.

Receipts contain a wealth of information that can be collected for your business's accounting system. A look at a receipt tells you the amount of cash collected, the type of products sold, the quantity of products sold and how much Value Added Tax (VAT) was collected.

HANDSON'S HARDWARE

Sales receipt 01/08/2012

| Item | Quantity | Price | Total |
|------|----------|-------|-------|
| Nails | 1 box | £8.99 | £8.99 |
| Picture hooks | 1 pack | £2.99 | £2.99 |
| Paint | 2 gallons | £10.00 | £10.00 |
| **Subtotal** | | | **£21.98** |
| **VAT @ 20%** | | | **£4.40** |
| **Total Sale** | | | **£26.38** |
| **Paid Cash** | | | **£26.38** |

**Figure 7-1:**
A sales receipt from Handson's Hardware.

We're assuming that your business operates some form of computerised accounting system, but it may be that you need to journal the sales information from your till into your accounting system (unless of course you have an automated process). Either way, as a reminder, the double entry required to enter your sales information is as follows:

|  | *Debit* | *Credit* |
|--|---------|----------|
| Bank account | £26.38 | |
| Sales | | £21.98 |
| VAT account | | £4.40 |

*Sales receipts for 1 August 2012*

In this example entry, the Bank account is an Asset account shown on the Balance Sheet (see Chapter 14 for more about the Balance Sheet), and its value increases with the debit. The Sales account is a Revenue account on the Profit and Loss statement (see Chapter 13 for more about the Profit and Loss statement), and its balance increases with a credit, showing additional revenue. (We talk more about debits and credits in Chapter 2.) The VAT Collected account is a Liability account that appears on the Balance Sheet, and its balance increases with this transaction.

Businesses pay VAT to HM Revenue & Customs monthly or quarterly, depending on rules set by HM Revenue & Customs. Therefore, your business must hold the money owed in a Liability account so that you're certain you can pay the VAT collected from customers when due. We talk more about VAT payments in Chapter 12.

## *Recording cash transactions in the books*

Assuming that you're using a computerised accounting system, you can enter more detail from the day's receipts and record stock sold as well. Most of the computerised accounting systems include the ability to record the sale of stock. Figure 7-2 shows you the Sage 50 Accounts Cash Sales screen that you can use to input data from each day's sales. Note that you need the Sage 50 Accounts Professional version to use the Sales Order Processing function to generate cash sales and automatically update your stock.

Note: A cheaper computerised option would be to use Sage One Cashbook, or Sage One Accounts, which is an online accounting service, but cheap to use. It's ideal for one-man bands and micro-businesses. Take a look at *Sage One For Dummies* by Jane Kelly (Wiley) to find out more.

**Figure 7-2:** Example of a cash sale in Sage 50 Accounts.

In addition to the information included in the Cash Receipts book, note that Sage 50 Accounts also collects information about the items sold in each transaction. Sage 50 Accounts then automatically updates stock information, reducing the amount of stock on hand when necessary. If the cash sale in Figure 7-2 is for an individual customer, you enter their name and address in the A/C field. At the bottom of the Cash Sales screen, the Print tab takes you to a further menu where you have the option to print or email the receipt. You can print the receipt and give it to the customer or, for a phone or Internet order, email it to the customer. Using this option, payment can be made by any method such as cheque, electronic payment or credit or debit card.

Sage 50 Accounts also gives you the ability to process card payments from customers over the phone and use real time authorisation and posting. To use Sage Pay, you need a Sage Pay account and a merchant bank account. For more information about this, please see www.sagepay.com.

If your business accepts credit cards, expect sales revenue to be reduced by the fees paid to credit card companies. Usually, you face monthly fees as well as fees per transaction; however, each business sets up individual arrangements with its bank regarding these fees. Sales volume impacts how much you pay in fees, so when researching bank services, ensure that you compare credit card transaction fees to find a good deal.

# Selling on Credit

Many businesses decide to sell to customers on credit, meaning credit that the business offers and not through a bank or credit card provider. This approach offers more flexibility in the type of terms you can offer your customers, and you don't have to pay bank fees. However, credit involves more work for you, the bookkeeper, and the risk of a customer not paying what he or she owes.

When you accept a customer's bank-issued credit card for a sale and the customer doesn't pay the bill, you get your money; the bank is responsible for collecting from the customer, taking the loss if he or she doesn't pay. This doesn't apply when you decide to offer credit to your customers directly. If a customer doesn't pay, your business takes the loss.

## Deciding whether to offer credit

The decision to set up your own credit system depends on what your competition is doing. For example, if you run an office supply store and all other office supply stores allow credit to make it easier for their customers to get supplies, you probably need to offer credit to stay competitive.

You need to set up some ground rules when you want to allow your customers to buy on credit. For personal customers, you have to decide:

- How to check a customer's credit history.

- What the customer's income level needs to be for credit approval.

- How long to give the customer to pay the bill before charging interest or late fees.

If you want to allow your trade or business customers to buy on credit, you need to set ground rules for them as well. The decisions you need to make include:

- Whether to deal only with established businesses. You may decide to give credit only to businesses that have been trading for at least two years.

- Whether to require *trade references,* which show that the business has been responsible and paid other businesses when they've taken credit. A customer usually provides you with the details of two suppliers that offered them credit. You then contact those suppliers directly to see whether the customer has been reliable and on time with payments.

- Whether to obtain credit rating information. You may decide to use a third-party credit-checking agency to provide a credit report on the business applying for credit. This report suggests a maximum credit limit and whether the business pays on time. Of course a fee is charged for this service, but using it may help you avoid making a terrible mistake. A similar service is available for individuals.

The harder you make getting credit and the stricter you make the bill-paying rules, the less chance you have of taking a loss. However, you may lose customers to a competitor with lighter credit rules.

You may require a minimum income level of £50,000 and make customers pay in 30 days to avoid late fees or interest charges. Your sales staff report that these rules are too rigid because your direct competitor down the street allows credit on a minimum income level of £30,000 and gives customers 60 days to pay before charging late fees and interest charges. Now you have to decide whether you want to change your credit rules to match those of the competition. If you do lower your credit standards to match your competitor, however, you may end up with more customers who can't pay on time (or at all) because you've qualified customers for credit at lower income levels and given them more time to pay. If you do loosen your qualification criteria and bill-paying requirements, monitor your customer accounts carefully to ensure that they're not falling behind.

The key risk you face is selling products for which you're never paid. For example, if you allow customers 30 days to pay and cut them off from buying goods when their accounts fall more than 30 days behind, the most you can lose is the amount purchased over a two-month period (60 days). But if you give customers more leniency, allowing them 60 days to pay and cutting them off after payment is 30 days late, you're faced with three months (90 days) of purchases for which you may never be paid.

## *Recording credit sales in the books*

When sales are made on credit, you have to enter specific information into the accounting system. In addition to inputting information regarding cash receipts (see 'Collecting on Cash Sales', earlier in this chapter), you update the customer accounts to make sure that each customer is billed and the money is collected. You debit the Trade Debtors account, an Asset account shown on the Balance Sheet (see Chapter 14), which shows money due from customers.

Figure 7-3 shows an example of a sales invoice from Simply Stationery.

When the bookkeeper for Simply Stationery enters this invoice, whether on a computer or in manual ledgers, the journal entry for a credit sale would look like this:

| | Debit | Credit |
|---|---|---|
| Trade Debtors | £48.00 | |
| Sales | | £40.00 |
| VAT Account | | £8.00 |

A computerised accounting system makes this journal entry automatically, but you still need to know what the bookkeeping entries are, just in case you need to correct something. In addition to making this journal entry, your accounts package will enter the information into the customer's account so that accurate statements can be sent out at the end of the month.

When the customer pays the bill, you update the individual customer's record to show that payment has been received. Sage 50 Accounts automatically enters the following into the bookkeeping records:

| | Debit | Credit |
|---|---|---|
| Trade Debtors | | £48.00 |
| Cash | £48.00 | |
| *Payment from The Village Shop* | | |

# Invoice

## Simply Stationery

32 High Street, Benton, Digbyshire. DG17 2LD
Tel: 01234 567890 Fax: 01234 567891
Email: Sales@simplystationery.co.uk
WWW.simplystationery .co.uk
VAT Reg: 862 113 49

**Invoice to:**                                                                      **Invoice No: 105**

The Village Shop,
69 Bradbury Way,
Benton,
Digbyshire
DG17 4LY

**Date: 21.04.12**

| Description | Qty | Price | Total | Discount | Net |
|---|---|---|---|---|---|
| A4 Copy Paper | 20 | £2.00 | £40.00 | 0.00 | £40.00 |
|  |  |  |  |  |  |
|  |  |  |  |  |  |
|  |  |  |  |  |  |

**Terms 30 Days**

| | |
|---|---|
| **Goods Total** | **£40.00** |
| **Less Discount** | **£00.00** |
| **Net Sales** | **£40.00** |
| **VAT @ 20%** | **£8.00** |
| **Total Sales** | **£48.00** |

**Figure 7-3:**
A sales
invoice
from Simply
Stationery.

If you're using Sage 50 Accounts, you can enter credit sales on an invoice form like the one in Figure 7-4. Most of the information on the invoice form is similar to the Cash Sales screen (see 'Collecting on Cash Sales', earlier in this chapter), but the invoice form also has space to enter a different address for shipping (the Delivery Address field) and includes payment terms (the Settlement Terms field).

Sage 50 Accounts uses the information on the invoice to update the following accounts:

✔ Trade Debtors

✔ Stock

✔ Customer's account

✔ VAT account

Print out the invoice and send it to the customer straight away. Depending on the payment terms you've negotiated with your customer, send out monthly statements to remind customers that their debt to your company is still outstanding. Regular monitoring of your Aged Debtor report ensures that you know who has not yet paid you. In order to keep these reports up to date, allocate the cash to each customer account on a regular basis.

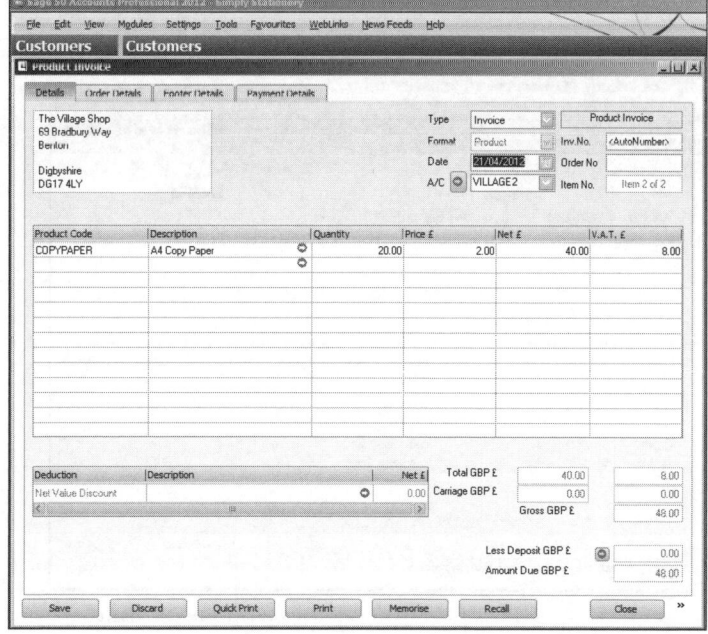

**Figure 7-4:**
Creating a sales invoice using Sage 50 Accounts for goods sold on credit.

When you receive payment from a customer, here's what to do:

1. **From the Bank module, click the Customer icon and select the customer account.**

2. **Sage 50 Accounts automatically lists all outstanding invoices. (See Figure 7-5.)**

3. **Enter how much the customer is paying in total.**

4. **Select the invoice or invoices paid.**

5. **Sage 50 Accounts updates the Trade Debtors account, the Cash account and the customer's individual account to show that payment has been received.**

TIP

If your customer is paying a lot of outstanding invoices, Sage 50 Accounts has two clever options that may save you some time. The first option, Pay in Full, marks every invoice as paid if the customer is settling up in full. The other option, Wizard, matches the payment to the outstanding invoices by starting with the oldest until it matches up the exact amount of the payment.

If your business uses a point-of-sale program integrated into the computerised accounting system, recording credit transactions is even easier for you. Sales details feed into the system as each sale is made, so that you don't have to enter the detail at the end of the day. These point-of-sale programs save a lot of time, but they can get really expensive.

**Figure 7-5:**
In Sage 50 Accounts, recording payments from customers who bought on credit starts with the Customer Receipt screen.

Even if customers don't buy on credit, point-of-sale programs provide businesses with an incredible amount of information about their customers and what they like to buy. This data can be used in the future for direct marketing and special sales to increase the likelihood of return business.

# Cashing Up the Cash Register

To ensure that cashiers don't pocket a business's cash, at the end of each day cashiers must *cash up* (show that they've the right amount of cash in the register based on the sales transactions during the day) the amount of cash, cheques and credit sales they took in during the day.

This process of cashing up a cash register actually starts at the end of the previous day, when cashier John Smith and his manager agree on the amount of cash left in John's register drawer. They record cash sitting in cash registers or cash drawers as part of the Cash in Hand account.

When John comes to work the next morning, he starts out with the amount of cash left in the drawer. At the end of the business day, he or his manager runs a summary of activity on the cash register for the day to produce a report of the total sales taken in by the cashier. John counts the amount of cash in his register as well as totals for the cheques, credit card receipts and credit account sales. He then completes a cash-out form that looks something like Table 7-1:

| Table 7-1 | Cash Register: John Smith, 25/4/2012 | |
|---|---|---|
| *Receipts* | *Sales* | *Total* |
| Opening Cash | | £100 |
| Cash Sales | £400 | |
| Credit Card Sales | £800 | |
| Credit Account Sales | £200 | |
| Total Sales | | £1,400 |
| Sales on Credit | | £1,000 |
| Cash Received | | £400 |
| Total Cash in Register | | £500 |

A manager reviews John Smith's cash register summary (produced by the actual register) and compares it to the cash-out form. If John's ending cash (the amount of cash remaining in the register) doesn't match the cash-out form, he and the manager try to pinpoint the mistake. If they can't find a mistake, they fill out a cash-overage or cash-shortage form. Some businesses charge the cashier directly for any shortages, whereas others take the position that the cashier's fired after a certain number of shortages of a certain amount (say, three shortages of more than £10).

The manager decides how much cash to leave in the cash drawer or register for the next day and deposits the remainder. He carries out this task for each of his cashiers and then deposits all the cash and cheques from the day in a night-deposit box at the bank. He sends a report with details of the deposit to the bookkeeper so that the data appears in the accounting system. The book-keeper enters the data on the Cash Sales screen (refer to Figure 7-2) if a computerised accounting system is being used, or into the Cash Receipts book if the books are being kept manually.

# Monitoring Sales Discounts

Most businesses offer discounts at some point in time to generate more sales. Discounts are usually in the form of a sale with 10 per cent, 20 per cent or even more off purchases.

When you offer discounts to customers, monitor your sales discounts in a separate account so that you can keep an eye on how much you discount sales each month. If you find that you're losing more and more money to discounting, look closely at your pricing structure and competition to find out why you're having to lower your prices frequently to make sales. You can monitor discount information easily by using the data found on a standard sales invoice. Figure 7-6 shows an invoice from Handson's Hardware, which shows a discount.

From this example, you can see clearly that the business takes in less cash when discounts are offered. When recording the sale in the Cash Receipts book, you record the discount as a debit. This debit increases the Sales Discount account, which the bookkeeper subtracts from the Sales account to calculate the net sales. (We walk you through all these steps and calculations when we discuss preparing the Profit and Loss statement in Chapter 13.) Here's what the bookkeeping entry would look like for Handson's Hardware. Remember, if you're using a computerised accounting system, this double entry is done automatically as you post the invoice onto the system.

# Invoice

## Handsons Hardware

Unit 10 Leestone Industrial Unit, Newtown, Digbyshire. DG14 7PQ
Tel: 01234 123456  Fax: 01234 123457
Email: Sales@handsonshardware.co.uk
WWW.handsonshardware.co.uk
VAT Reg: 987 654 49

**Invoice to:**

**Invoice No: 4567**
**Account No: 789**

Jo Tester,
74 Acacia Avenue,
Benton,
Digbyshire
DG 17 4GH

**Date: 25.02.12**

| Description | Qty | Price | Total |
|---|---|---|---|
| Hammer | 1 | £15.00 | £15.00 |
| Paint brushes | 5 | £5.00 | £25.00 |
| Paint | 2 Gall | £10.00 | £20.00 |
| | | | |

**Terms 30 Days**

| | |
|---|---|
| **Goods Total** | **£60.00** |
| **Less Discount** | **£6.00** |
| **Net Sales** | **£54.00** |
| **VAT @ 20%** | **£10.80** |
| **Total Sales** | **£64.80** |

**Figure 7-6:**
A sales
invoice from
Handson's
Hardware
showing
a sales
discount.

| | *Debit* | *Credit* |
|---|---|---|
| Bank account | £64.80 | |
| Sales Discounts | £6.00 | |
| Sales | | £60.00 |
| VAT | | £10.80 |

*Sales invoice no 4567*

If you use Sage 50 Accounts you can add the sales discount as a line item on the sales receipt or invoice, and the system automatically adjusts the sales figures and updates your Sales Discount account.

# Recording Sales Returns and Allowances

Most businesses deal with *sales returns* on a regular basis. Customers regularly return purchased items because the item is defective, they change their minds or for other reasons. Instituting a no-return policy is guaranteed to produce unhappy customers: ensure that you allow sales returns in order to maintain good customer relations.

Accepting sales returns can be a complicated process. Usually, a business posts a set of rules for returns that may include:

- ✔ Returns are allowed only within 30 days of purchase.

- ✔ You must have a receipt to return an item.

- ✔ When you return an item without a receipt, you can receive only a credit note.

You can set up whatever rules you want for returns. For internal control purposes, the key to returns is monitoring how your staff handle them. In most cases, ensure that a manager's approval is required on returns. Also, make sure that your employees pay close attention to how the customer originally paid for the item being returned. You certainly don't want to give a customer cash when they used credit – you're just handing over your money! After a return's approved, the cashier returns the amount paid by cash or credit card. Customers who bought the items on credit don't get any money back, because they didn't pay anything but expected to be billed later. Instead, a form is filled out so that the amount of the original purchase can be subtracted from the customer's credit account.

You use the information collected by the cashier who handled the return to input the sales return data into the books. For example, a customer returns an item worth £47 that was purchased with cash. You record the cash refund in the Cash Receipts book like this:

|  | **Debit** | **Credit** |
|---|---|---|
| Sales Returns and Allowances | £39.17 | |
| VAT @ 20% | £7.83 | |
| Bank account | | £47.00 |

*To record return of purchase*

If the item was bought with a discount, you list the discount as well and adjust the price to show that discount.

In this journal entry:

- ✔ The Sales Returns and Allowances account increases. This account normally carries a debit balance and is subtracted from the Sales account when preparing the Profit and Loss statement, thereby reducing revenue received from customers.

- ✔ The debit to the VAT account reduces the amount in that account because VAT is no longer due on the purchase.

- ✔ The credit to the Bank account reduces the amount of cash in that account.

*Sales allowances* (sales incentive programmes) are becoming more popular with businesses. Sales allowances are most often in the form of a gift card. A sold gift card is actually a liability for the business because the business has received cash, but no merchandise has gone out. For that reason, gift card sales are entered in the Gift Card Liability account. When a customer makes a purchase at a later date using the gift card, the Gift Card Liability account is reduced by the purchase amount. Monitoring the Gift Card Liability account allows businesses to keep track of how much is yet to be sold without receiving additional cash.

*Sales credit notes:* A business that sells goods on credit and then subsequently receives the goods back, needs to raise a credit note within their accounting system to reverse the effect of the sales invoice that has already been generated.

Figure 7-7 shows an example of a credit note that's been raised by Handson's Hardware, because the paint that was delivered was the wrong colour. The customer has returned the paint but needs a refund against their account.

# CREDIT NOTE

## Handsons Hardware

Unit 10 Leestone Industrial Unit, Newtown, Digbyshire. DG14 7PQ
Tel: 01234 123456    Fax: 01234 123457
Email: Sales@handsonshardware.co.uk
WWW.handsonshardware.co.uk
VAT Reg: 987 654 49

**Credit:**

Jo Tester,
74 Acacia Avenue,
Benton,
Digbyshire
DG17 4GH

**Invoice No: 4567**
**Account No: 789**

**Date: 25.02.12**

| Description | Qty | Price | Total |
|---|---|---|---|
| | | | |
| Paint | 2 | £10.00 | £20.00 |
| Reason: Wrong Colour | | | |

**Terms 30    Days**

| | |
|---|---|
| **Goods Total** | £20.00 |
| **Less Discount** | £2.00 |
| **Net Credit** | £18.00 |
| **VAT@ 20 %** | £3.60 |
| **Total Sales** | £21.60 |

**Figure 7-7:**
An example
of a credit
note raised,
annotated
with the
double-entry
transactions.

The double entry that occurs when a credit note is raised and entered into an accounting system is as follows:

|  | **Debit** | **Credit** |
|---|---|---|
| Sales Return account | £18.00 | |
| VAT account | £3.60 | |
| Debtors account | | £21.60 |

*Credit Note dated 25.02.12 to Jo Tester*

# Monitoring Trade Debtors

Making sure that customers pay their bills is a crucial responsibility of the bookkeeper. Before sending out the monthly bills, you should run an *Aged Debtor report*, which lists all customers who owe money to the business and the age of each debt, as shown in Figure 7-8.

**Figure 7-8:** An Aged Debtor report using Sage 50 software.

| Date: | 10/01/2012 | **Practice Company** | | Page: | 1 |
|---|---|---|---|---|---|
| Time: | 16:44:17 | **Aged Debtors Analysis (Detailed)** | | | |

| Date From: | 01/01/1980 | | | Customer From: | |
| Date To: | 10/01/2012 | | | Customer To: | ZZZZZZZZ |
| Include future transactions: | No | | | | |
| Exclude later payments: | No | | | | |

** NOTE: All report values are shown in Base Currency, unless otherwise indicated **

| A/C: | MAN | Name: | M Man | | Contact: | | | Tel: | | |
|---|---|---|---|---|---|---|---|---|---|---|

| No | Type | Date | Ref | Details | Balance | Future | Current | Period 1 | Period 2 | Period 3 | Older |
|---|---|---|---|---|---|---|---|---|---|---|---|
| 1 | SI | 05/11/2011 | 342 | Print Cartridge | 27.03 | 0.00 | 0.00 | 0.00 | 27.03 | 0.00 | 0.00 |
| | | | | Totals: | 27.03 | 0.00 | 0.00 | 0.00 | 27.03 | 0.00 | 0.00 |

Turnover: 0.00
Credit Limit £ 0.00

| A/C: | SMITH | Name: | J Smith | | Contact: | | | Tel: | | |
|---|---|---|---|---|---|---|---|---|---|---|

| No | Type | Date | Ref | Details | Balance | Future | Current | Period 1 | Period 2 | Period 3 | Older |
|---|---|---|---|---|---|---|---|---|---|---|---|
| 2 | SI | 02/11/2011 | 276 | Paper | 11.75 | 0.00 | 0.00 | 0.00 | 11.75 | 0.00 | 0.00 |
| | | | | Totals: | 11.75 | 0.00 | 0.00 | 0.00 | 11.75 | 0.00 | 0.00 |

Turnover: 0.00
Credit Limit £ 0.00

| | | | | Grand Totals: | 38.78 | 0.00 | 0.00 | 0.00 | 38.78 | 0.00 | 0.00 |

The Aged Debtor report quickly tells you which customers are behind in their bills. In this example, customers are put on stop when their payments are more than 60 days late, so J. Smith and M. Man can't buy on credit until their bills are paid in full. You can see that the 60 day plus invoices are shown in Period 2.

**REMEMBER**

Give a copy of your Aged Debtor report to the sales manager so he or she can alert staff to problem customers. The sales manager can also arrange for the appropriate collections procedures. Each business sets up its own specific collections process, usually starting with a phone call, followed by letters and possibly legal action, if necessary.

# Accepting Your Losses

You may encounter a situation in which a customer never pays your business, even after an aggressive collections process. In this case, you've no choice but to write off the purchase as a bad debt and accept the loss.

Most businesses review their Aged Debtor reports every 6 to 12 months and decide which accounts need to be written off as bad debt. Accounts written off are recorded in a Nominal Ledger account called *Bad Debt.* (See Chapter 4 for more information about the Nominal Ledger.) The Bad Debt account appears as an Expense account on the Profit and Loss statement. When you write off a customer's account as bad debt, the Bad Debt account increases, and the Trade Debtors account decreases.

To give you an idea of how you write off an account, assume that one of your customers never pays £105.75 due. Here's what your journal entry looks like for this debt:

|  | **Debit** | **Credit** |
|---|---|---|
| Bad Debt | £105.75 | |
| Trade Debtors | | £105.75 |

Sage 50 Accounts has a wizard that helps you write off individual transactions as a bad debt and does all the double entry for you, so you don't need to worry!

If the bad debt included VAT, you've suffered a double loss because you've paid over the VAT to HM Revenue & Customs, even though you never received it. Fortunately, you can reclaim this VAT when you do your next VAT return.

# Have a Go

The rest of this chapter gives you extra practice on double-entry bookkeeping, so that you're able to carry out adjustments to the accounts if you need to. More importantly, it means that you'll understand what your computerised accounting system is doing in the background every time you post an entry.

It may be worthwhile to refer back to the golden rules of bookkeeping mentioned in Chapter 2. You see, sticking the rules up on your wall doesn't seem so daft now, does it?!

1. **Take a look at the sales receipt in Figure 7-9. How would you record this transaction in your books, if you were the bookkeeper for a hardware business?**

2. **Take a look at the sales receipt in Figure 7-10. How would you record this transaction in your books, if you were a bookkeeper for this office supply business?**

HANDSON'S HARDWARE

Sales receipt 25/2/2012

| Item | Quantity | Price | Total |
|------|----------|-------|-------|
| Hammer | 1 | £15.00 | £15.00 |
| Paint Brushes | 5 | £5.00 | £5.00 |
| Paint | 2 gallons | £10.00 | £10.00 |
| **Subtotal** | | | **£60.00** |
| **VAT @ 20%** | | | **£12.00** |
| **Total Sale** | | | **£72.00** |
| **Paid Cash** | | | **£72.00** |

**Figure 7-9:** Sales Receipt for Handson's Hardware on 25/2/2012.

SIMPLY STATIONERY

Sales receipt 05/03/2012

| Item | Quantity | Price | Total |
|------|----------|-------|-------|
| Paper | 2 boxes | £10.00 | £20.00 |
| Print Cartridge | 1 | £15.00 | £15.00 |
| Hanging Files | 2 boxes | £5.00 | £10.00 |
| **Subtotal** | | | **£45.00** |
| **VAT @ 20%** | | | **£9.00** |
| **Total Sale** | | | **£54.00** |
| **Paid by VISA Credit Card** | | | **£54.00** |

**Figure 7-10:** Sales Receipt for Simply Stationery on 05/03/2012.

3. Using the invoice shown in Figure 7-11, how would you record this credit transaction in your books, if you were the bookkeeper for Handson's Hardware?

# Invoice

## Handsons Hardware

Unit 10 Leestone Industrial Unit ,Newtown, Digbyshire. DG14 7PQ

Tel: 01234 123456    Fax: 01234 123457

Email:  Sales@handsonshardware.co.uk

WWW.handsonshardware.co.uk

VAT Reg: 987 654 49

Invoice to:

Jo Tester,
74 Acacia Avenue,
Benton,
Digbyshire
DG17 4GH

Invoice No: 4673
Account No: 823

Date: 12.05.12

| Description | Qty | Price | Total | Discount | Net |
|---|---|---|---|---|---|
| Hammer | 1 | £15.00 | £15.00 | 0.00 | £15.00 |
| Nails | 1 box | £9.00 | £9.00 | 0.00 | £9.00 |
| Ladder | 1 | £90.00 | £90.00 | 0.00 | £90.00 |
|  |  |  |  |  |  |

**Terms 30 Days**

| | |
|---|---|
| Goods Total | £114.00 |
| Less Discount | £00.00 |
| Net Sales | £114.00 |
| VAT @ 20% | £22.80 |
| Total Sales | £136.80 |

**Figure 7-11:**
Sales invoice for Handson's Hardware.

4. **Using the invoice shown in Figure 7-12, how would you record this credit transaction in your books, if you were a bookkeeper for this office supply business?**

# Invoice

## Simply Stationery

32 High Street, Benton, Digbyshire. DG17 2LD
Tel: 01234 567890 Fax: 01234 567891
Email: Sales@simplystationery.co.uk
WWW.simplystationery .co.uk
VAT Reg: 862 113 49

Invoice to:                                                                    Invoice No: 124

Sues Insurance Agency
23 High Street
Benton
Digbyshire
DG17 4LU

                                                                                Date: 05.03.12

| Description | Qty | Price | Total | Discount | Net |
|---|---|---|---|---|---|
| A4 Copy Paper | 2 | £15.00 | £30.00 | 0.00 | £30.00 |
| Print cartridge | 1 | £25.00 | £25.00 | 0.00 | £25.00 |
| Hanging Files | 2 | £10.00 | £20.00 | 0.00 | £20.00 |
| | | | | | |

**Terms 30 Days**

| | |
|---|---|
| **Goods Total** | **£75.00** |
| **Less Discount** | **£00.00** |
| **Net Sales** | **£75.00** |
| **VAT@ 20 %** | **£15.00** |
| **Total Sales** | **£90.00** |

**Figure 7-12:**
Sales
invoice
for Simply
Stationery.

5. Use the information in the cash register summary shown below to complete the blank cash summary form. Also, assume that the cash register had £100 at the beginning of the day and £426 at the end of the day. Is there a difference between how much should be in the register and how much is actually in there?

### Cash Register Summary for Jane Doe on 15/3/2012

| Item | Quantity | Price | Total |
|------|----------|-------|-------|
| Paper | 20 boxes | £15.00 | £300.00 |
| Print cartridges | 10 | £25.00 | £250.00 |
| Envelopes | 10 boxes | £7.00 | £70.00 |
| Pens | 20 boxes | £8.00 | £160.00 |
| Subtotal | | | £780.00 |
| VAT @ 20 % | | | £156.00 |
| Total cash sales | | | £336.00 |
| Total credit card sales | | | £200.00 |
| Total credit account sales | | | £400.00 |
| Total sales | | | £936.00 |

### Cash Register: _____     Date: _____

| Receipts | Sales | Cash in Register |
|----------|-------|------------------|
| Beginning cash | | _____ |
| Cash sales | _____ | |
| Credit card sales | _____ | |
| Credit account sales | _____ | |
| Total sales | _____ | |
| Minus credit sales | _____ | |
| Total cash received | | _____ |
| Total cash that should be in register | | _____ |
| Actual cash in register | | _____ |
| Difference | | _____ |

6. How would you record the following transaction in your books, if you were a bookkeeper for an office supply business? Design a sales invoice using the information supplied and show the bookkeeping transactions. Be as creative as you like with the name and address of the office

supply business. Use the examples of previous sales invoices shown in Figures 7-3 and 7-6 to help you with the design of the invoice.

## Sales Receipt 05/03/2012

| Item | Quantity | Price | Total |
|------|----------|-------|-------|
| Paper | 2 box | £15.00 | £30.00 |
| Print cartridge | 1 | £15.00 | £15.00 |
| Hanging files | 2 boxes | £5.00 | £10.00 |
| Subtotal | | | £55.00 |
| Sales discount @ 20% | | | £11.00 |
| Sales after discount | | | £44.00 |
| VAT @ 20% | | | £8.80 |
| Total cash sale | | | £52.80 |

7. How would you record the following credit transaction in your books, if you were a bookkeeper for this office supply business?

## Sales Summary for 05/03/2012

| Item | Quantity | Price | Total |
|------|----------|-------|-------|
| Paper | 10 boxes | £15.00 | £150.00 |
| Print cartridges | 5 | £15.00 | £75.00 |
| Hanging files | 7 boxes | £5.00 | £35.00 |
| Envelopes | 10 boxes | £7.00 | £70.00 |
| Pens | 20 boxes | £8.00 | £160.00 |
| Subtotal | | | £490.00 |
| Sales discount @ 20% | | | £98.00 |
| Sales after discount | | | £392.00 |
| VAT @ 20% | | | £78.40 |
| Total cash sales | | | £145.40 |
| Total credit card sales | | | £150.00 |
| Total credit account sales | | | £175.00 |
| Total Sales | | | £470.40 |

8. A customer returns a pair of trousers he bought for £35 using a credit card. He has a receipt showing when he made the original purchase. The rate of VAT is 20 per cent. How would you record this transaction in the books?

9. On 15 December, Jean Jones, a customer of Simply Stationery, returns a filing cabinet she bought on 1 December for £75 on credit. She's already been issued with a sales invoice, but hasn't paid for it yet. Design a credit note for this transaction and state how you'd record the transaction in the books?

   Note: The rate of VAT is 20 per cent.

10. You discover, after compiling your Aged Debtors report for 30 June 2012, that you've an account that's more than six months past due for a total of £125.65. Your company policy is that you write off bad debt when an account is more than six months late. How would you record this transaction in your books?

# Answering the Have a Go Questions

1. **Handson's Hardware would record the sales receipts transactions as follows:**

   |  | *Debit* | *Credit* |
   | --- | --- | --- |
   | Bank account | £72.00 | |
   | Sales | | £60.00 |
   | VAT | | £12.00 |

   *Cash receipts for 25/2/2011*

2. **Simply Stationery would record the sales receipts information as follows:**

   |  | *Debit* | *Credit* |
   | --- | --- | --- |
   | Visa card Bank account | £54.00 | |
   | Sales | | £45.00 |
   | VAT | | £9.00 |

   *Cash receipts for 05/03/11*

3. **You'd record the sales invoice details as follows:**

   |  | *Debit* | *Credit* |
   | --- | --- | --- |
   | Debtors | £136.80 | |
   | Sales | | £114.00 |
   | VAT | | £22.80 |

   *Credit receipts for 12/05/2011*

**4. You'd record the sales invoice details as follows:**

|  | Debit | Credit |
|---|---|---|
| Debtors | £90.00 | |
| Sales | | £75.00 |
| VAT | | £15.00 |

*Credit receipts for 05/03/2011*

**5. Here's how you'd complete the cash out form.**

## Cash Register: Jane Doe, 15/3/2011

| Receipts | Sales | Cash in Register |
|---|---|---|
| Beginning cash | | £100.00 |
| Cash sales | £336.00 | |
| Credit card sales | £200.00 | |
| Business credit sales | £400.00 | |
| Total sales | £936.00 | |
| Minus sales on credit | (£600.00) | |
| Total cash received | | £336.00 |
| Total cash that should be in register | | £436.00 |
| Actual cash in register | | £426.00 |
| Difference | | Shortage of £10.00 |

The manager would need to investigate why the till was down by £10.

**6. You can use Figures 7-3 and 7-6 to guide you in designing your invoice for these transactions.**

The bookkeeping entry is as follows:

|  | Debit | Credit |
|---|---|---|
| Bank account | £52.80 | |
| Sales Discount | £11.00 | |
| Sales | | £55.00 |
| VAT | | £8.80 |

*Cash receipts for 05/03/11*

**7. The entry would be:**

|  | Debit | Credit |
|---|---|---|
| Bank account | £295.40 | |
| Debtors | £175.00 | |
| Sales Discount | £98.00 | |
| Sales | | £490.00 |
| VAT | | £78.40 |

*Cash receipts for 05/03/11*

8. **The entry would be:**

|  | Debit | Credit |
|---|---|---|
| Sales Returns and Allowance | £29.17 | |
| VAT | £5.83 | |
| Bank account | | £35.00 |

Even though the customer is receiving a credit on his credit card, you show this refund by crediting your Bank account. Remember, when a customer uses a credit card, the card is processed by the bank and cash is deposited in the business's Bank account.

9. **The double-entry bookkeeping would be:**

|  | Debit | Credit |
|---|---|---|
| Sales Returns and Allowances | £60.00 | |
| VAT | £15.00 | |
| Debtors | | £75.00 |

10. **The entry would look like this:**

|  | Debit | Credit |
|---|---|---|
| Bad Debt | £125.65 | |
| Debtors | | £125.65 |

*Accounts written-off for bad debt as at 30/06/11*

# Chapter 8

# Buying and Tracking Your Purchases

**In This Chapter**

▶ Tracking stock and monitoring costs

▶ Keeping your business supplied

▶ Paying your bills

*I*n order to make money, your business must have something to sell. Whether you sell products or offer services, you have to deal with costs directly related to the goods or services being sold. Those costs primarily come from the purchase or manufacturing of the products you plan to sell or the items you need in order to provide the services.

All businesses must keep careful watch over the cost of the products they sell or the services they offer. Ultimately, your business's profits depend on how well you manage those costs because, in most cases, costs increase over time rather than decrease. How often do you find a reduction in the price of needed items? It doesn't happen often. When costs increase but the price to the customer remains unchanged, the profit you make on each sale is less.

In addition to the costs to produce products or services, every business has additional expenses associated with purchasing supplies needed to run the business. The bookkeeper has primary responsibility for monitoring all these costs and expenses as invoices are paid and alerting business owners or managers when suppliers increase prices. This chapter covers how to track purchases and their costs, manage stock, buy and manage supplies, and pay the bills for the items your business buys.

## Keeping Track of Stock

Products to be sold are called *stock*. As a bookkeeper, you use two accounts to track stock:

- **Purchases:** Where you record the actual purchase of goods to be sold. This account is used to calculate the *Cost of Goods Sold,* which is an item on the Profit and Loss statement (see Chapter 13 for more on this statement).

- **Stock:** Where you track the value of stock on hand. This value is shown on the Balance Sheet as an asset in a line item called *Stock* (Chapter 14 addresses the Balance Sheet).

Businesses track physical stock on hand using one of two methods:

- **Periodic stock count:** Conducting a physical count of the stock in the stores and in the warehouse. This count can be done daily, monthly, yearly or for any other period that best matches your business needs. (Many businesses close for all or part of a day to count stock.)

- **Perpetual stock count:** Adjusting stock counts as each sale is made. In order to use this method, you must manage your stock using a computerised accounting system tied into your point of sale (usually cash registers).

Even if you use a perpetual stock method, periodically do a physical count of stock to ensure that the numbers match what's in your computer system. Because theft, damage and loss of stock aren't automatically entered in your computer system, the losses don't show up until you do a physical count of the stock you have on hand in your business.

When preparing your Profit and Loss statement at the end of an accounting period (whether that period is for a month, a quarter or a year), you need to calculate the Cost of Goods Sold in order to calculate the profit made.

In order to calculate the Cost of Goods Sold, you must first find out how many items of stock were sold. You start with the amount of stock on hand at the beginning of the month (called *Opening Stock*), as recorded in the Stock account, and add the amount of purchases, as recorded in the Purchases account, to find the Goods Available for Sale. Then you subtract the stock on hand at the end of the month *(Closing Stock),* which is determined by counting remaining stock.

Here's how you calculate the number of goods sold:

Opening Stock + Purchases = Goods Available for Sale − Closing Stock = Items Sold

After you determine the number of goods sold, compare that number to the actual number of items the business sold during that accounting period, which is based on sales figures collected through the month. When the numbers don't match, you've a problem. The mistake may be in the stock count, or items may be unaccounted for because someone has misplaced or damaged and discarded them. In the worst-case scenario, you may have a problem with customer or employee theft. These differences are usually tracked within the accounting system in a line item called *Stock Shortages*.

## Entering initial cost

When your business first receives stock, you enter the initial cost of that stock into the bookkeeping system based on the shipment's invoice. In some cases, invoices are sent separately, and only a delivery note is included in the order. When that situation applies, you still record the receipt of the goods, because the business incurs the cost from the day it receives the goods, and you must be sure that the money is available to pay for the goods when the invoice arrives and the bill comes due. You track outstanding bills in the Trade Creditors (Accounts Payable) account. Where you only have a delivery note, use the price agreed on your purchase order (if you use purchase orders) or the price from your last invoice from that supplier.

Entering the receipt of stock is a relatively easy entry in the bookkeeping system. For example, if your business buys £1,000 of stock to be sold, you normally receive a purchase invoice for those goods. The invoice is entered into your accounting system as described in Chapter 4. The following double entry takes place:

|                     | Debit  | Credit |
|---------------------|--------|--------|
| Materials Purchased | £1,000 |        |
| Trade Creditors     |        | £1,000 |

The Purchases account increases by £1,000 to reflect the additional costs, and the Trade Creditors account increases by the same amount to reflect the amount of the bill that needs to be paid in the future.

When stock enters your business, in addition to recording the actual costs, you need more detail about what you've bought, how much of each item you've bought and what each item cost. You also need to track:

✔ How much stock you have on hand.

✔ The value of the stock you have on hand.

✔ When you need to order more stock.

Tracking these details for each type of product bought can be a nightmare. However, a computerised accounting simplifies this process of tracking stock. Details about stock can be entered initially into your computer accounting system in several ways:

✔ If you pay by cheque or credit card when you receive the stock, you can enter the details about each item on the cheque counterfoil or credit card slip.

✔ If you use purchase orders, you can enter the detail about each item on the purchase order, record receipt of the items when they arrive and update the information when you receive the bill.

✔ If you don't use purchase orders, you can enter the detail about the items when you receive them and update the information when you receive the bill.

To give you an idea of how this information is collected in a computerised accounting software program, Figure 8-1 shows you how to enter the details in Sage 50 Accounts. This particular form is for the receipt of stock without a purchase order and can be used when you receive a supplier invoice.

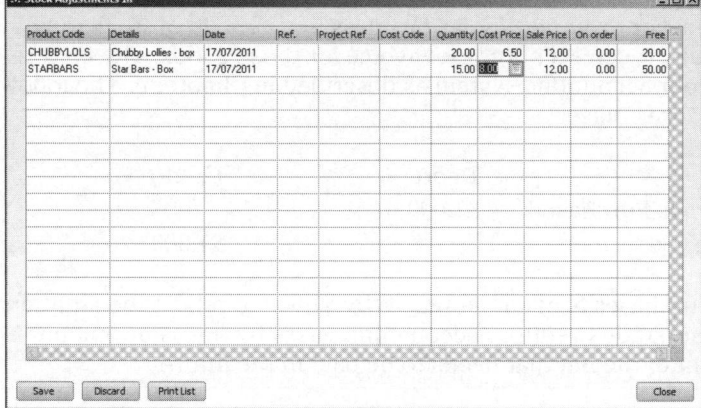

**Figure 8-1:**
Recording
of the
receipt of
stock using
Sage 50
Accounts.

Figure 8-2 shows a stock item record in the computerised accounting system. Note that you must give the item a product code and a description. The product code is a short unique name or code to identify the stock item internally. The longer description is a more user-friendly name that can appear on customer invoices (sales transactions). You can input a cost and sales price if you want, or you can leave them at zero and enter the cost and sales prices with each transaction.

If you've a set contract purchase price or sales price on a stock item, you can enter the price on this form to save time – you don't then have to enter the price each time you record a transaction. But, if the price changes frequently, leave the space blank so that you don't forget to enter the updated price when you enter a transaction.

**Figure 8-2:**
Setting up
a stock
item using
Sage 50
Accounts.

Notice in Figure 8-2 that you can also use this form to give you information about stock on hand and when stock needs to be reordered. To make sure that your shelves are never empty, enter a number for each item that indicates at what point you want to reorder stock. You can indicate the 'Reorder Level' in the section called 'Status'. (A nice feature of Sage 50 Accounts is that you can run a report to see which stock items have fallen below their reorder level and use that to place your next order.)

If you use the Purchase Order Processing routine and save the form that records the receipt of stock in Sage 50 Accounts, the software automatically:

✔ Adjusts the quantity of stock you have in stock.

✔ Increases the Asset account called Stock.

✔ Lowers the quantity of items on order (if you initially entered the information as a purchase order).

✔ Averages the cost of stock on hand.

✔ Increases the Trade Creditor account.

## Managing stock and its value

After you record the receipt of stock, you have the responsibility of managing the stock you have on hand. You must also know the value of that stock. You may think that as long as you know what you paid for the items, the value isn't difficult to calculate. Well, accountants can't let things be that simple, and so have five different ways to value stock:

- ✔ **LIFO (last in, first out):** You assume that the last items put on the shelves (the newest items) are the first items to be sold. Retail shops that sell non-perishable items, such as tools, are likely to use this type of system. For example, when a hardware store gets new hammers, workers probably don't unload the hammers on the shelves and put the newest items in the back. Instead, they put the new hammers in the front, so they're likely to be sold first.

- ✔ **FIFO (first in, first out):** You assume that the first items put on the shelves (the oldest items) are sold first. Shops that sell perishable goods, such as food shops, use this stock valuation method most often. For example, when new milk arrives at a shop, the person stocking the shelves unloads the older milk, puts the new milk at the back of the shelf, and then puts the older milk in front. Each carton of milk (or other perishable item) has a date indicating the last day it can be sold, so food shops always try to sell the oldest stuff first, while those items are still sellable. (They try, but how many times have you reached to the back of a food shelf to find items with the longest shelf life?)

- ✔ **Averaging:** You average the cost of goods received, to avoid worrying about which items are sold first or last. This method of stock is used most often in any retail or services environment where prices are constantly fluctuating and the business owner finds that an average cost works best for managing the Cost of Goods Sold.

- ✔ **Specific identification:** You maintain cost figures for each stock item individually. Retail outlets that sell big-ticket items such as cars, which often have a different set of extras on each item, use this type of stock valuation method.

- ✔ **LCM (lower of cost or market):** You set stock values based on whichever is lower: the amount you paid originally for the stock item (the cost), or the current market value of the item. Businesses that deal in precious metals, commodities, or publicly traded securities often use this method because the prices of their products can fluctuate wildly, sometimes even in the same day.

After you choose a stock valuation method, you need to use the same method each year on your financial reports and when you file your accounts. If you decide that you want to change the method, you need to explain the reasons for the change to both HM Revenue & Customs and to your financial backers. If you run an incorporated business in which shares have been sold, you need to explain the change to your shareholders. You also have to go back and show how the change in stock method impacts your prior financial reporting, and adjust your profit margins in previous years to reflect the new stock valuation method's impact on your long-term profit history.

### Figuring out the best method for you

We're sure that you're wondering why the stock valuation method you use matters so much. The key to the choice is the impact on your bottom line as well as the tax your business pays.

Because FIFO assumes the oldest (and most likely the lowest priced) items are sold first, this method results in a lower Cost of Goods Sold number. Because Cost of Goods Sold is subtracted from sales to determine profit, a lower Cost of Goods Sold number produces a higher profit. (For more on Cost of Goods Sold, see 'Keeping Track of Stock', earlier in this chapter.)

The opposite is true for LIFO, which uses cost figures based on the last price paid for the stock (and most likely the highest price). Using the LIFO method, the Cost of Goods Sold number is higher, which means a larger sum is subtracted from sales to determine profit. Thus, the profit margin is lower. The good news, however, is that the tax bill is also low.

The Averaging method gives a business the best picture of what's happening with stock costs and trends. Rather than constantly dealing with the ups and downs of stock costs, this method smooths out the numbers you use to calculate a business's profits. Cost of Goods Sold, taxes and profit margins for this method fall between those of LIFO and FIFO. Definitely choose this method when you're operating a business in which stock prices are constantly going up and down.

The Averaging method always falls between LIFO and FIFO as regards the Cost of Goods Sold, taxes and profit margin.

Sage 50 Accounts uses the LIFO method to calculate Cost of Goods Sold and stock line items on its financial reports, so if you choose this method, you can use Sage 50 Accounts and the financial reports it generates. However, if you choose to use one of the other four stock methods, you can't use the Sage 50 Accounts financial report numbers. Instead, you have to print out a report of purchases and calculate the accurate numbers to use on your financial reports for the Cost of Goods Sold and Stock accounts.

Check with your accountant to see which stock method is best for you given the type of business you're operating and which one is the most acceptable to HM Revenue & Customs.

### Comparing the methods

To show you how much of an impact stock valuation can have on profit margin, in this section we compare three of the most common methods: FIFO, LIFO and Averaging. In this example, we assume that Business A bought the stock in question at different prices on three different occasions. Opening Stock is valued at £500 (50 items at £10 each).

Here's the calculation to determine the number of items sold (from the earlier 'Keeping Track of Stock' section):

> Opening Stock + Purchases = Goods Available for Sale – Closing Stock = Items Sold
>
> 50 + 500 = 550 – 75 = 475

Here's what the business paid to purchase the stock:

| Date | Quantity | Unit Price |
|------|----------|-----------|
| 1 April | 150 | £10 |
| 15 April | 150 | £25 |
| 30 April | 200 | £30 |

Here's an example of how you calculate the Cost of Goods Sold using the Averaging method:

| Category | Quantity (Unit Price) | Total Cost |
|----------|----------------------|-----------|
| Opening Stock | 50 (£10) | £500 |
| Purchases | 150 (£10) | £1,500 |
| | 150 (£25) | £3,750 |
| | 200 (£30) | £6,000 |
| Total Stock | 550 | £11,750 |

Now you can do other calculations:

| | |
|---|---|
| Average Stock cost | £11,750 ÷ 550 = £21.36 |
| Cost of Goods Sold | 475 × £21.36 = £10,146 |
| Closing Stock | 75 @ £21.36 = £1,602 |

The Cost of Goods Sold number appears on the Profit and Loss statement and is subtracted from Sales. The Closing Stock number shows up as an asset on the Balance Sheet. This system applies to all three stock valuation methods.

Now, we demonstrate how you calculate the Cost of Goods Sold using the FIFO method. With this method, you assume that the first items you receive are the first ones you sell, and because the first items you receive here are those in Opening Stock, we start with them:

| Date | Quantity (Unit Price) | Total |
|------|----------------------|-------|
| Opening Stock | 50 (£10) | £500 |
| 1 April | 150 (£10) | £1,500 |
| 15 April | 150 (£25) | £3,750 |
| 30 April | 125 (£30) | £3,750 |
| Cost of Goods Sold | 475 | £9,500 |
| Closing Stock | 75 @ £30 | £2,250 |

*Note:* Only 125 of the 200 units purchased on 30 April are used in the FIFO method. Because this method assumes that the first items into stock are the first items you sell (or take out of stock), the first items you use are those on 1 April. Then you use the 15 April items, and finally you take the remaining needed items from those bought on April 30. Because you bought 200 on April 30 and you only needed 125, 75 of the items you bought on April 30 are left in Closing Stock. The Cost of Goods Sold figure, which is £9,500, is the sum of the total values of the units above which are deemed to have been sold to arrive at this figure (£500 + £1,500 + £3,750 + £3,750).

Next, calculate the Cost of Goods Sold using the LIFO method. With this method, you assume that the last items you receive are the first ones you sell, and because the last items you receive were those you purchased on April 30, we start with them:

| Date | Quantity (Unit Price) | Total |
|------|----------------------|-------|
| 30 April | 200 (£30) | £6,000 |
| 15 April | 150 (£25) | £3,750 |
| 1 April | 125 (£10) | £1,250 |
| Cost of Goods Sold | 475 | £11,000 |
| Closing Stock | 75 @ £10 | £750 |

*Note:* Because LIFO assumes the last items to arrive are sold first, the Closing Stock includes the 25 remaining units (150 purchased less 125 used/sold) from the 1 April purchase plus the 50 units in Opening Stock.

Here's how the use of stock under the LIFO method impacts the business profits. We assume that you sell the items to the customers for £40 per unit, which means total sales of £19,000 for the month (£40 × 475 units sold). In this example, we just look at the *Gross Profit,* which is the profit from Sales before considering expenses incurred for operating the business. We talk more about the different profit types and what they mean in Chapter 13. The following equation calculates Gross Profit:

Sales – Cost of Goods Sold = Gross Profit

Table 8-1 shows a comparison of Gross Profit for the three methods used in this example.

| Table 8-1 | Comparison of Gross Profit Based on Stock Valuation Method | | |
|---|---|---|---|
| *Profit and Loss Statement Line Item* | *FIFO* | *LIFO* | *Averaging* |
| Sales | £19,000 | £19,000 | £19,000 |
| Cost of Goods Sold | £9,500 | £11,000 | £10,146 |
| Gross Profit | £9,500 | £8,000 | £8,854 |

Looking at the comparisons of Gross Profit, you can see that stock valuation can have a major impact on your bottom line. LIFO is likely to give you the lowest profit because the last stock items bought are usually the most expensive. FIFO is likely to give you the highest profit because the first items bought are usually the cheapest. And the profit that the Averaging method produces is likely to fall somewhere in between the two.

# Buying and Monitoring Supplies

In addition to stock, all businesses must buy the supplies used to operate the business, such as paper, pens and paper clips. Supplies that businesses haven't bought in direct relationship to the manufacturing or purchasing of goods or services for sale fall into the category of *expenses.*

Just how closely you want to monitor the supplies you use depends on your business needs. The expense categories you establish may be as broad as Office Supplies and Retail Supplies, or you may want to set up accounts for each type of supply used. Each additional account is just one more thing that needs to be managed and monitored in the accounting system, so you need to determine whether keeping a particularly detailed record of supplies is worth your time.

Your best bet is to track supplies that make a big dent in your budget carefully with an individual account. For example, if you anticipate paper usage is going to be high, monitor that usage with a separate account called Paper Expenses.

Many businesses don't use the bookkeeping system to manage their supplies. Instead, they designate one or two people as office managers or supply managers and keep the number of accounts used for supplies to a minimum. Other businesses decide to monitor supplies by department or division, and set up a Supply account for each one. This system puts the burden of monitoring supplies in the hands of the department or division managers.

# Staying on Top of Your Bills

Eventually, you have to pay for both the stock and the supplies you purchase for your business. In most cases, you post the bills to the Trade Creditors account when they arrive, and they're paid when due. A large chunk of the cash you pay out of your Cash account (see Chapters 4 and 6 for more information on the Cash account and handling cash) is in the form of the cheques you send out to pay bills due in Trade Creditors, so you need to have careful controls over the five key functions of Trade Creditors:

- ✔ Entering bills you need to pay into the accounting system.
- ✔ Preparing cheques to pay the bills.
- ✔ Signing cheques to pay the bills.
- ✔ Sending out payment cheques to suppliers.
- ✔ Reconciling the Bank account.

In your business, the person who enters the bills to be paid into the system is likely to be the same person who also prepares the payment cheques. However, you must ensure that someone else does the other tasks. Never allow the person who prepares the cheques to review the bills to be paid and sign the cheques, unless of course that person's you, the business owner. (We talk more about cash control and the importance of separating duties in Chapter 6.)

Properly managing Trade Creditors allows you to avoid late fees or interest and take advantage of discounts offered for paying early, therefore saving your business a lot of money. If you're using a computerised accounting system, you need to enter the bill due date and any discount information at the time you receive the stock or supplies. (See Figure 8-1 for how you record this information.)

If you're working with a paper system rather than a computerised accounting system, you need to set up a way to ensure that you don't miss bill due dates. Many businesses use two accordion files: one set up by the month, and the other set up by the day. On receipt, you put a bill into the first accordion file according to the due month. On the first day of that month, the Purchase Ledger clerk pulls all the bills due that month and puts them in the daily accordion file based on the date the bill is due. The clerk then posts payment cheques in time to arrive in the supplier's office by the due date.

In some cases, businesses offer a discount if their customers pay bills early. Sage 50 Accounts allows you to set up for each supplier Settlement Due dates and Settlement Discount percentage figures. For example, if a supplier is set up as '10 days' and '2 per cent', it means that if the bill is paid in 10 days, the purchasing business can take a 2 per cent discount; otherwise, the amount due must be paid in full in 30 days. If the total amount due for a bill is £1,000 and the business pays the bill in 10 days, that business can take a 2 per cent discount, or £20. This discount may not seem like much, but if your business buys £100,000 of stock and supplies in a month and each supplier offers a similar discount, you can save £1,000. Over the course of a year, discounts on purchases can save your business a significant amount of money and improve your profits.

In addition, many businesses state that they charge interest or late fees if a bill isn't paid in 30 days (although in reality few dare make this charge if they want to retain the business).

# *Have a Go*

Here are some exercises for you to practise the principles discussed in this chapter.

1. **Harry's Hardware started the month with 25 wrenches on the shelf, with an average per unit value of £3.25. During the month, Harry made these additional purchases:**

   | | |
   |---|---|
   | 1 April | 100 wrenches @ £3.50 |
   | 10 April | 100 wrenches @ £3.75 |
   | 20 April | 150 wrenches @ £4.00 |

   At the end of the month, he had 100 wrenches on the shelf. Calculate the value of the Closing Stock and the Cost of Goods Sold using the Averaging method.

2. **Harry's Hardware started the month with 25 wrenches on the shelf, with an average per unit value of £3.25. During the month, he made these additional purchases:**

   | | |
   |---|---|
   | 1 April | 100 wrenches @ £3.50 |
   | 10 April | 100 wrenches @ £3.75 |
   | 20 April | 150 wrenches @ £4.00 |

   At the end of the month, he had 100 wrenches on the shelf. Calculate the value of the Closing Stock and the Cost of Goods Sold using the FIFO method.

3. **Harry's Hardware started the month with 25 wrenches on the shelf with an average per unit value of £3.25. During the month, he made these additional purchases:**

   | | |
   |---|---|
   | 1 April | 100 wrenches @ £3.50 |
   | 10 April | 100 wrenches @ £3.75 |
   | 20 April | 150 wrenches @ £4.00 |

   At the end of the month, he had 100 wrenches on the shelf. Calculate the value of the Closing Stock and the Cost of Goods Sold using the LIFO method.

4. **Suppose your company receives an invoice for £500,000 on 31 March that says, 'Settlement discount of 3 per cent if paid within 10 days of date of invoice.' How much discount would you receive and by what date should you pay the invoice to receive this discount?**

5. **Suppose your company receives an invoice for £100,000 on 31 March that said, 'Settlement discount of 2 per cent if paid within 15 days of the date of invoice.' How much discount would you receive and what date should you pay the invoice to receive this discount?**

6. **If you keep track of the amount of stock you have on hand by physically counting how much product is on your shop shelves and in your warehouse on a regular basis, what is this kind of stock system called?**

7. **If your stock is counted each time you ring up a sale on your register, what is this kind of stock system called?**

8. **If you work in a grocery shop and carefully place the newest loaves of bread at the back of the shelf and bring the older loaves of bread to the front, what type of stock system does your shop probably use?**

9. **If you work at a car dealership and you track the sale of a car using the original invoice price, what type of stock system does your dealership probably use?**

# Answering the Have a Go Questions

1. **Here's how you'd calculate the Closing Stock and Cost of Goods Sold using the Averaging method:**

| | | |
|---|---|---|
| Opening Stock | 25 wrenches @ ₤3.25 | ₤81.25 |
| 1 April | 100 wrenches @ ₤3.50 | ₤350.00 |
| 10 April | 100 wrenches @ ₤3.75 | ₤375.00 |
| 20 April | 150 wrenches @ ₤4.00 | ₤600.00 |
| Total Goods Available for Sale | 375 wrenches | ₤1,406.25 |
| Average Cost per Unit | ₤1,406.25/375 | ₤3.75 |
| Closing Stock | 100 @ ₤3.75 | ₤375.00 |
| Cost of Goods Sold | 275 @ ₤3.75 | ₤1,031.25 |

2. **Here's how you'd calculate the Closing Stock and Cost of Goods Sold using the FIFO method:**

| | | |
|---|---|---|
| Opening Stock: | 25 wrenches @ ₤3.25 | ₤81.25 |
| Next in: | | |
| 1 April | 100 wrenches @ ₤3.50 | ₤350.00 |
| 10 April | 100 wrenches @ ₤3.75 | ₤375.00 |
| 20 April | 50 wrenches @ ₤4.00 | ₤200.00 |
| Cost of Goods Sold | | ₤1,006.25 |
| Closing Stock | 100 wrenches @ ₤4.00 | ₤400.00 |

3. **Here's how you'd calculate the Closing Stock and Cost of Goods Sold using the LIFO method:**

| | | |
|---|---|---|
| First Sold purchased 20 April: | 150 @ ₤4.00 | ₤600.00 |
| Next Sold purchased 10 April: | 100 @ ₤3.75 | ₤375.00 |
| Next Sold purchased 1 April: | 25 @ ₤3.50 | ₤87.50 |
| Cost of Goods Sold | | ₤1,062.50 |
| Closing Stock | | |
| 75 from April 1 | @ ₤3.50 | ₤262.50 |
| 25 from Beginning @ ₤3.25 | ₤81.25 | ₤343.75 |

4. **The company receives a 3 per cent discount if it pays the invoice in 10 days – by 10 April.** The discount is ₤15,000 if paid by 10 April. So, you should pay the invoice by 10 April.

5. **The company receives a 2 per cent discount if it pays the invoice in 15 days – by 15 April.** The discount is ₤2,000 if paid by 15 April. So you should pay the invoice by 15 April.

6. **If you physically count your stock on a regular, monthly, quarterly or yearly basis, this is known as a periodic stock count system.**

7. **If your business operates a system whereby the till adjusts your stock each time a sale is made, this is a perpetual stock system.**

8. **A grocery shop would want the first product in (oldest item) to be the first product out (first sold).** So your grocery shop is using the FIFO method.

9. **A car dealership usually wants to maintain a specific identification system because each car in the stock probably has different options and a different cost.** So your car dealership is using the Specific identification method.

# Chapter 9

# Doing Your Banking

A ll business owners – whether the business is a small family-owned shop or a major international conglomerate – periodically like to test how well their businesses are doing. They also want to make sure that the numbers in their accounting systems actually match what's physically in their shops and offices. After they check out what's in the books, these business owners can prepare financial reports to determine the business's financial success or failure during the last month, quarter or year. This process of verifying the accuracy of your books is called *checking the books*.

The first step in checking the books involves counting the business's cash and verifying that the cash numbers in your books match the actual cash on hand at a particular point in time. This chapter explains how you can test that the cash counts are accurate, finalise the cash books for the accounting period, reconcile the bank accounts and post any adjustments or corrections to the Nominal Ledger.

## Checking the books: Why bother?

You're probably thinking that checking the books sounds like a huge task that takes lots of time. And you're right – but checking the books every now and then is essential to ensure that what's recorded in your accounting system realistically measures what's actually going on in your business.

Mistakes can be made with any accounting system and, unfortunately, any business can fall victim to theft or embezzlement. The only way to be sure that none of these problems exist in your business is to check the books periodically. Most businesses do this check every month.

# Making Sure that the Closing Cash Is Right

Checking your books starts with counting your cash. Why start with cash? Because the accounting process starts with transactions, and transactions occur when cash changes hands to buy things you need to run the business or to sell your products or services. Before you can even begin to test whether the books are right, you need to know whether your books have captured what's happened to your business's cash and if the amount of cash shown in your books actually matches the amount of cash you have on hand.

In Chapter 7, we discuss how a business cashes up the money taken in by each cashier. That daily process gives a business good control of the point at which cash comes into the business from customers who buy the business's products or services. The process also measures any cash refunds the business gives to customers who returned items.

## Producing a snapshot in time

The points of sale and return aren't the only times that cash comes into or goes out of the business. If your business sells products on credit (see Chapter 7), bookkeeping staff responsible for monitoring customer credit accounts collect some of the cash from customers at a later point in time. And when your business needs something, whether products to be sold or supplies for various departments, you must pay cash to suppliers and contractors. Sometimes cash is paid out on the spot, but often the bill is recorded in the Trade Creditors (Accounts Payable) account and paid at a later date. All these transactions involve the use of cash, so the amount of cash on hand in the business at any one time includes not only what's in the cash registers, but also what's on deposit in the business's bank accounts. You need to know the balances of those accounts and test those balances to ensure that they're accurate and match what's in your business's books. We talk more about how to do that in the section 'Reconciling Bank Accounts', later in this chapter.

So your snapshot in time includes not only the cash on hand in your cash registers, but also any cash you may have in the bank. Some departments may also have Petty Cash accounts, which you count as well. The total cash figure is what you show as an asset named 'Cash' in your business's financial statement, the *Balance Sheet.* The Balance Sheet shows all that the business owns (its assets) and owes (its liabilities), as well as the capital the owners have in the business. (We talk more about the Balance Sheet and how you prepare one in Chapter 14.)

The actual cash you have on hand is just one tiny piece of the cash moving through your business during the accounting period. Your cash books contain the full details of the cash that flowed into and out of the business.

## Closing the cash books

If you use a computerised accounting system, you don't have separate cash books: the money received into your business is recorded into the bank accounts. However, you can still check your cash received into the business by running various reports, such as Daybook reports, showing invoices paid on both the Customer and Supplier Ledgers. You can also run Aged Debtors reports to see who still owes you money, and also Aged Creditor reports to see how much money you owe to your suppliers. With Sage, you can run a month-end, which essentially automatically closes your cash books/bank for the period.

# Reconciling Bank Accounts

Part of checking out the cash involves checking that what you have in your bank accounts actually matches what the bank thinks you have in those accounts. This process is called *reconciling* the accounts.

If you've done everything right, your accounting records match the bank's records of how much cash you have in your accounts. The day you close your books probably isn't the same date as the bank sends its statements, so do your best to balance the books internally without actually reconciling your bank account. Correcting any problems during the process minimises problems you may face reconciling the Cash accounts when that bank statement actually arrives.

You've probably reconciled your personal bank account at least a few times over the years, and the good news is that reconciling business accounts is a similar process. Table 9-1 shows one common format for reconciling your bank account:

| Table 9-1 | | Bank Reconciliation | | |
|---|---|---|---|---|
| *Transactions* | *Beginning Balance* | *Deposits* | *Disbursements* | *Ending Balance* |
| Balance per bank statement | £ | £ | £ | £ |
| Deposits in transit (those not shown on statement) | | £ | | £ |
| Outstanding cheques (cheques that haven't shown up yet) | | | (£) | (£) |
| Total | £ | £ | £ | £ |
| Balance per cash book or Bank account (which should be the same) | | | | £ |

Below we show you an example of a bank reconciliation:

You've just received your bank statement in the post. You find that your balance at the bank is £1,200 beginning balance, £4,000 in deposits, £4,300 in payments, and your ending balance is £900. You review the deposits and find that a deposit of £1,000 doesn't show on the statement. You find that cheques totalling £600 have not yet cleared. The balance in your bank account is £1,300. Does your Bank account reconcile to the balance on your bank statement?

Using the bank reconciliation chart, Table 9-2 shows the answer.

| Table 9-2 | An Example of a Bank Reconciliation | | | |
|---|---|---|---|---|
| **Transactions** | **Beginning Balance** | **Deposits** | **Payments** | **Ending Balance** |
| Balance per bank statement | £1,200 | £4,000 | (£4,300) | £900 |
| Deposits in transit (those not shown on statement) | | | £1,000 | £1,000 |
| Outstanding cheques (cheques that haven't shown up yet) | | | (£600) | (£600) |
| Total | £1,200 | £5,000 | (£4,900) | £1,300 |
| Balance per cash book or Bank account (which should be the same) | | | | £1,300 |

The bank statement and your Bank account do reconcile.

After entering all the transactions into your accounts system, the books for the period you're looking at may still be incomplete. Sometimes, adjustments or corrections must be made to the bank account before it can be reconciled. For example, monthly credit card fees and interest received from the bank may not yet be recorded in your bank account. There may also be standing orders and direct debits that come out of your bank account, which need to be entered into your accounts system.

The best way to reconcile your bank account is to methodically enter all the cash you've received and cheques you've paid out using your source documents such as cheque books and paying-in books. Then, you need to work through a copy of your bank statements and see what else needs to be entered.

## Looking at a practical way to reconcile your bank account

Following is the method we adopt when we reconcile bank accounts. Most people reconcile the bank account on a monthly basis, so the chances are you have a month's worth of bank statements in front of you for this task.

Follow these steps:

1. **With your bank statements in front of you, place a tick against all the items already entered into your bookkeeping system, including all cheques and items paid in via paying-in books.**

   A number of items remain unticked.

2. **Now enter all the remaining entries into your system, ticking them once after you enter them.**

   These entries include all your electronic receipts and payments, such as direct debits and BACS payments. You should now have a tick placed against all the entries on your bank statement.

3. **Work through each transaction in your cash book and match them against the bank statement as a double-check.**

   For manual bookkeeping systems, you mark the Cashbook using a tick (or perhaps a *B* for bank statement). All items that are left on the Cashbook without a tick are items that have not appeared on the bank statement. These items are your un-presented cheques or outstanding lodgements (deposits in transit). You can now easily write up your bank reconciliation, as shown in the Table 9-1.

When you tick each item in the Cashbook against the bank statement entry, also place a cross against the original tick on the bank statement. You can then see at a glance on the bank statement that all transactions have been entered and also checked against the Cashbook.

The same reconciliation process can be applied to credit cards that the business receives. However, be sure that if you're using a computerised reconciliation process you correctly enter the credit card balance as a negative figure, because this balance is money owed.

## Considering credit card sales

If your business allows customers to buy your goods using a credit card, then you also need to reconcile the statements that you receive from the bank that handles your credit card sales.

You normally receive a statement listing:

✔ All your business's transactions for the month.

✔ The total amount your business sold through credit card sales.

✔ The total fees charged to your account.

If you find a difference between what the bank reports say you sold on credit cards and what the business's books show regarding credit card sales, you need to play detective and find the reason for the difference. In most cases, the error involves the charging back of one or more sales because a customer disputes the charge. In this case, an adjustment must be made to cash received, to reflect that loss of sale, so that the bank statement and business books match up.

For example, suppose £200 in credit card sales were disputed. The original entry of the transaction in the books looks like this:

|  | **Debit** | **Credit** |
|---|---|---|
| Sales | £200 | |
| Bank | | £200 |

*To reverse disputed credit sales recorded in June.*

This entry reduces the total Sales account for the month as well as the amount of the Cash account. If the dispute is resolved and the money is later retrieved, you can then re-enter the sale when the cash is received.

You also record any fees related to credit card fees as a bank payment. For example, if credit card fees for the month of June total £200, the entry in the books looks like this:

|  | *Debit* | *Credit* |
|---|---|---|
| Credit Card Fees | £200 | |
| Bank | | £200 |

*To post credit card fees for the month of June.*

## Tracking down errors

Ideally, your balance and the bank's balance, adjusted by transactions not yet shown on the statement, match. If they don't, you need to find out why.

- ✔ **If the bank balance is higher than your balance,** check to ensure that all the deposits listed by the bank appear in the Cash account in your books. If you find that the bank lists a deposit that you don't have, you need to do some detective work to work out what that deposit was for and add the detail to your accounting records. Also, check to make sure that all cheques you've issued have cleared. Your balance may be missing a cheque that should have been listed in outstanding cheques.

- ✔ **If the bank balance is lower than your balance,** check to ensure that all cheques listed by the bank are recorded in your Cash account. You may have missed one or two cheques that were written but not properly recorded. You also may have missed a deposit that you've listed in your Cash account and thought the bank should already have shown as a deposit, but that isn't yet on the statement. If you notice a missing deposit on the bank statement, make sure that you have your proof of deposit and check with the bank to ensure that the cash is in the account.

- ✔ **If all deposits and cheques are correct but you still see a difference,** your only option is to check your maths and make sure that all cheques and deposits were entered correctly.

Sometimes, you have to decide whether rooting out every little difference is really worthwhile. When the amount is just a few pence, don't waste your time trying to find the error, just adjust the balance in your books. But when the difference is a significant amount for your business, try to track it down. You never know exactly what accounts are impacted by an error or how that difference may impact your profit or loss.

# Using a computerised system

If you use a computerised accounting system, reconciliation is much easier than if you keep your books manually. In Sage 50 Accounts, for example, when you start the reconciliation process, a screen pops up in which you can add the ending bank statement balance and any bank fees or interest earned. Figure 9-1 shows you that screen. In this example, £930 is the ending balance

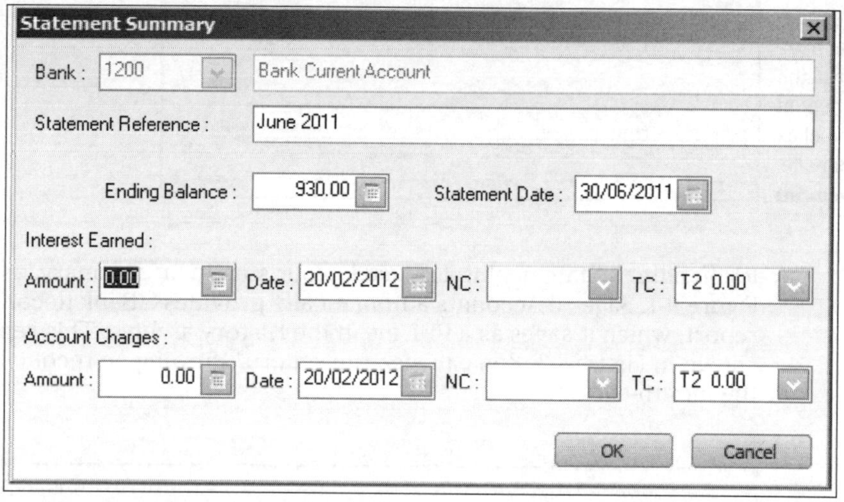

**Figure 9-1:**
When you start the reconciliation process in Sage 50 Accounts, you indicate the bank's ending balance and any bank service charges or interest earned on a particular account.

After you click OK, you get a screen that lists all cheques written since the last reconciliation as well as all deposits. Double-click on all the items listed in the top part of your Sage screen that are also shown on your bank statement, as in Figure 9-2. Ensure that the matched balance and the statement balance are the same and the difference is zero (see the bottom right corner of the Sage screen), and then click Reconcile.

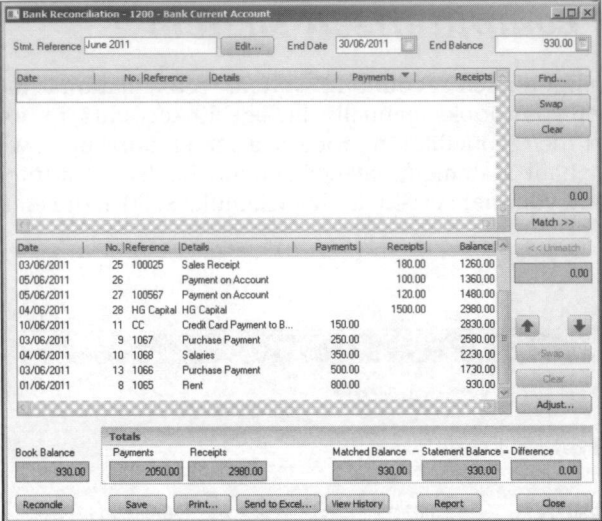

**Figure 9-2:**
To reconcile
cheques
using
Sage 50
Accounts,
double-
click all the
cheques
and depos-
its that have
cleared the
account
and click
Reconcile.

If you enter a Statement Reference in your statement summary, as shown in Figure 9-1, Sage 50 Accounts automatically provides a Bank Reconciliation report, which it saves as a PDF file in the History archive. This report is shown in Figure 9-3. You can also run reports showing un-reconciled items at the month-end.

**Figure 9-3:**
After recon-
ciling your
accounts,
Sage 50
Accounts
auto-
matically
provides
a Bank
Reconciliation
report.

| Date: | 20/02/2012 | | | | Page: 1 |
| Time: | 12:42:46 | | **Bank Reconciliation** | | |

1200
Bank Current Account
Currency:    Pound Sterling

Book Balance: £                930.00

| Statement Ref: June 2011 | | | Statement Date: 30/06/2011 | Reconciliation Date: 20/02/2012 |
|---|---|---|---|---|
| Date | Ref. | Details | Payments | Receipts |
| | | Opening Balance | | |
| 01/06/2011 | Cash Sales | Cash Sales | | 360.00 |
| 02/06/2011 | Cash Sales | Cash Sales | | 300.00 |
| 03/06/2011 | Cash Sales | Cash Sales | | 180.00 |
| 05/06/2011 | Cash Sales | Cash Sales | | 240.00 |
| 03/06/2011 | 100025 | Sales Receipt | | 180.00 |
| 05/06/2011 | | Payment on Account | | 100.00 |
| 05/06/2011 | 100567 | Payment on Account | | 120.00 |
| 04/06/2011 | HG Capital | HG Capital | | 1,500.00 |
| 10/06/2011 | CC | Credit Card Payment to Barclays | 150.00 | |
| 03/06/2011 | 1067 | Purchase Payment | 250.00 | |
| 04/06/2011 | 1068 | Salaries | 350.00 | |
| 03/06/2011 | 1066 | Purchase Payment | 500.00 | |
| 01/06/2011 | 1065 | Rent | 800.00 | |
| | | Totals: | 2,050.00 | 2,980.00 |
| | | **Closing Balance:** | | 930.00 |

# *Have a Go*

Your turn! Sharpen your pencil and test yourself on checking the books.

1. **Make a list of all the accounts in your business that you need to reconcile at the end of each accounting period. Remember to include all bank accounts and Petty Cash accounts, as well as any credit card accounts that have been used in the month.** (We provide a general answer at the end of this chapter.)

2. **What's the purpose of a Petty Cash account? List a few typical items that you might pay through petty cash.**

3. **If you allow customers to pay by credit card, check your system to ensure that you understand how to account for monies received by the credit card company. Have you got a system in place to be able to identify which customers are paying you?**

   For example, the credit card company probably just deposit a lump sum from credit card payments into your bank account. You need to ensure that you've a method of identifying which customers have paid you via credit card, so that you may update your accounts.

   If you don't have procedures in place, write some now.

4. **When you get your credit card sales statement, you find a total of £225 was charged in fees and you find three chargebacks for customer disputes totalling £165. How do you record this information in your books?**

5. **When you get your credit card sales statement, you find a total of £275 in chargebacks from customer disputes and £320 in fees. How do you record this information in your books?**

6. **You've just received your bank statement in the post. You find your balance at the bank is £1,500 beginning balance – £6,000 in deposits, £6,500 in payments and your ending balance is £1,000. You review the deposits and find that a deposit of £2,000 does not show on the statement. You find that cheques totalling £1,700 haven't cleared yet. The balance in your Bank account is £1,300. Does your Bank account reconcile to the balance on your bank statement?**

7. **You've just received your bank statement in the post. You find your balance at the bank is £1,800 beginning balance – £7,000 in deposits, £6,500 in payments and your ending balance is £2,300. You review the deposits and find that a deposit of £1,000 does not show on the statement. You find that cheques totalling £2,500 haven't cleared yet. The balance in your Bank account is £1,200. Does your Bank account reconcile to the balance on your bank statement?**

8. Suppose that you can't reconcile your bank statement. As you review the cheques, you see one written for £2,500 that you haven't recorded in your books. As you research the cheque, you find that it's a payment made to Olive's Office Supplies. How would you record that in the books?

9. Suppose you can't reconcile your bank statement and you find that a deposit of £5,300 isn't recorded. As you research the deposit, you find that the sales receipts weren't recorded for 15 May. How would you record that in the books?

# Answering the Have a Go Questions

1. **The following accounts are normally reconciled:**

   • Bank Current account

   • Bank Deposit account

   • Petty Cash account

   • Credit Card accounts

2. **Usually, small cash needs are handled using a petty cash fund. Often, an office manager handles this.** You may want to send a memo to your staff to advise them of the typical items of expenditure that are expected to be paid through petty cash. Typical petty cash items include:

   • Tea, coffee, milk.

   • Postage.

   • Keys cut.

   • Small stationery items.

   • Sundry cleaning supplies.

   This list just offers a sample of the kinds of expenditure that may be posted through the Petty Cash account.

3. **Not all companies take payment via credit card from their customers.** If yours does, take the time now to reflect on the procedures surrounding the credit card receipts. Can they be improved?

4. **The bookkeeping entry to show the credit card fee is as follows:**

   |  | *Debit* | *Credit* |
   |---|---|---|
   | Credit Card Fee | £225 | |
   | Bank | | £225 |

**5. The bookkeeping entry for the disputed sales items is as follows:**

|        | Debit | Credit |
|--------|-------|--------|
| Sales  | £165  |        |
| Bank   |       | £165   |

The bookkeeping entry to show the credit card fee is as follows:

|                 | Debit | Credit |
|-----------------|-------|--------|
| Credit Card Fee | £320  |        |
| Cash            |       | £320   |

The bookkeeping entry for the sales adjustment is as follows:

|       | Debit | Credit |
|-------|-------|--------|
| Sales | £275  |        |
| *Cash* |       | *£275* |

**6. The bank statement does reconcile to the cheque book. Here's the proof:**

| Transactions | Beginning Balance | Deposits | Payments | Ending Balance |
|--------------|-------------------|----------|----------|----------------|
| Balance per bank statement | £1,500 | £6,000 | (£6,500) | £1,000 |
| Deposits in transit (those not shown on statement) | | £2,000 | | £2,000 |
| Outstanding cheques (cheques that haven't shown up yet) | | | (£1,700) | (£1,700) |
| Total | £1,500 | £8,000 | (£8,200) | £1,300 |
| Balance per Bank account or Cashbook (which should be the same) | | | | £1,300 |

7. **The bank statement doesn't reconcile to the Bank account. A difference is shown of £400.** You must review the Bank account for possible errors. Here's the proof:

| Transactions | Beginning Balance | Deposits | Payments | Ending Balance |
|---|---|---|---|---|
| Balance per bank statement | £1,800 | £7,000 | (£6,500) | £2,300 |
| Deposits in transit (those not shown on statement) | | £1,000 | | £1,000 |
| Outstanding cheques (cheques that haven't shown up yet) | | | (£2,500) | (£2,500) |
| Total | £1,800 | £8,000 | (£9,000) | £800 |
| Balance per Bank account or Cashbook (which should be the same) | | | | £1,200 |

In the situation where the bank reconciliation doesn't balance, try the following:

- Check that you've ticked off every item on the bank statement and matched off each entry to the Cashbook.

- Ensure that you've entered the correct bank statement balance.

- Check your maths on the reconciliation.

- Check that you've entered all the items into your accounts system correctly.

Check all these things, and you'll most likely have found the problem.

8. **You need to record the office supplies expense and you need to reflect the use of cash.**

   If using a computerised accounting system, you enter the invoice as a purchase invoice, to record the liability. Then you need to pay the invoice, using the Bank account. The system does the double entry for you, as shown below:

   The bookkeeping for the initial entry of the invoice is as follows:

   |  | *Debit* | *Credit* |
   |---|---|---|
   | Office Supplies Expenses | £2,500 | |
   | Creditors Ledger | | £2,500 |

   You then need to process the payment, and the bookkeeping is as follows:

   |  | *Debit* | *Credit* |
   |---|---|---|
   | Creditors Ledger | £2500 | |
   | Bank | | £2500 |

9. **You need to record the missing sales as follows:**

   |  | *Debit* | *Credit* |
   |---|---|---|
   | Bank | £5,300 | |
   | Sales | | £5,300 |

# Part III
# Preparing the Books for Year- (Or Month-) End

'Brother Cedric's doing the abbey's books now – They should be ready for your inspection in five years.'

## In this part . . .

*E*ventually, every accounting period comes to an end. You need to check your work and get ready to close down the period, whether at the end of a month, a quarter or a year.

This part introduces you to the process of preparing your books for closing an accounting period. You find out about the key adjustments needed to record depreciation of your assets, such as cars and buildings. This part also shows you how to post accruals and prepayments.

To round off the closing process, we show you how to check your books by reviewing the Trial Balance and checking individual accounts for any errors before making any required adjustments or corrections.

# Chapter 10

# Adjusting Your Books

. . . . . . . . . . . . . . . . . . . . . . . . . . . . . . . . . . . . . . . .

## *In This Chapter*

▶ Making adjustments for non-cash transactions

▶ Checking your Trial Balance

▶ Adding to and deleting from the Chart of Accounts

. . . . . . . . . . . . . . . . . . . . . . . . . . . . . . . . . . . . . . . .

**D**uring an accounting period, your bookkeeping duties focus on your business's day-to-day transactions. When the time comes to report those transactions in financial statements, you must make adjustments to your books. Your financial reports are supposed to show your business's financial health, so your books must reflect any significant change in the value of your assets, even if that change doesn't involve the exchange of cash.

If you use cash-based accounting, these adjustments aren't necessary because you only record transactions when cash changes hands. We talk about accrual and cash-based accounting in Chapter 2.

If you're following the checklist we suggest in Chapter 6, we assume, in this chapter, that you've already entered/completed the following:

✔ Sale invoices

✔ Purchase invoices

✔ Bank receipts

✔ Bank payments

✔ Reconciled the bank accounts

All the above entries are routine transactions for the month. However, you also need to make some other types of adjustments. This chapter reviews the types of adjustments you need to make to the books before preparing the financial statements, including calculating depreciation, posting accruals and prepayments, updating stock figures and dealing with bad debts.

When you've posted all the necessary adjustments outlined above, print out a Trial Balance to check all the accounts and review for accuracy. We show you in the later section 'Checking your Trial Balance' how you can do this review using Sage 50 as an example.

# Adjusting All the Right Areas

We look at each of the adjustments that you need to make to your books in turn. These include the following areas:

- ✔ **Asset depreciation:** To recognise the use of assets during the accounting period.

- ✔ **Accruals:** Where goods or services have been received but not invoiced, and an accrual has to be made in the accounts, so that they can be matched with revenue for the month.

- ✔ **Prepaid expenses:** To match a portion of expenses that were paid at one point during the year, but for which the benefits are used throughout the year, such as an annual insurance premium. The benefit needs to be apportioned out against expenses for each month.

- ✔ **Stock:** To update stock to reflect what you have on hand.

- ✔ **Bad debts:** To acknowledge that some customers never pay and to write off those accounts.

## Depreciating assets

The largest non-cash expense for most businesses is depreciation. *Depreciation* is an important accounting exercise for every business to undertake because it reflects the use and ageing of assets. Older assets need more maintenance and repair, and eventually need to be replaced. As the depreciation of an asset increases and the value of the asset dwindles, the need for more maintenance or replacement becomes apparent. (For more on depreciation and why to do it, check out Chapter 11.)

The actual time to make this adjustment to the books is when you close the books for an accounting period. (Some businesses record depreciation expenses every month to match monthly expenses with monthly revenues more accurately, but most business owners only worry about depreciation adjustments on a yearly basis, when they prepare their annual financial statements.)

Depreciation doesn't involve the use of cash. By accumulating depreciation expenses on an asset, you're reducing the value of the asset as shown on the Balance Sheet (see Chapter 14 for the low-down on Balance Sheets).

Readers of your financial statements can get a good idea of the health of your assets by reviewing your accumulated depreciation. If financial report readers see that assets are close to being fully depreciated, they know that you probably need to spend significant funds on replacing or repairing those assets soon. As they evaluate the financial health of the business, they take that future obligation into consideration before making a decision to lend money to the business or possibly invest in it.

Usually, you calculate depreciation for accounting purposes using the *Straight-Line depreciation method.* This method is used to calculate an equal amount to be depreciated each year, based on the anticipated useful life of the asset. For example, suppose that your business purchases a car for business purposes that costs £25,000. You anticipate that the car is going to have a useful lifespan of five years and be worth £5,000 after five years. Using the Straight-Line depreciation method, you subtract £5,000 from the total car cost of £25,000 to find the value of the car during its five-year useful lifespan (£20,000). Then, you divide £20,000 by five to find your depreciation charge for the car (£4,000 per year). When adjusting the assets at the end of each year in the car's five-year lifespan, your entry to the books looks like this:

|  | *Debit* | *Credit* |
|---|---|---|
| Depreciation Charge | £4,000 | |
| Accumulated Depreciation: Vehicles | | £4,000 |
| *To record depreciation for Vehicles.* | | |

This entry increases depreciation charges, which appear on the Profit and Loss statement (see Chapter 13). The entry also increases Accumulated Depreciation, which is the use of the asset and appears on the Balance Sheet directly under the Vehicles asset line. The Vehicles asset line always shows the value of the asset at the time of purchase.

You can accelerate depreciation if you believe that the business isn't going to use the asset evenly over its lifespan – namely, that the business is going to use the asset more heavily in the early years of ownership. We talk more about alternative depreciation methods in Chapter 11.

If you use a computerised accounting system as opposed to keeping your books manually, you may or may not need to make this adjustment at the end of an accounting period. If your system is set up with an asset register feature, depreciation is automatically calculated, and you don't have to worry about it. Check with your accountant (the person who sets up the asset register feature) before calculating and recording depreciation expenses.

## Accruing the costs

Goods and services may have been received by the business but may not have been invoiced. These costs need to be *accrued*, which means recorded in the books, so that they can be matched to the revenue for the month. These accruals are necessary only if you use the accrual accounting method. If you use the cash-based accounting method, you need to record the bills only when cash is actually paid. For more on the accrual and cash-based methods, refer to Chapter 2.

You accrue bills yet to be received. For example, suppose that your business prints and mails flyers to advertise a sale during the last week of the month. A bill for the flyers totalling £500 hasn't been received yet. Here's how you enter the bill in the books:

|  | *Debit* | *Credit* |
|---|---|---|
| Advertising | £500 | |
| Accruals | | £500 |

*To accrue the bill from Jack's Printing for June sales flyers.*

This entry increases advertising expenses for the month and increases the amount due in the Accruals account. When you receive and pay the bill later, the Accruals account is debited rather than the Advertising account (to reduce the liability), and the Cash account is credited (to reduce the amount in the Cash account). You make the actual entry in the Cash Payments book when the cash is paid out.

When checking out the cash, also review any accounts in which expenses are accrued for later payment, such as Value Added Tax Collected, to ensure that all Accrual accounts are up to date. This Tax account is actually a Liability account for taxes that you need to pay in the future. If you use the accrual accounting method, you must match the expenses related to these taxes to the revenues collected for the month in which they're incurred.

## Allocating prepaid expenses

Most businesses have to pay certain expenses at the beginning of the year even though they benefit from that expense throughout the year. Insurance is a prime example of this type of expense. Most insurance businesses require you to pay the premium annually at the start of the year even though the value of that insurance protects the business throughout the year.

For example, suppose that your business's annual car insurance premium is £1,200. You pay that premium in January in order to maintain insurance cover throughout the year. Showing the full cash expense of your insurance when you prepare your January financial reports greatly reduces any profit that month and makes your financial results look worse than they actually are, which is no good. Instead, you record a large expense such as insurance or prepaid rent as an asset called *Prepaid Expenses*, and then you adjust the value to reflect that the asset is being used up.

When you record the initial invoice, you record the expense to prepayments. The double entry is as follows:

|  | *Debit* | *Credit* |
| --- | --- | --- |
| Prepayments | £1200 | |
| Bank | | £1200 |

This double entry shows that you paid the original invoice by cheque and that you've coded the whole value of the invoice to prepayments.

Your £1,200 annual insurance premium is actually valuable to the business for 12 months, so you calculate the actual expense for insurance by dividing £1,200 by 12, giving you £100 per month.

Each month the Prepayment account is reduced by £100 and the cost is transferred to the Insurance Expenses account as shown in the double entry below.

|  | *Debit* | *Credit* |
| --- | --- | --- |
| Insurance Expenses | £100 | |
| Prepaid Expenses | | £100 |

*To record insurance expenses for March.*

This entry increases Insurance Expenses on the Profit and Loss statement and decreases the asset Prepaid Expenses on the Balance Sheet. No cash changes hands in this entry because you laid cash out when the insurance bill was paid, and the Asset account Prepaid Expenses was increased in value at the time the cash was paid.

## Counting stock

Stock is a Balance Sheet asset that you need to adjust at the end of an accounting period. During the accounting period, your business buys stock and records those purchases in a Purchases account without indicating any change to stock. When the business sells the products, you record the sales in the Sales account but don't make any adjustment to the value of the stock. Instead, you adjust the stock value at the end of the accounting period because adjusting with each purchase and sale is much too time-consuming.

The steps for making proper adjustments to stock in your books are as follows:

1. **Determine the stock remaining.**

   In addition to calculating closing stock using the purchases and sales numbers in the books, also do a physical count of stock to make sure that what's on the shelves matches what's in the books.

2. **Set a value for that stock.**

   The value of closing stock varies depending on the method your business chooses for valuing stock. We talk more about stock value and how to calculate the value of closing stock in Chapter 8.

3. **Adjust the number of items remaining in stock in the Stock account and adjust the value of that account based on the information collected in Steps 1 and 2.**

If you record stock using your computerised accounting system, the system makes adjustments to stock as you record sales. At the end of the accounting period, the computer has already adjusted the value of your business's closing stock in the books. Although the work's done for you, still do a physical count of the stock to make sure that your computer records match the physical stock at the end of the accounting period.

## Allowing for bad debts

No business likes to accept that money owed by some of its customers is never going to be received, but this situation is a reality for most businesses that sell items on credit. When your business determines that a customer who bought products on credit is never going to pay for them, you record the value of that purchase as a *bad debt*. (For an explanation of credit, check out Chapter 7.)

At the end of an accounting period, list all outstanding customer accounts in an *Aged Debtor report,* which is covered in Chapter 7. This report shows which customers owe how much and for how long. After a certain amount of time, you have to admit that some customers simply aren't going to pay. Each business sets its own policy of how long to wait before tagging an account as a bad debt. For example, your business may decide that when a customer is six months late with a payment, you're unlikely to ever see the money.

After you decide that an account is a bad debt, don't include its value as part of your assets in Trade Debtors (Accounts Receivable). Including bad debt value doesn't paint a realistic picture of your situation for the readers of your financial reports. Because the bad debt is no longer an asset, you adjust the value of your Trade Debtors to reflect the loss of that asset.

You can record bad debts in a couple of ways:

✔ **By customer:** Some businesses identify the specific customers whose accounts are bad debts and calculate the bad-debt expense for each accounting period based on specified customer accounts.

✔ **By percentage:** Other businesses look at their bad-debts histories and develop percentages that reflect those experiences. Instead of taking the time to identify each specific account that may be a bad debt, these businesses record bad debt expenses as a percentage of their Trade Debtors.

✔ **By using a bit of both:** You can identify specific customers and write them off and apply a percentage to cover the rest.

However you decide to record bad debts, you need to prepare an adjusting entry at the end of each accounting period to record bad-debt expenses. Here's an adjusting entry to record bad-debt expenses of £1,000:

|  | *Debit* | *Credit* |
|---|---|---|
| Bad Debt Expense | £1,000 | |
| Trade Debtors | | £1,000 |

*To write off customer accounts.*

You can't have bad-debt expenses if you don't sell to your customers on credit. You only need to worry about bad debt if you offer your customers the convenience of buying your products on credit.

If you use a computerised accounting system, check the system's instructions for how to write off bad debts. To write off a bad debt using Sage 50 Accounts, follow these steps:

1. **Open the Customers screen and select Customer Write Off/Refund from the Tasks on the left-hand side of the screen.** This screen brings up the Write Offs, Refunds and Returns Wizard (see Figure 10-1). Select the task you wish to perform, such as Write Off and then select the customer account, using the drop-down arrow. Click Next to continue.

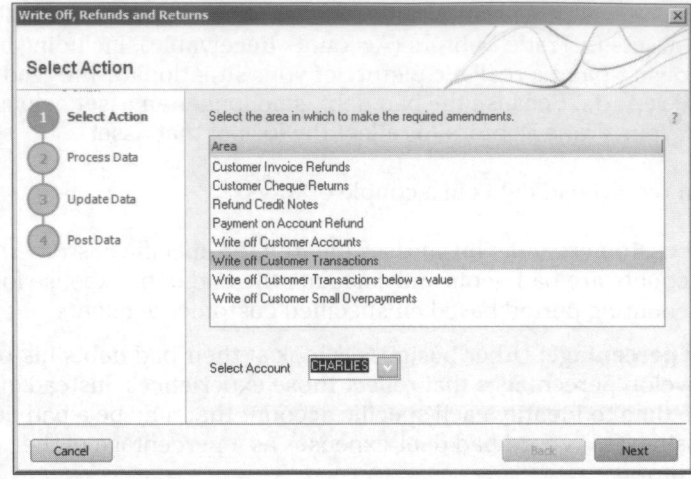

**Figure 10-1:** In Sage 50 Accounts, use the Write Offs, Refunds and Returns Wizard to write off bad debts.

2. **Highlight the invoices you're writing off and click Next (see Figure 10-2).**

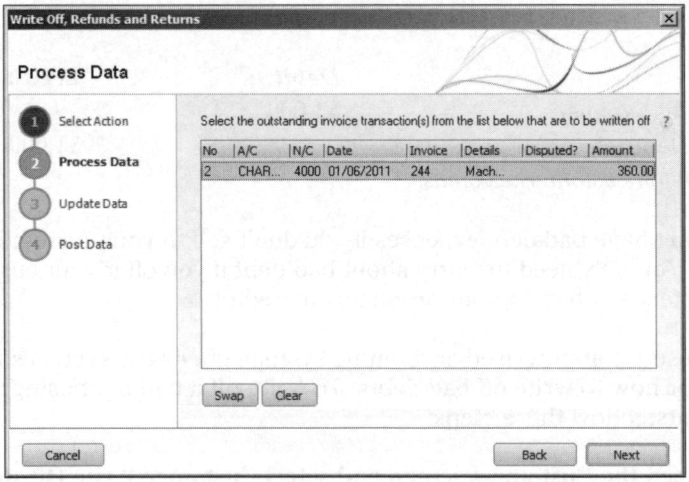

**Figure 10-2:** Selecting the customer account in which you're writing off debt in Sage 50 Accounts.

3. **Enter the date of the write off and any reference you may wish to use (see Figure 10-3). Click Next to continue.**

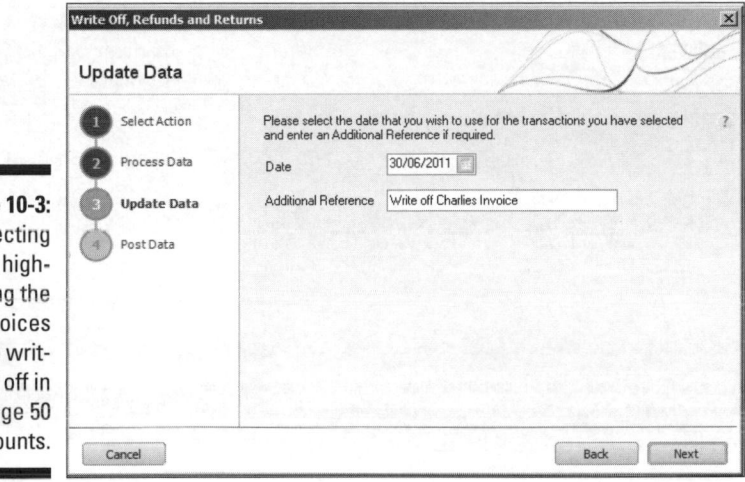

**Figure 10-3:**
Selecting and high-lighting the invoices you're writing off in Sage 50 Accounts.

4. **Check the data that's about to be written off (Figure 10-4). If you're happy that the details are correct, click Post. Otherwise, click Back and redo.**

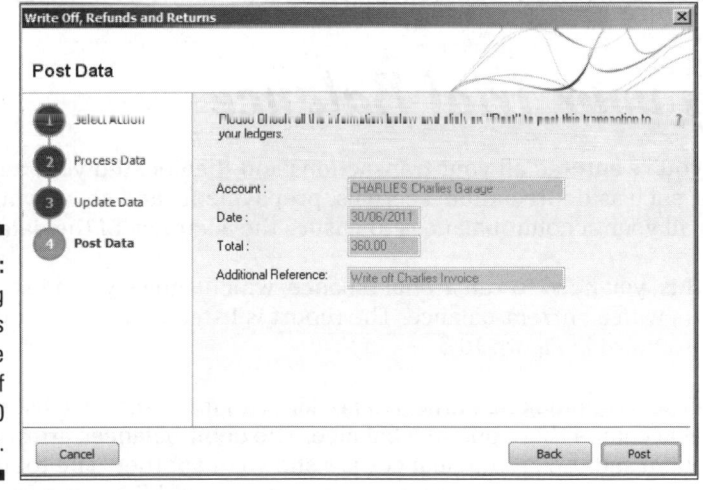

**Figure 10-4:**
Confirming the details of the write-off in Sage 50 Accounts.

5. **Double-click on the customer account and click the Activity tab to check that the write-off has been done (see Figure 10-5).**

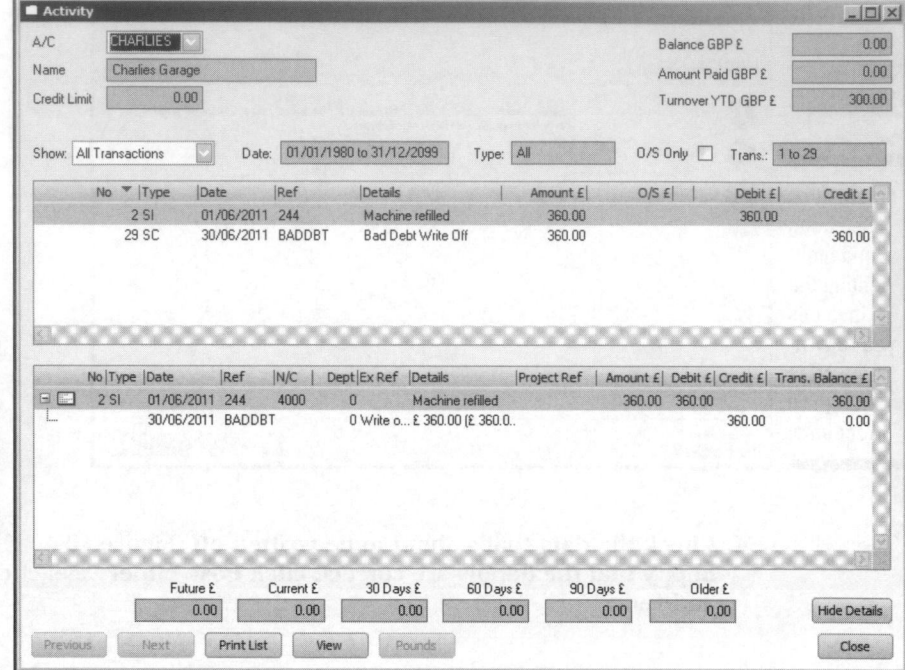

**Figure 10-5:**
Check that
the write-off
has been
posted
properly by
viewing the
Customer
Activity
screen.

# Checking your Trial Balance

When you've entered all your transactions and then posted your adjusting entries, such as depreciation, accruals, prepayments and so on, you need to review all your account balances to ensure the accuracy of the data.

To do this, you need to run a Trial Balance, which shows you a list of all accounts with a current balance. The report is listed in account number order as shown in Figure 10-6.

You can see from looking at the Trial Balance that it's simply a list of all the nominal accounts that contain a balance. The debit balances are shown in one column and the credit balances are shown in another. The totals of each of the columns must always equal. If they don't, this difference means that there's a major problem with your accounts. Computerised trial balances are always going to balance, unless there's serious corruption of data. If you're maintaining a manual Trial Balance, you must check all your figures again.

| Date: | 22/02/2012 | | **Sweet Dreams** | | Page: | 1 |
|-------|-----------|--|------------------|--|--------|---|
| Time: | 16:42:16 | | **Period Trial Balance** | | | |

**To Period:** Month 3, June 2011

| N/C | Name | Debit | Credit |
|------|---------------------------|-----------|-----------|
| 0050 | Motor Vehicles | 10,000.00 | |
| 1100 | Debtors Control Account | 140.00 | |
| 1200 | Bank Current Account | 930.00 | |
| 2100 | Creditors Control Account | | 725.00 |
| 2200 | Sales Tax Control Account | | 330.00 |
| 2201 | Purchase Tax Control Account | 270.84 | |
| 3010 | Capital Introduced | | 11,500.00 |
| 4000 | Sweet Sales | | 1,650.00 |
| 5000 | Materials Purchased | 1,354.16 | |
| 7003 | Staff Salaries | 350.00 | |
| 7100 | Rent | 800.00 | |
| 8100 | Bad Debt Write Off | 360.00 | |
| | **Totals:** | 14,205.00 | 14,205.00 |

Page 1 of 1    100%

**Fig 10-6:**
An example
of a Trial
Balance in
Sage 50.

You may want to make further adjustments after you've reviewed your Trial Balance. Perhaps you posted items to the wrong nominal code. You need to write out correcting entries to sort this mistake out. This is where your double-entry rules come back into play.

You may want to investigate an account because the balance seems high. For example, Kate the bookkeeper wants to see what's been coded to Capital Introduced, as at £11,500 the amount seems quite high.

In order to investigate this account, Kate would have to run a Nominal Activity report in Sage. This report would show her all the items that have been posted to the nominal code she's investigating.

See Figure 10-7 for the Nominal Activity report that Kate has run for Capital Introduced.

Kate can see from the report that two items have been posted to Capital Introduced; one for £10,000, which relates to the company vehicle that was bought using owner funds, and the other, which was cash lent to the business by the owner. Kate is happy with her findings and doesn't need to make any adjustments.

## Moving beyond the catch-all Miscellaneous Expenses account

When new accounts are added to the Chart of Accounts, the account most commonly adjusted is the Miscellaneous Expenses account. In many cases, you may expect to incur an expense only one or two times during the year, therefore making it unnecessary to create a new account specifically for that expense. But after a while, you find that your 'rare' expense is adding up, and you'd be better off with a designated account, meaning that you need to create adjusting entries to move expenses out of the Miscellaneous Expenses account.

For example, suppose you think that you're going to need to rent a car for the business just once before you buy a new vehicle, and so you enter the rental cost in the books as a Miscellaneous Expense. However, after renting cars three times, you decide to start a Rental Expense account mid-year. When you add the Rental Expense account to your Chart of Accounts, you need to use an adjusting entry to transfer any expenses incurred and recorded in the Miscellaneous Expense account prior to the creation of the new account.

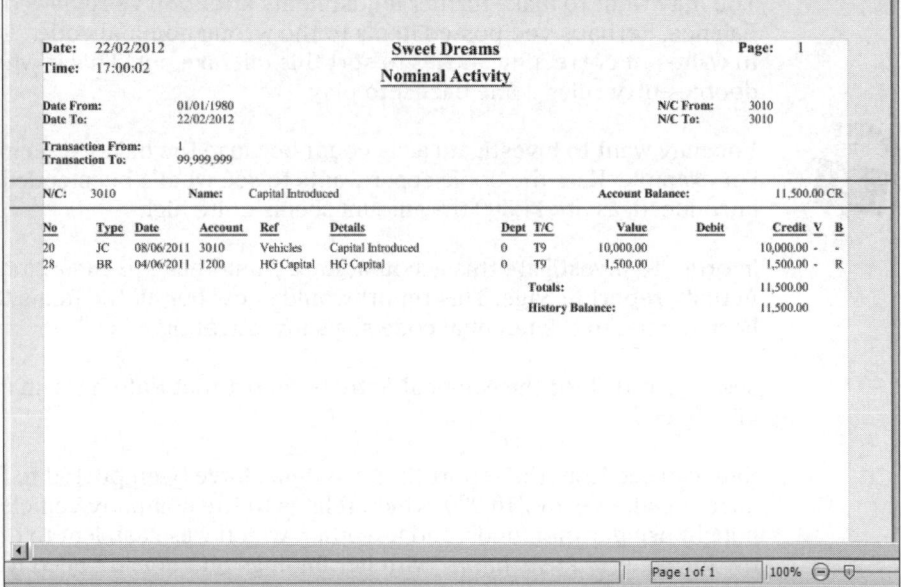

**Figure 10-7:** Showing a Nominal Activity report for Capital Introduced.

# Changing Your Chart of Accounts

After you finalise your Nominal Ledger for the year, you may want to make changes to your Chart of Accounts, which lists all the accounts in your accounting system. (For the full story on the Chart of Accounts, see Chapter 3.) You may need to add accounts if you think that you need additional ones or delete accounts if you think that they're no longer needed.

Delete accounts from your Chart of Accounts only at the end of the year. If you delete an account in the middle of the year, your annual financial statements don't reflect the activities in that account prior to its deletion. So even if you decide halfway through the year not to use an account, leave it on the books until the end of the year and then delete it.

You can add accounts to your Chart of Accounts throughout the year, but if you decide to add an account in the middle of the year in order to more closely track certain assets, liabilities, revenues or expenses, you may need to adjust some related entries.

Suppose that you start the year recording paper expenses in the Office Supplies Expenses account, but paper usage and its expense keeps increasing and you decide to track the expense in a separate account beginning in July.

First, you add the new account, Paper Expenses, to your Chart of Accounts. Then you prepare an adjusting entry to move all the paper expenses that were recorded in the Office Supplies Expenses account to the Paper Expenses account. In the interest of space and to avoid boring you, the adjusting entry below is an abbreviated one. In your actual entry, you probably detail the specific dates on which paper was bought as an office supplies expense rather than just tally one summary total.

|  | *Debit* | *Credit* |
|---|---|---|
| Paper Expenses | £1,000 | |
| Office Supplies Expenses | | £1,000 |

*To move expenses for paper from the Office Supplies Expenses account to the Paper Expenses account.*

# Have a Go

The following section allows you to have a practise with bookkeeping questions.

1. **Using the information below, and using Figure 10-6 (a Sage 50 Trial Balance) as an example of how it should look, reconstruct a Trial Balance for the end of June.**

   Your totals for each of the accounts at the end of June are:

   | Account | Debit | Credit |
   |---------|-------|--------|
   | Cash Debit | £2,500 | |
   | Debtors Debit | £1,500 | |
   | Stock Debit | £1,000 | |
   | Equipment Debit | £5,050 | |
   | Vehicle Debit | £25,000 | |
   | Furniture Debit | £5,600 | |
   | Creditors Credit | | £2,000 |
   | Loans Payable Credit | | £28,150 |
   | Owner's Capital Credit | | £5,000 |
   | Sales Credit | | £27,000 |
   | Purchases Debit | £12,500 | |
   | Advertising Debit | £2,625 | |
   | Interest Expenses Debit | £345 | |
   | Office Expenses Debit | £550 | |
   | Payroll Taxes Debit | £425 | |
   | Rent Expense Debit | £800 | |
   | Salaries and Wages Debit | £3,500 | |
   | Telephone Expenses Debit | £500 | |
   | Utilities Expenses Debit | £255 | |

2. **Your company owns a copier that cost £30,000. Assume a useful life of five years. How much should you record for depreciation expenses for the year? What is your bookkeeping entry?**

3. **Your offices have furniture that cost £200,000. Assume a useful life of five years. How much should you record for depreciation expenses for the year? What is your adjusting entry?**

4. **Suppose that your company pays £6,000 for an advertising campaign that covers the period 1 January to 31 December. You have already received an invoice dated 15 January, which you've paid at the end of January. You are closing the books for the month of May. How much should you have charged to the Profit and Loss account for the period to 31 May and what balance should remain in prepayments?**

5. Your accountant has prepared your year-end accounts, but hasn't sent you a bill yet! From past experience, you know that you should accrue about £2,400. What journal entry do you need to make to enter this situation into the books?

6. At the end of the month, you find that you've £9,000 in Closing Stock. You started the month with £8,000 in Opening Stock. What adjusting entry would you make to the books?

7. At the end of the month you calculate your Closing Stock and find that the value is £250 more than your Opening Stock value, which means that you purchased stock during the month that was not used. What adjusting entry should you make to the books?

8. You identify six customers that are more than six months late paying their bills, and the total amount due from these customers is £2,000. You decide to write off the debt. What adjusting entry would you make to the books?

9. Your company has determined that, historically, 5 per cent of its debtors never pay. What adjusting entry should you make to the books if your Debtors account at the end of the month is £10,000?

10. You decide that you want to track the amount that you spend on postage separately. Prior to this, you were entering these transactions in the Office Expense account. You make this decision in May, five months into your accounting year. You've already entered £1,000 for postage expenses. What would you need to do to start the account in the middle of the accounting year?

11. You decide that you want to track telephone expenses separately from other utilities. Prior to this, you were entering these transactions in the Utilities Expense account. You make this decision in July, but have already recorded transactions totalling £1,400 in your books. What do you need to do to start this new account in the middle of the accounting year?

# Answering the Have a Go Questions

1. Here's how the completed Trial Balance should look:

| Account | Debit | Credit |
|---|---|---|
| Cash | | £2,500 |
| Debtors | £1,500 | |
| Stock | £1,000 | |
| Equipment | £5,050 | |
| Vehicle | £25,000 | |

| | | |
|---|---|---|
| Furniture | £5,600 | |
| Creditors | | £2,000 |
| Loans Payable | | £28,150 |
| Owner's Capital | | £5,000 |
| Sales | | £27,000 |
| Purchases | £12,500 | |
| Advertising | £2,625 | |
| Interest Expenses | £345 | |
| Office Expenses | | £550 |
| Payroll Taxes | | £425 |
| Rent Expense | | £800 |
| Salaries and Wages | £3,500 | |
| Telephone Expenses | £500 | |
| Utilities Expenses | £255 | |
| TOTALS | £62,150 | £62,150 |

2. **Annual depreciation expense = £30,000 ÷ 5 = £6,000**

| | Debit | Credit |
|---|---|---|
| Depreciation expense | £6,000 | |
| Accumulated depreciation: Office Machines | | £6,000 |

3. **Annual depreciation expense = (£200,000) ÷ 5 = £40,000**

| | Debit | Credit |
|---|---|---|
| Depreciation expense | £40,000 | |
| Accumulated depreciation: Furniture & Fittings | | £40,000 |

4. **The original invoice should be coded to Prepaid Expenses.** You need to calculate the monthly charge for advertising which would be £6,000 ÷ 12 months = £500 per month. Each month, you must do the following journal:

| | Debit | Credit |
|---|---|---|
| Advertising Costs | £500 | |
| Prepaid Expenses | | £500 |

This journal has the effect of charging the Profit and Loss account with £500 each month and reducing the prepayment in the Balance Sheet.

Therefore, in May the following balances are:

Advertising Expenses (in Profit & Loss)   £2,500 (£500 × 5 months)

Prepayment in Balance Sheet   £3,500 (£6,000 – £2,500)

**5. The journal entry should be as follows:**

| | Debit | Credit |
|---|---|---|
| Accountancy Costs | £2,400 | |
| Accruals | | £2,400 |

You could, if you wish, prepare a monthly accrual and post a monthly charge through the accounts. To do this, simply split the £2,400 by 12 and post £200 per month. When the actual invoice comes in, it should be coded to Accruals rather than Accounting Fees.

**6. You ended the month with £1,000 more stock than you started with.** So you need to increase the Stock on hand by £1,000 and decrease the Purchases expense by £1,000, because some of the stock purchased won't be used until the next month. The entry would be:

| | Debit | Credit |
|---|---|---|
| Stock | £1,000 | |
| Purchases | | £1,000 |

**7. Your entry would be:**

| | Debit | Credit |
|---|---|---|
| Stock | £250 | |
| Purchases | | £250 |

This entry decreases the amount of the Purchases expenses because you purchased some of the Stock which you then didn't use.

**8. Your entry would be:**

| | Debit | Credit |
|---|---|---|
| Bad Debt Expense | £2,000 | |
| Debtors (Accounts Receivable) | | £2,000 |

**9. First you need to calculate the amount of the Bad Debt Expense:**

Bad Debt Expense = £10,000 × 0.05 = £500

Your entry would be:

| | Debit | Credit |
|---|---|---|
| Bad Debt Expense | £500 | |
| Debtors | | £500 |

10. **First you need to establish a new account called Postage Expenses to your Chart of Accounts.**

    Then you need to transfer the amount of transactions involving the payment of postage from your Office Expenses account to your new Postage Expenses account. The transaction looks like this:

    |  | *Debit* | *Credit* |
    |---|---|---|
    | Postage Expense | £1,000 | |
    | Office Expense | | £1,000 |

11. **First you need to establish a new account called Telephone Expenses in your Chart of Accounts.** Then you need to transfer the amount of transactions involving the payment of telephone bills from your Utilities Expenses account to your Telephone Expenses account. The transaction looks like this:

    |  | *Debit* | *Credit* |
    |---|---|---|
    | Telephone Expenses | £1,400 | |
    | Utilities Expenses | | £1,400 |

# Chapter 11

# Depreciating Your Assets

. . . . . . . . . . . . . . . . . . . . . . . . . . . . . . . . . . . . . . . . . . . . . . . . . . . . . . .

. . . . . . . . . . . . . . . . . . . . . . . . . . . . . . . . . . . . . . . . . . . . . . . . . . . . . . .

*A*ll businesses use equipment, furnishings and vehicles that last more than a year. Any asset that has a lifespan of more than a year is called a *fixed asset*. They may last longer than other assets, but even fixed assets eventually get old and need replacing.

And because your business needs to match expenses with revenue, you don't want to *write off* (set off against profits) the full expense of a fixed asset in one year. After all, you're sure to make use of the asset for more than one year.

Imagine how bad your Profit and Loss statement looks when you write off the cost of a £100,000 piece of equipment in just one year. You can give the impression that your business isn't doing well. Imagine the impact on a small business – £100,000 can eat up its entire profit or maybe even put the business in the position of reporting a loss.

Instead of writing off the full amount of a fixed asset in one year, you use an accounting method called *depreciation* to write off the asset as it gets used up. In this chapter, we introduce you to the various ways you can depreciate your assets and explain how to calculate depreciation, how depreciation impacts the Profit and Loss statement and how to record depreciation in your books.

# Defining Depreciation

You may think of depreciation as something that happens to your car as it loses value. In fact, most new cars depreciate 20 to 30 per cent or even more as soon as you drive them off the garage forecourt. But when you're talking about accounting, the definition of depreciation is a bit different.

Essentially, accountants use *depreciation* as a way to allocate the costs of a fixed asset over the period in which the asset is useable to the business. You, the bookkeeper, record the full transaction when the asset is bought, but then subtract a portion of that value as a Depreciation expense each year to reduce the value of the asset gradually. Depreciation expenses don't involve the exchange of cash; they're solely done for accounting purposes. Most businesses enter Depreciation expenses into the books once a year just before preparing their annual reports, but others calculate depreciation expenses monthly or quarterly.

Although you can decide how much depreciation to charge your business and thereby reduce your business profits, HM Revenue & Customs isn't quite so obliging. Instead, it gives you Capital Allowances (which are a bit like depreciation), but strict rules exist about how you can write off assets as tax-deductible expenses. We talk more about HM Revenue & Customs rules in the section 'Tackling Taxes and Depreciation', later in this chapter.

## Knowing what you can and can't depreciate

Businesses don't depreciate all assets. Low-cost items or items that aren't expected to last more than one year are recorded in Expense accounts rather than Asset accounts. For example, office supplies are expense items and not depreciated, but the office copier, which you're going to use for more than one year, is recorded in the books as a fixed asset and depreciated each year.

Lifespan isn't the deciding factor for depreciation, however. Some assets that last many years suffer really low depreciation. One good example is land and buildings; you can always make use of these, so their value seldom depreciates (you always hope that property prices will go up, but they can and do go down as well). You also can't depreciate any property that you lease or rent, but if you make improvements to leased property, you can depreciate the cost of those improvements. In that case, you write off the lease or rent as an expense item and depreciate the lease improvements over their estimated useful life.

You can't depreciate any items that you use outside your business, such as your personal car or home computer. However, if you use these assets for both personal needs and business needs, you can claim a proportion of their Capital Allowances on your tax return. We talk more about this subject in the section 'Tackling Taxes and Depreciation', later in this chapter.

## Figuring out the useful life of a fixed asset

You're probably wondering how you figure out the useful life of a fixed asset. Your accountant can advise you about common practice and any peculiarities of your business or trade. As one example, computer equipment is usually depreciated at a rate of 33.3 per cent per annum. However, if your computers have to be replaced every year, the appropriate depreciation rate is 100 per cent.

Table 11-1 gives you initial guidance on common depreciation rates.

| Table 11-1 | Depreciation Rates for Business Assets |
| --- | --- |
| *Life ÷ Depreciation Rate* | *Business Equipment* |
| 40 years ÷ 2.5% per annum | Land and buildings |
| 10 years ÷ 10% per annum | Long-life plant and machinery |
| 5 years ÷ 20% to 4 years ÷ 25% per annum | Office furniture and fixtures, equipment, motor vehicles |
| 3 years ÷ 33.3% per annum | Computer equipment |

## Delving into cost basis

In order to calculate depreciation for an asset, you need to know the cost basis of that asset. The equation for cost basis is:

Cost of the fixed asset + Disallowed Value Added Tax + Shipping and delivery costs + Installation charges + Other costs = Cost basis

- **Cost of the fixed asset:** What you paid for the equipment, furniture, structure, vehicle or other asset.
- **Disallowed VAT:** Any VAT charged on the purchase of the asset that you're unable to reclaim.
- **Shipping and delivery:** Any shipping or delivery charges you paid to get the fixed asset.

> ✔ **Installation charges:** Any charges you paid in order to have the equipment, furniture or other fixed asset installed on your business's premises.
>
> ✔ **Other costs:** Any other charges you need to pay to make the fixed asset usable for your business. For example, if you buy a new computer and need to set up certain hardware in order to use that computer for your business, those set-up costs can be added as part of the cost basis of the fixed asset (the computer).

# Depreciating the Value of Assets

After you decide on the useful life of an asset and calculate its cost basis (see the preceding sections), you have to decide how to go about reducing the asset's value according to accounting standards.

## Evaluating your depreciation options

When calculating depreciation of your assets each year, you've a choice of two main methods: Straight-Line and Reducing Balance. In this section, we explain these methods as well as the pros and cons of using each one.

Although other methods of calculating depreciation are available, for accounting purposes the two main methods are Straight-Line and Reducing Balance. Both methods are acceptable, and it does not matter to HM Revenue & Customs which you use. In practice, a business chooses one method and sticks with it. Straight-Line suits those businesses that want to write off their assets more quickly.

To show you how the methods handle assets differently, we calculate the first year's depreciation expense using the purchase of a piece of equipment on 1 January 2011, with a cost basis of £25,000. We have assumed the equipment has a useful life of five years, so the annual depreciation rate is 20 per cent.

### Straight-Line depreciation

When depreciating assets using the *Straight-Line method,* you spread the cost of the asset evenly over the number of years that your business is going to use the asset. Straight-Line is the most common method used for depreciation of assets, and the easiest one to use. The formula for calculating Straight-Line depreciation is:

Cost of fixed asset × Annual depreciation rate = Annual depreciation expense

For the piece of equipment in this example, the cost basis is £25,000 and the annual depreciation rate is 20 per cent. With these figures, the calculation for finding the annual depreciation expense of this equipment based on the Straight-Line depreciation method is:

£25,000 × 20% = £5,000 per annum

Each year, the business's Profit and Loss statement includes £5,000 as a depreciation expense for this piece of equipment. You add this £5,000 depreciation expense to the Accumulated Depreciation account for this asset. This Accumulated Depreciation account is shown below the asset's original value on the Balance Sheet. You subtract the accumulated depreciation from the value of the asset to show a net asset value, which is the value remaining on the asset.

### Reducing Balance depreciation

The *Reducing Balance method* of depreciation works well because it comes closest to matching the calculation of Capital Allowances, HM Revenue & Customs' version of depreciation.

The peculiarity of this method is that, unlike Straight-Line, the annual depreciation expense varies, and in theory the asset is never fully depreciated. Each year, the calculated depreciation figure is deducted from the previous year's value to calculate the new brought-forward figure. As time goes on, the annual depreciation figure gets smaller and the new brought-forward figure for the asset gets gradually smaller and smaller – but the item never fully depreciates.

Using the same asset as in the preceding section at a cost of £25,000 and depreciating at an annual rate of 20 per cent, calculating depreciation using the Reducing Balance method is as follows:

| | |
|---|---|
| Cost | 25,000 |
| First Year: depreciation (20%) | 5,000 |
| **Balance** | **20,000** |
| Second Year: depreciation (20% of £20,000) | 4,000 |
| **Balance** | **16,000** |
| Third Year: deprecation (20% of £16,000) | 3,200 |
| **Balance** | **12,800** |
| Fourth Year: depreciation (20% of £12,800) | 2,560 |
| **Balance** | **10,240** |

And so on, for ever.

## *Using Sage 50 Accounts to calculate depreciation*

With two different methods for depreciating your business's assets, you're probably wondering which method to use. Your accountant is the best person to answer that question. He can look at the way your business operates and determine which method makes the most sense for presenting your financial data.

Depreciation doesn't involve the use of cash. When talking about accounting, depreciation's purely a way to show how quickly you're using up an asset.

If you're using Sage 50 Accounts, the good news is that you don't have to calculate depreciation expense amounts manually. The system has a Fixed Asset Register that takes care of the management of your fixed assets and the calculation of depreciation for you. All you need to do is enter the asset details in the Fixed Asset Record, and determine the depreciation method and the depreciation rate, by selecting the appropriate boxes and entering the desired information. Each month, the accounts system posts depreciation for you, as part of the month-end routine. Figure 11-1 shows the Fixed Asset Record that needs to be completed for each asset.

After you enter asset information, the system automatically calculates the depreciation expense using the Straight-Line method or the Reducing Balance method, as shown in Figure 11-2. You select the method you want to use and save the information about each asset, which you can then refer to at the end of each year when you need to record the depreciation expense for that year.

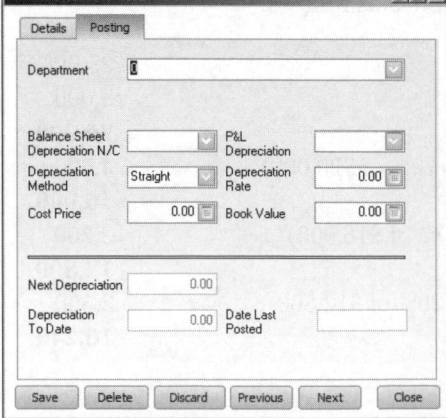

**Figure 11-1:** You can enter information about your fixed assets in Sage 50 Accounts.

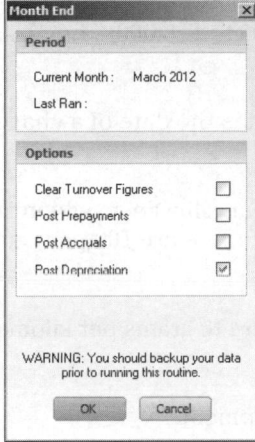

**Figure 11-2:**
Sage 50
Accounts
calculates
the depre-
ciation
expense
using your
chosen
method.

Make sure that you check on how to enter data correctly based on your system. We don't give you lengthy instructions for Sage 50 Accounts here because it depends on how you or your accountant initially set up the system.

# Tackling Taxes and Depreciation

Depreciation calculations for tax purposes are a completely different animal compared with the calculations used to record depreciation for accounting purposes.

HM Revenue & Customs doesn't recognise depreciation as a valid business expense because a business can set the rates it wants for any category of asset. In an extreme example, a business may choose to depreciate 100 per cent of a very expensive computer in one year. In fact, HM Revenue & Customs *adds back* your depreciation figures to your profit as their starting point for calculating your business tax bill.

The good news is that HM Revenue & Customs gives Capital Allowances instead of depreciation, which you can set off against your business profits. Capital Allowances are a simplified tax allowance that you can offset against profits and thereby reduce your taxable profits.

HM Revenue & Customs keeps things simple. Many business assets are described as plant and machinery, including vans, cars, tools, furniture and computers.

You can also include items of plant and machinery that you used privately before using them in your business and items that you only partly use for business purposes.

Most businesses have an annual investment allowance (AIA), which from 6 April 2012 is planned to reduce from £100,000 to £25,000. The AIA can't be claimed on cars.

For businesses whose accounting period spans the date of a change in allowances, transitional rules apply.

Businesses may also be able to claim first year allowance, which is available on certain specific types of assets. Currently there are 100 per cent first year allowances available on assets such as:

- ✔ New cars with $CO_2$ emissions of less than 110 grams per kilometre driven.
- ✔ Certain energy efficient equipment.
- ✔ Certain environmentally beneficial equipment.
- ✔ Equipment for refuelling vehicles with natural gas, biogas or hydrogen fuel.
- ✔ New zero emission vehicles (such as electric vans).

A temporary 40 per cent first year allowance also exists, but isn't available for cars.

As the rules for Capital Allowances change from time to time, make sure that you check the HM Revenue & Customs' website (www.hmrc.gov.uk) for further details, or talk to your friendly accountant, who'll be able to advise you.

If you'd like further detailed guidance on capital allowances, including case studies and methods of calculation, then you can also refer to the Business Link website (www.businesslink.gov.uk).

# Setting Up Depreciation Schedules

In order to keep good accounting records, you need to track how much you depreciate each of your assets in some form of a schedule. After all, your financial statements only include a total value for all your assets and a total accumulated depreciation amount. Most businesses maintain depreciation schedules in some type of spreadsheet program that exists outside their accounting systems. Usually, one person is responsible for managing assets and their depreciation. However, in a large business, these tasks can turn into full-time jobs for several people.

The best way to keep track of depreciation is to prepare a separate schedule for each Asset account that you depreciate. For example, set up depreciation schedules for Buildings, Furniture and Fixtures, Office Equipment accounts and so on. Your depreciation schedule must include all the information you need to determine annual depreciation, such as the original purchase date, original cost basis and recovery period. You can add columns to track the actual depreciation expenses and calculate the current value of each asset. Table 11-2 shows a sample depreciation schedule for vehicles.

| Table 11-2 | Depreciation Schedule: Vehicles | | | |
|---|---|---|---|---|
| Date Put in Service | Description | Cost | Useful Life | Annual Depreciation |
| 1/5/2011 | Black car | £30,000 | 5 years | £6,000 |
| 1/1/2012 | Blue van | £25,000 | 5 years | £5,000 |

Depreciation can be more than just a mathematical exercise. Keeping track of depreciation is a good way to monitor the age of your assets and know when to plan for their replacement. As your assets age, they incur greater repair costs, so keeping depreciation schedules can help you plan repair and maintenance budgets as well.

# Recording Depreciation Expenses

Recording a depreciation expense calls for a rather simple entry into your accounting system.

After calculating your depreciation expense, no matter which method you use, you record a depreciation expense the same way. Recording a depreciation expense of £4,000 for a vehicle (or vehicles) looks like this:

| | Debit | Credit |
|---|---|---|
| Depreciation Expense | £4,000 | |
| Accumulated Depreciation: Vehicles | | £4,000 |

The Depreciation Expense account increases by the amount of the debit, and the Accumulated Depreciation: Vehicles account increases by the credit. On the Profit and Loss statement, you treat depreciation as an expense, and on the Balance Sheet, you subtract the Accumulated Depreciation: Vehicles from the value of Vehicles.

# Have a Go

1. List three categories of assets that can be depreciated. Note: If you want to be more specific about an asset – then also state which category it would be included in.

2. List three types of assets that can't be depreciated.

3. Calculate the cost basis of a new piece of machinery for your factory. You bought the machine for £25,000, paid £2,000 for its transportation and a further £3,000 for setting it up in your factory.

4. Calculate the cost basis for the renovations of the office space you just leased. You paid £20,000 for new carpet, £30,000 for new office furniture, £5,000 for painting the space, and you paid a contractor £15,000 to install dry wall.

5. Calculate the annual depreciation expense for a copier with a cost basis of £5,000 and a depreciation rate of 20 per cent using the Straight-Line depreciation method.

6. Calculate the annual depreciation expense for a computer with a cost basis of £1,500 and a useful life of three years using the Straight-Line method of depreciation.

7. John has just bought a photocopier costing £8,000. He intends to depreciate it at a rate of 20 per cent, using the Reducing Balance method. Calculate the depreciation charges for the next three years and then write down the net book value at the end of the three-year period.

8. Deborah has calculated that the depreciation for her white transit van is £5,000 per annum (£20,000 cost, depreciated on a Straight-Line basis over four years). What is the double entry that she needs to post to ensure that the depreciation is posted into her accounting records? (Note: We're assuming that she's posting the journal manually and not relying on depreciation to be calculated automatically via her accounting system.)

9. What is the purpose of depreciating assets?

10. If you wanted to apply an even amount of depreciation each year against your asset, which depreciation method would you use?

11. If you have a machine with a useful life of four years, what depreciation rate would you use?

12. How do you calculate net book value?

13. Which method of depreciation uses net book value in its calculations?

# Answering the Have a Go Questions

1. **The following assets are ones that can be depreciated (this list isn't exhaustive):**

    - Plant and machinery

    - Motor vehicles

    - Office equipment

    - Furniture and fittings

    - Computers

2. **The following items aren't normally depreciated:**

    - Small value assets – for example under £1,000. Treat these assets as expenses for that year

    - Land

    - Treat any asset with a short-term life of less than one year as an expense for that year.

    - Any type of current asset wouldn't be depreciated (for example, Stock, Debtors & Cash).

3. **The cost basis for the new piece of machinery is:**

    | | |
    |---|---|
    | Purchase price of machinery: | £25,000 |
    | Transportation costs | £2,000 |
    | Installation costs | £3,000 |
    | Total cost of asset | **£30,000** |

4. **The cost basis for office renovations would be:**

    | | |
    |---|---|
    | New carpet | £20,000 |
    | Painting | £5,000 |
    | Dry wall installation | £15,000 |
    | Total cost | **£40,000** |

    New office furniture should be set up in a separate depreciation schedule with a cost basis of £30,000.

5. **The annual depreciation cost for the copier is:**

    | | |
    |---|---|
    | Cost price of photocopier | £5,000 |
    | Depreciation (0.20 × £5,000) | **£1,000** |

6. **The annual depreciation expense for the computer is:**

   Cost price of computer        £1,500

   Depreciation (£1,500/3 years)     £500

   *This equates to a depreciation rate of 33.33 per cent (100 per cent/3 years)*

7. **Using the Reducing Balance method, here's what to do:**

   *Year 1*

   Cost of photocopier        £8,000

   Depreciation at 20 per cent     £1,600 (0.20 × £8,000)

   Net Book Value         £6,400

   *Year 2*

   Depreciation at 20 per cent     £1,280 (20 per cent of £6,400)

   Net Book Value         £5,120 (£6,400–£1,280)

   *Year 3*

   Depreciation at 20 per cent     £1,024 (20 per cent of £5,120)

   Net Book Value         £4,096 (£5,120–£1,024)

8. **The bookkeeping entry for posting the annual depreciation is:**

   | | *Debit* | *Credit* |
   |---|---|---|
   | Depreciation account (P&L) | £5,000 | |
   | Accumulated depreciation account (B/S) | | £5,000 |

   The Balance Sheet now shows a net book value of £15,000, which is the original cost of the asset at £20,000, less the depreciation charge of £5,000 for the first year.

   The Profit and Loss account now shows a charge of £5,000, which is the depreciation of the white van for one year.

9. **The purpose of depreciation is to spread the cost of the fixed assets across their useful lives.** The value of a fixed asset is shown as decreasing gradually in the accounts.

10. **Straight-Line.**

11. **25 per cent (100 per cent ÷ four years).**

12. **Cost of fixed assets less accumulated depreciation.**

13. **Reducing balance.**

# Chapter 12

# Adding the Cost of Value Added Tax (VAT)

• • • • • • • • • • • • • • • • • • • • • • • • • • • • • • • • • • • • • • • • • • • • • • •

## In This Chapter

▶ Examining the nuts and bolts of VAT

▶ Setting up for VAT

▶ Getting the return right

▶ Paying and reclaiming VAT

• • • • • • • • • • • • • • • • • • • • • • • • • • • • • • • • • • • • • • • • • • • • • • •

A lot of mystery and tales of horror surround the subject of Value Added Tax (VAT). Now that HM Revenue & Customs administers both tax and VAT, the average business person is facing an even more powerful organisation with a right to know even more about your business.

The rules governing which goods and services are subject to VAT and which items of VAT are reclaimable can be quite complex. This chapter can only scratch the surface and give a broad understanding. Contact both HM Revenue & Customs and your accountant/auditor at an early stage to find out whether all your sales are subject to VAT and how you can ensure that you're only reclaiming allowable VAT. Remember the following – get it right from the beginning.

## Looking into VAT

*VAT* is a tax charged on most business transactions made in the UK or the Isle of Man. VAT is also charged on goods and some services imported from certain places outside the European Union and on some goods and services coming into the UK from other EU countries. VAT applies to all businesses – sole traders, partnerships, limited companies, charities and so on. In simple terms, all VAT-registered businesses act as unpaid collectors of VAT for HM Revenue & Customs.

Examples of taxable transactions are:

✔ Selling new and used goods, including hire purchase.

✔ Renting and hiring out goods.

✔ Using business stock for private purposes.

✔ Providing a service, for example plumbing or manicure.

✔ Charging admission to enter buildings.

As you can see, this list covers most business activities.

Certain services are exempt from VAT, including insurance, finance and credit, some property transactions, certain types of education and training, fundraising charity events and subscriptions to membership organisations. Supplies exempt from VAT don't form part of your turnover for VAT purposes.

VAT is a tax on the difference between what you buy (inputs) and what you sell (outputs), as long as these items fall within the definition of taxable transactions (see the following sections). At the end of a VAT reporting period, you pay over to HM Revenue & Customs the difference between all your output tax and input tax.

✔ **Input tax** is the VAT you pay out to your suppliers for goods and services you purchase for your business. You can reclaim the VAT on these goods or services coming *in* to your business. (See 'Getting VAT back', later in this chapter.) Input tax is, in effect, a tax added to all your purchases.

✔ **Output tax** is the VAT that you must charge on your goods and services when you make each sale. You collect output tax from your customers on each sale you make of items or services going *out* of your business. Output tax is, in effect, a tax added to all your sales.

*Notice 700: The VAT Guide* needs to be your bible in determining how much you need to pay and what you can reclaim. (You can find this guide at www. hmrc.gov.uk.)

## Knowing what to charge

In addition to the obvious trading activities, you need to charge VAT on a whole range of other activities, including the following:

- **Business assets:** If you sell off any unneeded business assets, such as office equipment, commercial vehicles and so on, you must charge VAT.

- **Sales to staff:** Sales to staff are treated no differently than sales to other customers. Therefore you must charge VAT on sales such as canteen meals, goods at reduced prices, vending machines and so on.

- **Hire or loans:** If you make a charge for the use of a business asset, this amount must incur VAT.

- **Gifts:** If you give away goods that cost more than £50, you must add VAT. Treat gifts as if they're a sale for your VAT records.

- **Goods for own use:** Anything you or your family take out of the business must go on the VAT return. HM Revenue & Customs doesn't let you reclaim the VAT on goods or services that aren't used for the complete benefit of the business.

  HM Revenue & Customs is really hot on using business stock for your own use, which is common in restaurants, for example. HM Revenue & Customs knows that you do it and has statistics to show how much on average businesses 'take out' this way. If you don't declare this item when you've used business stock, be prepared to have HM Revenue & Customs jump on you from a great height.

- **Commission earned:** If you sell someone else's goods or services and get paid by means of a commission, you must include VAT on this income.

- **Bartered goods:** If you swap your goods or services for someone else's goods or services, you must account for VAT on the full value of your goods or services that are part of this arrangement.

- **Advance payments:** If a customer gives you any sum of money, you must account for VAT on this amount and the balance when he or she collects the goods. If, for example, you accept payment by instalments, you collect VAT on each instalment.

- **Credit notes:** These items are treated exactly like negative sales invoices, so make sure that you include VAT so you can effectively reclaim the VAT on the output that you're going to, or may have already, paid.

In general you don't have to charge VAT on goods you sell to a VAT-registered business in another European Community (EC) member state. However, you must charge UK VAT if you sell goods to private individuals.

## Knowing how much to charge

The rate of VAT applicable to any transaction is determined by the nature of that transaction. The 20 per cent rate applies to most transactions. The type of business (size or sector) generally has no bearing on the VAT rates. Three rates of VAT currently exist in the UK:

- ✔ A standard rate is 20 per cent from 1 January 2011. This is the rate at which most businesses should add VAT to products and services that they sell.

- ✔ A reduced rate, currently 5 per cent. Some products and services have a lower rate of VAT, including domestic fuel, energy-saving installations and the renovation of dwellings.

- ✔ A zero per cent rate. Many products and services are given a zero rating, including some foods, books and children's clothing. A zero rating for a product or service isn't the same as a total exemption.

You can view a list of business areas where sales are reduced-rated or zero-rated in *Notice 700,* which you can download from `www.hmrc.gov.uk`. You can call the VAT helpline on 0845 010 9000 if you have queries about the list.

# Registering for VAT

First of all you need to register for VAT so that you can charge VAT on your sales and reclaim VAT on your purchases.

The current VAT registration threshold is £73,000 (this threshold changes each year, so check with HM Revenue & Customs for the current threshold). So, if your annual turnover (sales, not profit) is less than this figure, you don't have to register for VAT.

You may find it advantageous to register for VAT even though your sales fall below the VAT registration threshold (and may never exceed it). Registering for VAT gives your business increased credibility – if your customers are large businesses, they expect their suppliers to be VAT registered. Also, you can't reclaim VAT if you're not registered. If your business makes zero-rated supplies but buys in goods and services on which you pay VAT, you want to be able to reclaim this VAT.

As your business grows, it may be difficult to know whether you've broken through the VAT registration threshold. HM Revenue & Customs states that you must register for VAT if:

✔ At the end of any month the total value of the sales you made in the past 12 months (or less) is more than the current threshold.

✔ At any time you have reasonable grounds to expect your sales to be more than the threshold in the next 30 days.

After you register for VAT, you're on the VAT treadmill and have to account for output tax on all your sales, keep proper VAT records and accounts and send in VAT returns regularly.

# Paying in and Reclaiming VAT

HM Revenue & Customs adopts a simple process, laying down and policing the rules in two ways:

✔ Businesses must file periodic returns to the VAT Central Unit (see the later section 'Completing Your VAT Return', for when to file VAT payments).

✔ Businesses receive periodic enquiries and visits from HM Revenue & Customs to verify that these returns are correct.

VAT returns must be completed by the due date, which is shown on the form, and is usually one month after the period covered by the return. Yes, this schedule means that you've one month to complete your VAT return. Any payment due to HM Revenue & Customs must be sent electronically. As long as you complete your VAT return on time and don't arouse the suspicions of HM Revenue & Customs, you may not meet the staff for many years.

You face a financial penalty if your return is late and/or seriously inaccurate. HM Revenue & Customs can and does impose hefty fines on businesses that transgress. Also, offenders who previously had the luxury of quarterly VAT returns often find themselves having to complete monthly VAT returns. Don't mess around with HM Revenue & Customs!

HM Revenue & Customs targets certain business sectors. In general, businesses structured in a complex manner (such as offshore companies) that involve a lot of cash are likely to come in for extra scrutiny. Experience tells HM Revenue & Customs that looking closely at certain types of businesses often yields extra revenues. Also, businesses that submit VAT returns late on a regular basis attract fines and may be forced to submit monthly VAT returns together with payments on account.

## Paying VAT online

HM Revenue & Customs has phased out paper VAT returns, and from April 2012 (apart from a small number of exceptions) you need to file your VAT return online and pay your VAT electronically. The advantage of paying online is that you qualify for seven additional calendar days after the date shown on your return to pay. Visit the HM Revenue & Customs website at www.hmrc.gov.uk and click VAT Online Services to find out about doing your VAT return online:

- ✔ Fill in the appropriate boxes on your VAT return, using 0.00 for nil amounts.

- ✔ Make any payment due by electronic methods (BACS, CHAPS or bank giro).

- ✔ Wait for the acknowledgement that your electronic return was received.

- ✔ Keep a copy of the electronic acknowledgement page for your records.

## Getting help for small businesses

HM Revenue & Customs has some arrangements to make VAT accounting easier for small businesses. The accounting method that your business uses determines when you pay VAT:

- ✔ **Annual Accounting:** If you use the Annual Accounting scheme, you make interim payments, either three or nine, spread across the year, towards an estimated annual VAT bill. This arrangement evens out VAT payments and helps to smooth cash flow. At the end of the year, you submit a single annual return and settle up for any balance due (or maybe receive a cheque back from HM Revenue & Customs). In effect, you complete one annual VAT return at the end of the year but make periodic payments on account (you agree with HM Revenue & Customs how many payments per year you want).

This arrangement may suit the disorganised business that struggles to complete the more traditional four quarterly VAT returns.

You can use this scheme if you don't expect your annual sales (excluding VAT) to exceed £1,350,000 (or in special cases £1,600,000).

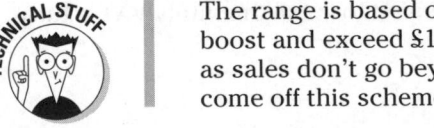

The range is based on estimates of your total sales. If your sales have a boost and exceed £1,350,000, you can stay on this scheme just as long as sales don't go beyond £1,600,000. If sales exceed £1,600,000, you must come off this scheme.

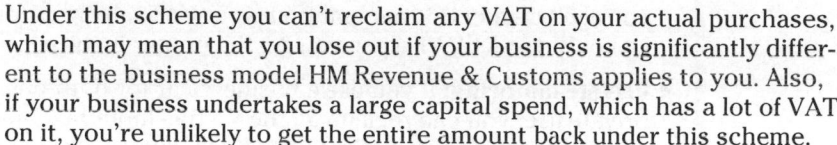

- ✔ **Cash Accounting:** If you use the Cash Accounting scheme, your business accounts for income and expenses when they're actually incurred. Therefore, you don't pay HM Revenue & Customs VAT until your customers pay you. This arrangement may suit a business that has regular slow-paying customers. You can use this scheme if your estimated VAT taxable turnover isn't more than £1,350,000.

- ✔ **Flat Rate Scheme:** This arrangement makes VAT much simpler by allowing you to calculate your VAT payment as a flat percentage of your turnover. The percentage is determined according to the trade sector in which your business operates.

  Under this scheme you can't reclaim any VAT on your actual purchases, which may mean that you lose out if your business is significantly different to the business model HM Revenue & Customs applies to you. Also, if your business undertakes a large capital spend, which has a lot of VAT on it, you're unlikely to get the entire amount back under this scheme.

  You can use this scheme if your annual sales (excluding VAT) aren't expected to exceed £150,000.

- ✔ **Retail Schemes:** If you make lots of quite small sales to the public, you may find it difficult to issue a VAT invoice for each sale. Several available retail schemes may help. For example, you can use a simpler receipt that a till can print out.

  To find out more about the numerous retail schemes, visit the HM Revenue & Customs website www.hmrc.gov.uk and click the link to VAT, under Businesses and Corporations. You must then follow the next steps:

Click on 'Getting Started with VAT', followed by 'Accounting schemes' to simplify VAT accounting or save money, and then scroll down the screen and select 'VAT retail scheme'.

## Getting VAT back

When you're completing your VAT return, you want to reclaim the VAT on every legitimate business purchase. However, you must make sure that you only reclaim legitimate business purchases. The following is the guidance that HM Revenue & Customs gives:

- ✔ **Business purchases:** You can reclaim the VAT on all business purchases and expenses, not just on the raw materials and goods you buy for resale. These purchases include things like business equipment, telephone and utility bills, and payments for other services such as accountants and solicitors' fees.

You can't deduct your input tax for certain purchases, including cars, business entertainment and second-hand goods that you bought under one of the VAT second-hand schemes.

✔ **Business/private use:** If you use services for both business and private purposes, such as your telephone, you can reclaim VAT only on the business use. No hard and fast rules exist on how you split the bill – your local HM Revenue & Customs office is likely to consider any reasonable method.

✔ **Pro-forma invoice:** If a supplier issues a pro-forma invoice, which includes VAT that you have to pay before you're supplied with the goods or service, you can't deduct this amount from your VAT bill on your next return. You can only deduct VAT when you get the proper invoice.

✔ **Private motoring:** If you use a business car for both business and private use, you can reclaim all the VAT as input tax, but you have to account for tax on any private motoring using a scale charge (see the later section 'Using fuel for private motoring').

✔ **Lost invoices:** You can't reclaim any VAT on non-existent invoices. If you do and you get a VAT visit, you're in for the high jump!

✔ **Bad-debt relief:** Occasionally customers don't pay you, and if you've already paid over to HM Revenue & Customs the output VAT on this sale, you're going to be doubly annoyed. Fortunately, HM Revenue & Customs isn't totally heartless – you can reclaim this VAT on a later VAT return.

# Completing Your VAT Return

You need to submit your VAT return online. To do so, go to www.hmrc.gov.uk and click on the link 'Register (new users)', in the box called 'Do it Online' on the top-left side of the page. The site guides you through the setup process. Ensure that you allow plenty of time to register, as it involves receiving user IDs and passwords through the post.

Letting your accounting software complete your VAT return is the easiest method. Sage 50 Accounts does VAT returns as a matter of routine, picking up all the necessary information automatically. You just need to tell the program when to start and when to stop picking up the invoice information. Sage 50 Accounts even prints out the VAT return in a format similar to HM Revenue & Customs' own VAT return form. Figure 12-1 shows the Sage 50 Accounts VAT return.

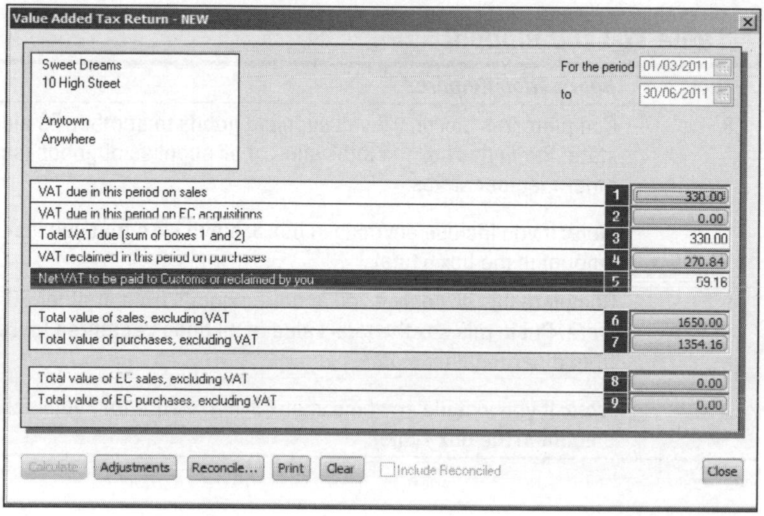

**Figure 12-1:**
The Sage 50 Accounts VAT return.

## Filling in the boxes

At last we come to the nitty-gritty of what figures go into each of the nine boxes on the VAT return. Table 12-1 helps keep the process simple.

| **Table 12-1** | **VAT Return Boxes** |
|---|---|
| **Box** | **Information Required** |
| 1 | VAT due on sales and other outputs in the period. *Notice 700: The VAT Guide* gives further help. |
| 2 | VAT due from you on acquisitions of goods from other EC Member States. *Notice 725 VAT: The Single Market* gives further help. |
| 3 | For paper returns, enter the sum of boxes 1 and 2. The electronic form handles all the maths needed in completing the form. |
| 4 | The input tax you're entitled to claim for the period. |
| 5 | The difference between the figures from boxes 3 and 4. Deduct the smaller from the larger. If the figure in box 3 is more than the figure in box 4, you owe this amount to HM Revenue & Customs. <br><br> If the figure in box 3 is less than the figure in box 4, HM Revenue & Customs owes you this amount. |
| 6 | Your total sales/outputs excluding any VAT. |
| 7 | Your total purchases/inputs excluding any VAT. |

*(continued)*

| Box | Information Required |
|-----|---------------------|
| | **Table 12-1** *(continued)* |
| 8 | Complete this box only if you supplied goods to another EC member state. Put in this box the total value of all supplies of goods (sales) to other member states.<br><br>*Note:* If you include anything in box 8, make sure that you include the amount in the box 6 total. |
| 9 | Complete this box only if you acquired goods from another EC member state. Put in this box the total value of all goods acquired (purchases) from other member states.<br><br>*Note:* If you include anything in box 9, make sure that you include the amount in the box 7 total. |

We deliberately keep this process simple, but remember that behind every box is a multitude of traps set to ensnare you. The HM Revenue & Customs website, www.hmrc.gov.uk has detailed notes to help you complete your VAT return.

## Glancing at problem areas

Not all businesses are entirely straightforward for VAT purposes. Some business activities have their own unique rules and regulations. The list below outlines the exceptions to the rule:

- **Building developer:** See *VAT Notice 708: Buildings and construction* about non-deductible input tax on fixtures and fittings. Also *Notice 742 Land and Property*, regarding land and new-build property sales.

- **Tour operator:** See *VAT Notice 709/5: Tour operators' margin scheme* about VAT you can't reclaim on margin scheme supplies.

- **Second-hand dealer:** See *VAT Notice 718: margin schemes for second-hand goods, works of art, antiques, and collectors' items* about VAT you can't reclaim on second-hand dealing.

### Using fuel for private motoring

If your business pays for non-business fuel for company car users, you must reduce the amount of VAT you reclaim on fuel by means of the scale charge.

*Notice 700/64: Motoring expenses* gives full details. If you use the scale charge, you can recover all the VAT charged on road fuel without having to split your mileage between business and private use. A *scale charge* is a method of accounting for output VAT on road fuel bought by a business that is then used for private mileage. The scale charge is based on the $CO_2$ emissions of each vehicle. You can obtain your $CO_2$ emissions from your vehicle registration certificate (for cars registered after 2001). The HMRC website offers full details of all $CO_2$ emissions and the associated fuel scale charge. See www. hmrc.gov.uk for further details.

### Leasing a motor car

You may find that you're able to claim only 50 per cent of the input tax on contract hire rentals in certain situations. If you lease a car for business purposes, you normally can't recover 50 per cent of the VAT charged. The 50 per cent block is to cover the private use of the car. You can reclaim the remaining 50 per cent of the VAT charged. If you lease a qualifying car that you use exclusively for business purposes and not available for private use, you can recover the input tax in full.

## Filing under special circumstances

If you're filing your first VAT return, your final return or a return with no payment, bear a few things in mind:

- ✔ **First return:** On your first return, you may want to reclaim VAT on money you spent prior to the period covered by your first VAT return. In general, you can recover VAT on capital and pre-start up costs and expenses incurred before you registered for VAT as long as they're VAT qualifying. For further help on this, refer to *Notice 700: The VAT Guide*, available from HM Revenue & Customs.

  If you're completing a VAT return for the first time, go onto the HM Revenue & Customs website for help (www.hmrc.gov.uk) and/or speak with your accountant. You may be missing a trick in not reclaiming VAT on something you bought but didn't reclaim the VAT on. More importantly, you may be reclaiming VAT on something that the taxman doesn't permit you to reclaim.

- ✔ **Final return:** For help with your final return, read *Notice 700/11: Cancelling your registration*. If you've any business assets, such as equipment, vehicles or stock on which you previously reclaimed VAT, you must include these items in your final VAT return. In effect, HM Revenue & Customs wants to recover this VAT (unless the amount is less than £1,000) in your last return.

As soon as your business circumstances change, you must inform HM Revenue & Customs, which has specified time limits, depending on the circumstances. If you ignore these time limits, you may incur penalties. If in doubt, contact the VAT helpline on 0845-0109000.

✔ **Nil return:** You can file a Nil return if you:

- Have not traded in the period covered by the VAT return *and*

- No VAT exists on purchases (inputs) to recover *or*

- No VAT exists on sales (outputs) to declare.

Complete all boxes on the return as 'None' on your paper-based return or '0.00' on your electronic return.

## Correcting mistakes

HM Revenue & Customs accepts the fact that people make mistakes (after all, we're only human!) and they don't expect perfection. However, they do have strict rules concerning mistakes. If you find a mistake on a previous return, you may be able to adjust your VAT account and include the value of that adjustment on your current VAT return. You can only do this if the mistake is found to be genuine and not deliberate, and is also below the error-correcting threshold (currently £10,000). If the amount is payable to HM Revenue & Customs, include it in the total for box 1 or box 2 (acquisitions). If the amount is repayable to you, include it in the total for box 4.

If you make a bigger mistake (the net value of the mistake is more than £10,000), *do not* include the amount on your current return. Inform your local VAT Business Advice Centre by letter or on form *VAT 652: Voluntary disclosure of errors on VAT returns*. The Centre then issues a Notice of Voluntary Disclosure showing only the corrections to the period in question, and you become liable to the under-declared VAT and interest. Under these circumstances, no mis-declaration penalty is applied. Form *Notice 700/45: How to correct VAT errors and make adjustments or claims* helps you.

If you discover that an error has been made, you must disclose it to HM Revenue & Customs immediately. You cannot adjust these errors in a later VAT return.

## Pursuing Payments and Repayments

Your completed VAT return results in one of two outcomes: you owe HM Revenue & Customs money or it owes you money – unless of course you complete a Nil return, in which case you and HM Revenue & Customs are quits.

If you owe VAT but can't afford to pay by the due date, still send in your completed VAT return, and then contact the Business Payment Support Service on 0845-3021435. This service was set up on 24 November 2008 to meet the needs of businesses and individuals affected by the current economic downturn. You can discuss temporary options with them, such as extending the period of payment.

If you're owed money, you should receive a repayment about two weeks after you submit your VAT return. If, after three weeks, you haven't received your repayment, contact the Customs and Excise National Advice Service on 0845-0109000.

If your business is due a repayment of VAT on a regular basis and you're on quarterly VAT returns, switch to monthly VAT returns at the earliest opportunity. Under a monthly system, you wait only two weeks for your VAT repayment rather than an additional two months.

If for any reason you receive a 'Notice of assessment and/or over-declaration' as a result of a mistake found by a visiting officer, don't wait until your next VAT return to rectify the issue. If you owe VAT, send your payment and the remittance advice in the envelope provided. If they owe you, suppress a large smile and pay in the cheque, or check your bank account if you normally pay electronically.

# Part IV
# Reporting Results and Starting Over

'I hate the end of the financial year.'

## In this part . . .

Now's the time to show off all the hard work you and your employees have put into keeping your business operating and making a profit. This part instructs you in how to use all the information you collect throughout the accounting period to prepare financial reports that give investors, lenders, suppliers, HM Revenue & Customs, and your employees a clear picture of how well your business did during the month, the quarter or the year.

Finally, we guide you through the process of closing the books at year-end and getting ready for the next year.

# Chapter 13

# Producing a Profit and Loss Statement

*In This Chapter*

▶ Sorting out the elements of a Profit and Loss statement

▶ Preparing the statement

▶ Analysing statement data

▶ Zeroing in on profitability

*W*ithout one very important financial report tool, you can never know for sure whether or not your business is making a profit. This tool is called the *Profit and Loss statement,* and most businesses prepare this statement on a monthly basis, as well as quarterly and annually, in order to get periodic pictures of how well the business is doing financially.

Analysing the Profit and Loss statement and the details behind it can reveal lots of useful information to help you make decisions for improving your profits and business overall. This chapter covers the various parts of a Profit and Loss statement, how you develop one and examples of how you can use it to make business decisions.

## Lining Up the Profit and Loss Statement

Did your business make any profit? You can find the answer in your *Profit and Loss statement,* the financial report that summarises all the sales activities, costs of producing or buying the products or services sold and expenses incurred in order to run the business.

Profit and Loss statements summarise the financial activities of a business during a particular accounting period (which can be a month, quarter, year or some other period of time that makes sense for a business's needs).

Normal practice is to include two accounting periods on a Profit and Loss statement: the current period plus the year to date. The five key lines that make up a Profit and Loss statement are:

- **Sales or Revenue:** The total amount of invoiced sales you take in from selling the business's products or services. You calculate this amount by totalling all the sales or revenue accounts. The top line of the Profit and Loss statement is Sales or Revenue; either is okay.

- **Cost of Goods Sold:** How much you spent in order to buy or make the goods or services that your business sold during the accounting period under review. The section 'Finding Cost of Goods Sold' below shows you how to calculate Cost of Goods Sold.

- **Gross Profit:** How much your business made before taking into account operations expenses; calculated by subtracting the Cost of Goods Sold from the Sales or Revenue.

- **Operating Expenses:** How much you spent on operating the business; these expenses include administrative fees, salaries, advertising, utilities and other operations expenses. You add all your expenses accounts on your Profit and Loss statement to get this total.

- **Net Profit or Loss:** Whether or not your business made a profit or loss during the accounting period in review; calculated by subtracting total expenses from Gross Profit.

# Formatting the Profit and Loss Statement

Here, we show you a simplified UK format for the Profit and Loss statement:

*Revenues*

| | |
|---|---|
| Turnover | £10,000 |
| Cost of Goods Sold | <u>£5,000</u> |
| *Gross Profit* | £5,000 |
| ***Operating Expenses*** | |
| Advertising | £700 |
| Salaries | £1,200 |
| Supplies | £1,500 |
| Depreciation | £500 |
| Interest Expenses | <u>£500</u> |
| *Total Operating Expenses* | £4,400 |
| Operating Profit | £600 |

*Other Income*

| Interest Income | £200 |
|---|---|
| Total Profit | £800 |

# Preparing the Profit and Loss Statement

If you're using a computerised accounting system, the Profit and Loss report is generated at the press of a button. However, if you're operating a manual system, you need to use the figures from your Trial Balance to construct the Profit and Loss statement.

## Finding Net Sales

*Net Sales* is a total of all your sales minus any discounts. In order to calculate Net Sales, you look at the sales account, discounts and any sales fees on your Trial Balance. For example, suppose that you have Total Sales at £20,000, discounts of £1,000, as well as credit card fees on sales of £125. To find your Net Sales, you subtract the discounts and credit card fees from your Total Sales amount, leaving you with £18,875.

## Finding Cost of Goods Sold

*Cost of Goods Sold* is the total amount your business spent to buy or make the goods or services that you sold. To calculate this amount for a business that buys its finished products from another business in order to sell them to customers, you start with the value of the business's Opening Stock (the amount in the Stock account at the beginning of the accounting period), add all purchases of new stock and then subtract any Closing Stock (stock that's still on the shelves or in the warehouse; it appears on the Balance Sheet, which is covered in Chapter 14).

The following is a basic Cost of Goods Sold calculation:

Opening Stock + Purchases = Goods Available for Sale

£100 + £1,000 = £1,100

Goods Available for Sale − Closing Stock = Cost of Goods Sold

£1,100 − £200 = £900

To simplify the example for calculating Cost of Goods Sold, these numbers assume the Opening Stock (the value of the stock at the beginning of the accounting period) and Closing Stock (the value of the stock at the end of the accounting period) values are the same. See Chapter 8 for details about calculating stock value. So to calculate Cost of Goods Sold, you need just two key lines: the purchases made and the discounts received to lower the purchase cost, as in the following example.

Purchases – Purchases Discounts = Cost of Goods Sold

£8,000 – £1,500 = £6,500

## Drawing remaining amounts from your Trial Balance

After you calculate Net Sales and Cost of Goods Sold (see the preceding sections), you can use the rest of the numbers, usually overheads, from your Trial Balance to prepare your business's Profit and Loss statement. Figure 13-1 shows a sample Profit and Loss statement.

You and anyone else in-house are likely to want to see the type of detail shown in the example in Figure 13-1, but most business owners prefer not to show all their operating detail to outsiders: they like to keep the detail private. Fortunately, if you operate as a sole trader or partnership, only HM Revenue & Customs needs to see your detailed Profit and Loss figures. If your turnover is less than £73,000 per annum, HM Revenue & Customs allow you to file an abbreviated set of accounts for the purpose of completing your Self Assessment Tax return (SA103S), only requesting the following headings:

- Turnover
- Other Income
- Cost of Goods Sold
- Car, Van and Travel Expenses (after private-use deduction)
- Wages, Salaries and Other Staff Costs
- Rent, Rates, Power and Insurance Costs
- Repairs and Renewals of Property and Equipment
- Accountancy, Legal and Other Professional Fees
- Interest, Bank and Credit Card Financial Charges
- Phone, Fax, Stationery and Other Office Costs
- Other Allowable Business Expenses

**Profit and Loss Statement**

**May 2012**

| Month Ended | May |
|---|---|
| Revenues: | |
| Net Sales | £ 18,875 |
| Cost of Goods Sold | (£ 6,500) |
| Gross Profit | £ 12,375 |
| Operating Expenses: | |
| Advertising | £ 1,500 |
| Bank Service Charges | £ 120 |
| Insurance Expenses | £ 100 |
| Interest Expenses | £ 125 |
| Legal & Accounting Fees | £ 300 |
| Office Expenses | £ 250 |
| Payroll Taxes Expenses | £ 350 |
| Postage Expenses | £ 75 |
| Rent Expenses | £ 800 |
| Salaries | £ 3,500 |
| Supplies | £ 300 |
| Telephone Expenses | £ 200 |
| Utilities | £ 255 |
| Total Operating Expenses | £ 7,875 |
| Net Profit | £ 4,500 |

**Figure 13-1:** A sample Profit and Loss statement.

Also, if you're a small limited company, when you file your accounts at Companies House you can file abbreviated accounts, which means that you can keep your detailed Profit and Loss figures secret. Speak with your external accountant about whether you qualify as a small company because the exemption levels do change from time to time.

# Gauging your Cost of Goods Sold

Businesses that make their own products rather than buy them for future sale must record stock at three different levels:

- **Raw materials:** This line item includes purchases of all items used to make your business's products. For example, a fudge shop buys all the ingredients to make the fudge it sells, so the value of any stock on hand that hasn't been used to make fudge yet needs to appear in the raw materials line item.

> ✔ **Work-in-progress stock:** This line item shows the value of any products being made but that aren't yet ready for sale. A fudge shop is unlikely to have anything in this line item because fudge doesn't take more than a few hours to make. However, many manufacturing businesses take weeks or months to produce products and therefore usually have some portion of the stock value in this line item.
>
> Valuing work in progress can be very complex. As well as the raw material content, you need to add in direct wages and production overheads consumed to produce the products to the stage they're at. In reality, most small businesses do not attempt to value work in progress.
>
> ✔ **Finished-goods stock:** This line item lists the value of stock that's ready for sale. (For a business that doesn't make its own products, finished-goods stock is the same as the stock line item.)

If you keep the books for a business that manufactures its own products, you can use a computerised accounting system to record the various stock accounts described here. However, your basic accounting system software won't cut it – you need a more advanced package in order to record multiple stock types. One such system is Sage 50 Accounts.

# Deciphering Gross Profit

Business owners must carefully watch their Gross Profit trends on monthly Profit and Loss statements. Gross Profit trends that appear lower from one month to the next can mean one of two things: sales revenue is down, or Cost of Goods Sold is up.

If revenue is down month to month, you may need to find out quickly why and fix the problem in order to meet your sales goals for the year. Or, by examining sales figures for the same month in previous years, you may determine that the drop is just a normal sales slowdown given the time of year and isn't cause to hit the panic button.

If the downward trend isn't normal, it may be a sign that a competitor's successfully drawing customers away from your business, or it may indicate that customers are dissatisfied with some aspect of the products or services you supply. Whatever the reason, preparing a monthly Profit and Loss statement gives you the ammunition you need to find and fix a problem quickly, thereby minimising any negative hit to your yearly profits.

The other key element of Gross Profit – Cost of Goods Sold – can also be a big factor in a downward profit trend. For example, if the amount you spend to purchase products that you sell goes up, your Gross Profit goes down. As a business owner, you need to do one of five things if the Cost of Goods Sold is reducing your Gross Profit:

- ✔ Find a new supplier who can provide the goods cheaper.

- ✔ Increase your prices, as long as you don't lose sales because of the increase.

- ✔ Find a way to increase your volume of sales so that you can sell more products and meet your annual profit goals.

- ✔ Find a way to reduce other expenses to offset the additional product costs.

- ✔ Accept the fact that your annual profit is going to be lower than expected.

The sooner you find out that you have a problem with costs, the faster you can find a solution and minimise any reduction in your annual profit goals.

# Monitoring Expenses

The Expenses section of your Profit and Loss statement gives you a good summary of how much you spent to keep your business operating that wasn't directly related to the sale of an individual product or service. For example, businesses usually use advertising both to bring customers in and with the hopes of selling many different types of products. That's why you need to list advertising as an expense rather than a Cost of Goods Sold. After all, rarely can you link an advertisement to the sale of an individual product. The same is true of all the administrative expenses that go into running a business, such as rent, wages and salaries, office costs and so on.

Business owners watch their expense trends closely to be sure that they don't creep upwards and lower the business's bottom lines. Any cost-cutting you can do on the expense side is guaranteed to increase your bottom-line profit.

# Using the Profit and Loss Statement to Make Business Decisions

Many business owners find it easier to compare their Profit and Loss statement trends using percentages rather than the actual numbers. Calculating these percentages is easy enough – you simply divide each line item by Net Sales. Figure 13-2 shows a business's percentage breakdown for one month.

### Profit and Loss Statement

### May 2012

| Month Ended | May | |
|---|---|---|
| Net Sales | £ 18,875 | 100.0% |
| Cost of Goods Sold | (£ 6,500) | 34.4% |
| Gross Profit | £ 12,375 | 65.6% |
| Operating Expenses: | | |
| Advertising | £ 1,500 | 7.9% |
| Bank Service Charges | £ 120 | 0.6% |
| Insurance Expenses | £ 100 | 0.5% |
| Interest Expenses | £ 125 | 0.7% |
| Legal & Accounting Fees | £ 300 | 1.6% |
| Office Expenses | £ 250 | 1.3% |
| Payroll Taxes Expenses | £ 350 | 1.9% |
| Postage Expenses | £ 75 | 0.4% |
| Rent Expenses | £ 800 | 4.2% |
| Salaries | £ 3,500 | 18.5% |
| Supplies | £ 300 | 1.6% |
| Telephone Expenses | £ 200 | 1.1% |
| Utilities | £ 255 | 1.4% |
| Total Operating Expenses | £ 7,875 | 41.7% |
| Net Profit | £ 4,500 | 23.8% |

**Figure 13-2:** Percentage breakdown of a Profit and Loss statement.

Looking at this percentage breakdown, you can see that the business had a Gross Profit of 65.6 per cent, and its Cost of Goods Sold, at 34.4 per cent, accounted for just over one-third of the revenue. If the prior month's Cost of Goods Sold was only 32 per cent, the business owner needs to find out why the cost of the goods used to make this product seems to have increased. If this trend of increased Cost of Goods Sold continues through the year without some kind of fix, the business makes at least 2.2 per cent less Net Profit.

You may find it helpful to see how your Profit and Loss statement results compare to industry trends for similar businesses with similar revenues, a process called *benchmarking*. By comparing results, you can find out whether your costs and expenses are reasonable for the type of business you operate, and you can identify areas with room to improve your profitability. You also may spot red flags for line items upon which you spend much more than the national average.

To find industry trends for businesses similar to yours with similar revenues, visit www.bvdinfo.com. The FAME database contains full financial data on approximately two million companies in the UK and Ireland that file their accounts at Companies House. A word of warning though: small companies are required to file very little financial information – typically just a Balance Sheet. This fact means that if you want to see detailed Profit and Loss information, you have to look at the big businesses with turnover above £5.6 million and a Balance Sheet greater than £2.8 million.

However, the information available for all the companies on this database is useful and can be searched in a number of ways. For example, you can compile industry-average statistics, which can be a useful way to see how your business compares with others in the same line of business. You can take this compilation a stage further and compare your business to other businesses that you already know or have found on this database.

You can also find out how your business looks to the outside world if you use FAME to dig out the financials for your business. A credit rating, details of any court judgements and other interesting information are all included in the reports.

FAME is available by subscription, which may make it expensive for the occasional user. You may find that a regional library has FAME available to the public on a free basis or through a per-session cost. Most of the UK universities have FAME, so if you can access one of their library services you can also use this facility. This service may be available through an annual library subscription.

Another source of financial information is your local business link (www.businesslink.gov.uk). Business link acts as a signpost to help small and medium-sized businesses. They can help you access your trade association and other business support agencies and consultancies that run benchmarking.

# Testing Profits

With a completed Profit and Loss statement, you can do a number of quick ratio tests of your business's profitability. You certainly want to know how well your business did compared to other similar businesses. You also want to be able to measure your *return* (the percentage you made) on your business.

Three common tests are Return on Sales, Return on Assets and Return on Shareholders' Capital. These ratios have much more meaning if you can find industry averages for your particular type of business, so that you can compare your results. Check with your local Chamber of Commerce to see whether it has figures for local businesses or order a report for your industry online from FAME.

# Return on Sales

The Return on Sales (ROS) ratio tells you how efficiently your business runs its operations. Using the information on your Profit and Loss statement, you can measure how much profit your business produced per pound of sales and how much extra cash you brought in per sale.

You calculate ROS by dividing Net Profit before taxes by Sales. For example, suppose that your business had a Net Profit of £4,500 and Sales of £18,875. The following shows your calculation of ROS.

Net Profit before taxes ÷ Sales = Return on Sales

£4,500 ÷ £18,875 = 23.8%

As you can see, your business made 23.8 per cent on each pound of sales. To determine whether that amount calls for celebration, you need to find the ROS ratios for similar businesses. You may be able to get such information from your local Chamber of Commerce, or you can order an industry report online from FAME.

# Return on Assets

The Return on Assets (ROA) ratio tests how well you're using your business's assets to generate profits. If your business's ROA is the same or higher than other similar companies, you're doing a good job of managing your assets.

To calculate ROA, you divide Net Profit by Total Assets. You find Total Assets on your Balance Sheet, which you can read more about in Chapter 14. Suppose that your business's Net Profit was £4,500 and Total Assets were £40,050. The following shows your calculation of ROA.

Net Profit ÷ Total Assets = Return on Assets

£4,500 ÷ £40,050 = 11.2%

Your calculation shows that your business made 11.2 per cent on each pound of assets it held.

ROA can vary significantly depending on the type of industry in which you operate. For example, if your business requires you to maintain lots of expensive equipment, such as a manufacturing firm, your ROA is much lower than a service business that doesn't need as many assets. ROA can range from below 5 per cent, for manufacturing businesses that require a large investment in machinery and factories, to as high as 20 per cent or even higher for service businesses with few assets.

## Return on Shareholders' Capital

To measure how successfully your business earned money for the owners or investors, calculate the Return on Shareholders' Capital (ROSC) ratio. This ratio often looks better than Return on Assets (see the preceding section) because ROSC doesn't take debt into consideration.

You calculate ROSC by dividing Net Profit by Shareholders' or Owners' Capital. (You find capital amounts on your Balance Sheet; see Chapter 14.) Suppose that your business's Net Profit was £4,500 and the Shareholders' or Owners' Capital was £9,500. Here is the formula:

Net Profit ÷ Shareholders' or Owners' Capital = Return on Shareholders' Capital

£4,500 ÷ £9,500 = 47.3%

Most business owners put in a lot of cash upfront to get a business started, so seeing a business whose liabilities and capital are split close to 50 per cent each is fairly common.

## Branching Out with Profit and Loss Statement Data

The Profit and Loss statement you produce for external use – financial institutions and investors – may be very different from the one you produce for in-house use by your managers. Most business owners prefer to provide the minimum amount of detail necessary to satisfy external users of their financial statements, such as summaries of expenses instead of line-by-line expense details, a Net Sales figure without reporting all the detail about discounts and fees, and a Cost of Goods Sold number without reporting all the detail about how that was calculated.

Internally, the contents of the Profit and Loss statement are a very different story. With more detail, your managers are better able to make accurate business decisions. Most businesses develop detailed reports based on the data collected to develop the Profit and Loss statement. Items such as discounts, returns and allowances are commonly pulled out of Profit and Loss statements and broken down into more detail:

- ✔ **Discounts** are reductions on the selling price as part of a special sale. They may also be in the form of volume discounts provided to customers who buy large amounts of the business's products. For example, a business may offer a 10 per cent discount to customers who buy 20 or more of the same item at one time. In order to put their Net Sales numbers in perspective, business owners and managers must monitor how much they reduce their revenues to attract sales.

- ✔ **Returns** are transactions in which the buyer returns items for any reason – not the right size, damaged, defective and so on. If a business's number of returns increases dramatically, a larger problem may be the cause; therefore business owners need to monitor these numbers carefully in order to identify and resolve any problems with the items they sell.

- ✔ **Allowances** cover gifts cards and other accounts that customers pay for upfront without taking any merchandise. Allowances are actually a liability for a business because the customer (or the person who was given the gift card) eventually comes back to get merchandise and doesn't have to pay any cash in return.

Another section of the Profit and Loss statement that you're likely to break down into more detail for internal use is the Cost of Goods Sold. Basically, you take the detail collected to calculate that line item, including Opening Stock, Closing Stock, Purchases and Purchase discounts, and present it in a separate report. (We explain how to calculate Cost of Goods Sold in the section 'Finding Cost of Goods Sold', earlier in this chapter.)

No limit exists to the number of internal reports you can generate from the detail that goes into your Profit and Loss statement and other financial statements. For example, many businesses design a report that looks at month-to-month trends in revenue, Cost of Goods Sold and profit. In fact, you can set up your computerised accounting system (if you use one) to generate this and other custom-designed reports automatically. Using your computerised system, you can produce these reports at any time during the month if you want to see how close you are to meeting your month-end, quarter-end or year-end goal.

Many businesses also design a report that compares actual spending to the budget. On this report, each of the Profit and Loss statement line items appear with their accompanying planned budget figures and the actual figures. When reviewing this report, you flag any line item that's considerably higher or lower than expected and then research them to find a reason for the difference.

# Have a Go

The following section tests your knowledge about the Profit and Loss statements:

1. **Your Purchases account shows that you purchased £10,000 worth of paper goods to be sold during the accounting period. In which section of the Profit and Loss Statement would you include that account?**

2. **Your Telephone Expenses account shows that you paid a total of £2,000 for your company's telephones during the accounting period. In which section of the Profit and Loss Statement would you show that account?**

3. **Your Sales Discounts account shows that you offered customers a total of £1,500 in discounts during the accounting period. In which section of the Profit and Loss Statement would you put that information?**

4. **Describe how you would calculate Gross Profit. Show the calculation required if it helps.**

5. **Explain how you would calculate Net Profit. Show the calculation required if it helps.**

6. **Using the figures given below, prepare a Profit and Loss statement using the format shown earlier in this chapter.**

| | |
|---|---|
| Net Sales | £50,000 |
| Interest Profit and Loss | £1,200 |
| Cost of Goods Sold | £20,000 |
| Advertising | £3,000 |
| Salaries | £5,000 |
| Supplies | £2,500 |
| Interest Expenses | £1,300 |
| Depreciation | £1,500 |

7. **Looking at your accounts, you find that you've the following balances at the end of an accounting period:**

| | |
|---|---|
| Sales of Goods | £20,000 |
| Sales Discounts | £2,000 |
| Sales Returns | £1,500 |

   **Using these figures, calculate your Net Sales.**

8. **Suppose that you started the month of June with £200 of stock in hand. You purchased £2,000 of stock during June and you've £500 of stock left to sell at the end of June. You're preparing a Profit and Loss statement for the month of June. What would your Cost of Goods Sold be for the month of June?**

9. Suppose that you started the month of July with £500 of stock on hand. You purchased £1,500 of stock during July and you've £100 of stock left to sell at the end of July. You're preparing a Profit and Loss statement for the month of July. What would your Cost of Goods Sold be for the month of July?

10. Suppose that your company had a net Profit and Loss of £10,595 and sales of £40,500 for the month of June. Calculate the ROS ratio.

11. Suppose that your company had a net Profit and Loss of £13,565 and sales of £75,725 for the month of July. Calculate the ROS ratio.

12. Your company's net profit for the month of May is £5,300 and its total assets are £75,040. What's the ROA ratio?

13. Your company's Net Profit for the month of May is £10,700 and its Total Assets are £49,650. What's the ROA ratio?

14. Your company earned a Net Profit of £75,750 and its Shareholders' or Owner's Equity is £500,000. Calculate the Return on Equity ratio.

15. Your company earned a net profit of £52,500 and its owner's equity is £375,000. Calculate the Return on Equity ratio.

# Answering the Have a Go Questions

1. Purchases are included as part of your calculation for Cost of Goods Sold.

2. Telephone Expenses are part of Operating Expenses for a business.

3. Sales Discounts are included as part of your calculation for Net Sales.

4. Gross Profit is calculated as follows:

| | |
|---|---|
| Sales Revenue | X |
| Less Cost of Goods Sold | (X) |
| Gross Profit | X |

The actual Gross Profit figure is often expressed as a percentage of sales to provide you with a Gross Profit margin.

For example:

| | |
|---|---|
| Sales Revenue | £100,000 |
| Cost of Goods Sold | (£75,000) |
| Gross Profit | £25,000 |

*Gross Profit margin would be 25,000 ÷ 100,000 = 0.25 (25 per cent expressed as a percentage)*

5. **Net Profit is often described as the 'bottom line', as it's the profit after all Operating Expenses have been taken from your Gross Profit.**

   You can express the Net Profit as a percentage of sales to provide you with a Net Profit margin.

   For example:

   | | | |
   |---|---|---|
   | Sales Revenue | | £100,000 |
   | Cost of Goods Sold | (£75,000) | |
   | Gross Profit | | £25,000 |
   | Operating Expenses | (£15,000) | |
   | Net Profit | | £10,000 |

   The Net Profit margin would be 10,000 ÷ 100,000 = 0.10 (10 per cent expressed as a percentage)

6. **Using the figures given in the example, the Profit and Loss statement would appear as follows:**

   | | | |
   |---|---|---|
   | ***Revenues*** | | |
   | Sales | | £50,000 |
   | Cost of Goods Sold | (£20,000) | |
   | *Gross Profit* | | £30,000 |
   | Operating Expenses | | |
   | Advertising | | £3,000 |
   | Salaries | | £5,000 |
   | Supplies | | £2,500 |
   | Interest Expenses | | £1,300 |
   | Depreciation | | £1,500 |
   | Total Operating Expenses | | £13,300 |
   | Operating Profit | | £16,700 |
   | Other Income | | |
   | Interest income | | £1,200 |
   | Net Profit | | £17,900 |

7. **The net sales are calculated as follows:**

   | | |
   |---|---|
   | Sales of Goods Sold | £20,000 |
   | Sales Discounts | (2,000) |
   | Sales Returns | (1,500) |
   | Net Sales | £16,500 |

8. **Your Cost of Goods Sold for the month of June would be:**

| | |
|---|---|
| Opening Stock | £200 |
| Add Purchases | £2,000 |
| Goods Available for Sale | £2,200 |
| Less Closing Stock | (£500) |
| Cost of Goods Sold | £1,700 |

9. **Your Cost of Goods Sold for the month of July would be:**

| | |
|---|---|
| Opening Stock | £500 |
| Add Purchases | £1,500 |
| Goods Available for Sale | £2,000 |
| Less Closing Stock | (£100) |
| Cost of Goods Sold | £1,900 |

10. **The ROS ratio would be:**

    £10,595/£40,500 = 26.2 per cent

    So, in this case the company made 26.2 per cent for each pound of sales.

11. **The ROS ratio would be:**

    £13,565/£75,725 = 17.9 per cent

    So, in this case the company made 17.9 per cent for each pound of sales.

12. **The ROA ratio is:**

    £5,300/£75,040 = 7.06 per cent

13. **The ROA ratio is:**

    £10,700/£49,650 = 21.55 per cent

14. **The Return on Equity ratio would be:**

    £75,750/£500,000 = 15.15 per cent

    So the owner's return on his investment is 15.15 per cent.

15. **The Return on Equity ratio would be:**

    £52,500/£375,000 = 14 per cent

    So the owner's return on his investment is 14 per cent.

# Chapter 14

# Developing a Balance Sheet

. . . . . . . . . . . . . . . . . . . . . . . . . . . . . . . . . . . . . . .

### In This Chapter

▶ Tackling the Balance Sheet

▶ Pulling together your Balance Sheet accounts

▶ Choosing a format

▶ Drawing conclusions from your Balance Sheet

▶ Polishing your electronically produced Balance Sheet

. . . . . . . . . . . . . . . . . . . . . . . . . . . . . . . . . . . . . . .

*P*eriodically, you want to know how well your business is doing. Therefore, at the end of each accounting period, you draw up a Balance Sheet – a snapshot of your business's condition. This snapshot gives you a picture of where your business stands – its assets, its liabilities and how much the owners have invested in the business at a particular point in time.

This chapter explains the key ingredients of a Balance Sheet and tells you how to pull them all together. You also find out how to use analytical tools called ratios to see how well your business is doing.

## Breaking Down the Balance Sheet

Basically, creating a Balance Sheet is like taking a picture of the financial aspects of your business.

The business name appears at the top of the Balance Sheet along with the ending date for the accounting period being reported. The rest of the report summarises:

  ✔ **The business's assets,** which include everything the business owns in order to stay in operation.

  ✔ **The business's debts,** which include any outstanding bills and loans that it must pay.

  ✔ **The owners' capital,** which is basically how much the business's owners have invested in the business.

---

## Generating Balance Sheets electronically

If you use a computerised accounting system, you can take advantage of its report function to generate your Balance Sheets automatically. These Balance Sheets give you quick snapshots of the business's financial position, but may require adjustments before you prepare your financial reports for external use.

One key adjustment you're likely to make involves the value of your stock. Most computerised accounting systems use the averaging method to value stock. This method totals all the stock purchased and then calculates an average price for the stock (see Chapter 8 for more information on stock valuation). However, your accountant may recommend a different valuation method that works better for your business. We discuss the options in Chapter 8. Therefore, if you use a method other than the default averaging method to value your stock, you need to adjust the stock value that appears on the Balance Sheet generated from your computerised accounting system.

---

Assets, liabilities and capital probably sound familiar – they're the key elements that show whether or not your books are in balance. If your liabilities plus capital equal assets, your books are in balance. All your bookkeeping efforts are an attempt to keep the books in balance based on this formula, which we talk more about in Chapter 2.

# *Gathering Balance Sheet Ingredients*

Most people now operate a computerised accounting system and the Balance Sheet is achieved simply by pressing a few buttons. However, you'll find it useful to know how the Balance Sheet is constructed, and this chapter shows you how, with the aid of a fictitious set of accounts.

To keep this example simple, we've selected the following key accounts from the company's Trial Balance as shown in Table 14-1:

| Table 14-1 | Balance Sheet Accounts | |
|---|---|---|
| *Account Name* | *Balance in Account* | |
| | Debit | Credit |
| Cash | £2,500 | |
| Petty Cash | £500 | |

| Account Name | Balance in Account | |
| --- | --- | --- |
| Trade Debtors (Accounts Receivable) | £1,000 | |
| Stock | £1,200 | |
| Equipment | £5,050 | |
| Vehicles | £25,000 | |
| Furniture | £5,600 | |
| Drawings | £10,000 | |
| Trade Creditors (Accounts Payable) | | £2,200 |
| Loans Payable | | £29,150 |
| Capital | | £5,000 |
| Net Profit for the Year | | £14,500 |
| Total | £50,850 | £50,850 |

# Dividing and listing your assets

The first part of the Balance Sheet is the assets section. The first step in developing this section is dividing your assets into two categories: current assets and fixed assets.

### Current assets

*Current assets* are things your business owns that you can easily convert to cash and expect to use in the next 12 months to pay your bills and your employees. Current assets include cash, Trade Debtors (money due from customers) and stock. (We cover Trade Debtors in Chapter 7 and stock in Chapter 8.)

When you see Cash as the first line item on a Balance Sheet, that account includes what you have on hand in the tills and what you have in the bank, including current accounts, savings accounts and petty cash. In most cases, you simply list all these accounts as one item, Cash, on the Balance Sheet.

The current assets for the fictional business are:

| | |
| --- | --- |
| Cash | £2,500 |
| Petty Cash | £500 |
| Trade Debtors | £1,000 |
| Stock | £1,200 |

You total the Cash and Petty Cash accounts, giving you £3,000, and list that amount on the Balance Sheet as a line item called Cash.

### Fixed assets

*Fixed assets* are things your business owns that you expect to have for more than 12 months. Fixed assets include land, buildings, equipment, furniture, vehicles and anything else that you expect to have for longer than a year.

The fixed assets for the fictional business are:

| | |
|---|---|
| Equipment | £5,050 |
| Vehicles | £25,000 |
| Furniture | £5,600 |

Most businesses have more items in the fixed assets section of a Balance Sheet than the few fixed assets we show here for the fictional business. For example:

- A manufacturing business that has a lot of tools, dies or moulds created specifically for its manufacturing processes needs to have a line item called Tools, Dies and Moulds.

- A business that owns one or more buildings needs to have a line item labelled Land and Buildings.

- A business may lease its business space and then spend lots of money doing it up. For example, a restaurant may rent a large space and then furnish it according to a desired theme. Money the restaurant spends on doing up the space becomes a fixed asset called Leasehold Improvements and is listed on the Balance Sheet in the fixed assets section.

Everything mentioned so far in this section – land, buildings, leasehold improvements and so on – is a *tangible asset*. These items are ones that you can actually touch or hold. Another type of fixed asset is the *intangible asset*. Intangible assets aren't physical objects; common examples are patents, copyrights and trademarks.

- A **patent** gives a business the right to dominate the markets for the patented product. When a patent expires (usually after 20 years), competitors can enter the marketplace for the product that was patented, and the competition helps to lower the price to consumers. For example, pharmaceutical businesses patent all their new drugs and therefore are protected as the sole providers of those drugs. When your doctor prescribes a brand-name drug, you're getting a patented product. Generic drugs are products whose patents have run out, meaning that any pharmaceutical business can produce and sell its own version of the same product.

✔ A **copyright** protects original works, including books, magazines, articles, newspapers, television shows, movies, music, poetry and plays, from being copied by anyone other than the creator(s). For example, this book is copyrighted, so no one can make a copy of any of its contents without the permission of the publisher, John Wiley & Sons, Ltd.

✔ A **trademark** gives a business ownership of distinguishing words, phrases, symbols or designs. For example, check out this book's cover to see the registered trademark, *For Dummies*, for this brand. Trademarks can last forever, as long as a business continues to use the trademark and files the proper paperwork periodically.

In order to show in financial statements that their values are being used up, all fixed assets are depreciated or amortised. Tangible assets are depreciated; see Chapter 11 for details on how to depreciate. Intangible assets such as patents and copyrights are amortised (amortisation is similar to depreciation). Each intangible asset has a lifespan based on the number of years for which the rights are granted. After setting an initial value for the intangible asset, a business then divides that value by the number of years it has protection, and the resulting amount is then written off each year as an Amortisation Expense, which is shown on the Profit and Loss statement. You can find the total amortisation or depreciation expenses that have been written off during the life of the asset on the Balance Sheet in a line item called Accumulated Depreciation or Accumulated Amortisation, whichever is appropriate for the type of asset.

## Acknowledging your debts

The liabilities section of the Balance Sheet comes after the assets section and shows all the money that your business owes to others, including banks, suppliers, contractors, financial institutions and individuals. Like assets, you divide your liabilities into two categories on the Balance Sheet:

✔ **Current liabilities section:** All bills and debts that you plan to pay within the next 12 months. Accounts appearing in this section include Trade Creditors (bills due to suppliers, contractors and others), Credit Cards Payable and the current portion of a long-term debt (for example, if you've a mortgage on your premises, the payments due in the next 12 months appear in the current liabilities section).

✔ **Long-term liabilities section:** All debts you owe to lenders that are to be paid over a period longer than 12 months. Mortgages Payable and Loans Payable are common accounts in the long-term liabilities section of the Balance Sheet.

Most businesses try to minimise their current liabilities because the interest rates on short-term loans, such as credit cards, are usually much higher than those on loans with longer terms. As you manage your business's liabilities, always look for ways to minimise your interest payments by seeking longer-term loans with lower interest rates than you can get on a credit card or short-term loan.

The fictional business used for the example Balance Sheets in this chapter has only one account in each liabilities section:

**Current liabilities:**

Trade Creditors                    £2,200

**Long-term liabilities:**

Loans Payable                    £29,150

## Naming your investments

Every business has investors. Even a small family business requires money upfront to get the business on its feet. Investments are reflected on the Balance Sheet as *capital*. The line items that appear in a Balance Sheet's capital section vary depending upon whether or not the business is incorporated. (Businesses incorporate primarily to minimise their personal legal liabilities; we talk more about incorporation in Chapter 5.)

If you're preparing the books for a business that isn't incorporated, the capital section of your Balance Sheet contains these accounts:

✔ **Capital:** All money invested by the owners to start up the business as well as any additional contributions made after the start-up phase. If the business has more than one owner, the Balance Sheet usually has a Capital account for each owner so that individual stakes in the business can be recorded.

✔ **Drawings:** All money taken out of the business by the business's owners. Balance Sheets usually have a Drawing account for each owner in order to record individual withdrawal amounts.

✔ **Retained Earnings:** All profits left in the business.

## Sorting out share investments

You're probably most familiar with the sale of shares on the open market through the various stock market exchanges, such as the London Stock Exchange (LSE) and the Alternative Investment Market (AIM). However, not all companies sell their shares through public exchanges; in fact, most companies aren't public companies but rather remain private operations.

Whether public or private, people become owners in a business by buying shares. If the business isn't publicly traded, the owners buy and sell shares privately. In most small businesses, family members, close friends and occasionally outside investors buy shares, having been approached individually as a means to raise additional money to build the business.

The value of each share is set at the time the share is sold. Many businesses set the initial share value at £1 to £10.

For an incorporated business, the capital section of the Balance Sheet contains the following accounts:

✔ **Shares:** Portions of ownership in the business, purchased as investments by business owners.

✔ **Retained Earnings:** All profits that have been reinvested in the business.

Because the fictional business isn't incorporated, the accounts appearing in the capital section of its Balance Sheet are:

| | |
|---|---|
| Capital | £5,000 |
| Retained Earnings | £4,500 |

# Pulling Together the Final Balance Sheet

After you group together all your accounts (see the preceding section 'Gathering Balance Sheet Ingredients'), you're ready to produce a Balance Sheet. Businesses in the UK usually choose between two common formats for their Balance Sheets: the Horizontal format or the Vertical format, with the Vertical format preferred. The actual line items appearing in both formats are the same; the only difference is the way in which you lay out the information on the page.

## Horizontal format

The Horizontal format is a two-column layout with assets on one side and liabilities and capital on the other side.

Figure 14-1 shows the elements of a sample Balance Sheet in the Horizontal format.

Balance Sheet
As of 31 May 2012

| **Fixed Assets** | | | **Capital** | | |
|---|---|---|---|---|---|
| Equipment | £ 5,050 | | Opening balance | £ 5,000 | |
| Furniture | £ 5,600 | | Net Profit for year | £ 14,500 | |
| Vehicles | £ 25,000 | | | £ 19,500 | |
| | | £ 35,650 | Less Drawings | £ 10,000 | |
| | | | | | £ 9,500 |
| | | | **Long-term Liabilities** | | |
| | | | Loans Payable | | £ 29,150 |
| **Current Assets** | | | **Current Liabilities** | | |
| Stock | £ 1,200 | | Trade Creditors | | £ 2,200 |
| Trade Debtors | £ 1,000 | | | | |
| Cash | £ 3,000 | | | | |
| | £ 5,200 | | | | |
| | | £ 40,850 | | | £ 40,850 |

**Figure 14-1:** A sample Balance Sheet using the Horizontal format.

## Vertical format

The Vertical format is a one-column layout showing assets first, followed by liabilities and then capital.

Using the Vertical Format, Figure 14-2 shows the Balance Sheet for a fictional business.

Whether you prepare your Balance Sheet as per Figure 14-1 or Figure 14-2, remember that Assets = Liabilities + Capital, so both sides of the Balance Sheet must balance to reflect this.

Balance Sheet
As of 31 May 2012

**Fixed Assets**
| | | |
|---|---|---|
| Equipment | £ 5,050 | |
| Furniture | £ 5,600 | |
| Vehicles | £ 25,000 | |
| | | £ 35,650 |

**Current Assets**
| | | |
|---|---|---|
| Stock | £ 1,200 | |
| Trade Debtors | £ 1,000 | |
| Cash | £ 3,000 | |
| | £ 5,200 | |

**Less: Current Liabilities**
| | | |
|---|---|---|
| Trade Creditors | £ 2,200 | |
| **Net Current Assets** | | £ 3,000 |
| **Total Assets Less Current Liabilities** | | £ 38,650 |
| **Long-term Liabilities** | | |
| Loans Payable | | £ 29,150 |
| | | £ 9,500 |

**Capital**
| | | |
|---|---|---|
| Opening Balance | | £ 5,000 |
| Net Profit for Year | | £ 14,500 |
| | | £ 19,500 |
| Less Drawings | | £ 10,000 |
| | | £ 9,500 |

**Figure 14-2:**
A sample Balance Sheet using the Vertical format.

The Vertical format includes:

- ✔ **Net current assets:** Calculated by subtracting current assets from current liabilities – a quick test to see whether or not a business has the money on hand to pay bills. Net current assets is sometimes referred to as *working capital.*

- ✔ **Total assets less current liabilities:** What's left over for a business's owners after all liabilities have been subtracted from total assets. Total assets less current liabilities is sometimes referred to as *net assets.*

# Putting Your Balance Sheet to Work

With a complete Balance Sheet in your hands, you can analyse the numbers through a series of ratio tests to check your cash status and monitor your debt. These tests are the type of tests that financial institutions and potential investors use to determine whether or not to lend money to or invest in your business. Therefore, a good idea is to run these tests yourself before seeking loans or investors. Ultimately, the ratio tests in this section can help you determine whether or not your business is in a strong cash position.

## Testing your cash

When you approach a bank or other financial institution for a loan, you can expect the lender to use one of two ratios to test your cash flow: the *current ratio* and the *acid test ratio* (also known as the *quick ratio*).

### Current ratio

This ratio compares your current assets to your current liabilities and provides a quick glimpse of your business's ability to pay its bills in the short term.

The formula for calculating the current ratio is:

Current assets ÷ Current liabilities = Current ratio

The following is an example of a current ratio calculation:

£5,200 ÷ £2,200 = 2.36 (current ratio)

Lenders usually look for current ratios of 1.2 to 2, so any financial institution considers a current ratio of 2.36 a good sign. A current ratio under 1 is considered a danger sign because it indicates that the business doesn't have enough cash to pay its current bills. This rule is only a rough guide and some business sectors may require a higher or lower current ratio figure. Get advice to see what the norm is for your business sector.

A current ratio over 2.0 may indicate that your business isn't investing its assets well and may be able to make better use of its current assets. For example, if your business is holding a lot of cash, you may want to invest that money in some long-term assets, such as additional equipment, that you can use to help grow the business.

### Acid test (quick) ratio

The acid test ratio uses only the Cash account and Trade Debtors in its calculation – otherwise known as *liquid assets*. Although similar to the current ratio in that it examines current assets and liabilities, the acid test ratio is a stricter test of a business's ability to pay bills. The assets part of this calculation doesn't take stock into account because it can't always be converted to cash as quickly as other current assets and because, in a slow market, selling your stock may take a while.

Many lenders prefer the acid test ratio when determining whether or not to give a business a loan because of its strictness.

Calculating the acid test ratio is a two-step process:

1. **Determine your quick assets.**

   Cash + Trade Debtors = Quick assets

2. **Calculate your quick ratio.**

   Quick assets ÷ Current liabilities = Quick ratio

The following is an example of an acid test ratio calculation:

£3,000 + £1,000 = £4,000 (quick assets)

£4,000 ÷ £2,200 = 1.8 (acid test ratio)

Lenders consider that a business with an acid test ratio around 1 is in good condition. An acid test ratio of less than 1 indicates that the business cannot currently pay back its current liabilities.

## Assessing your debt

Before you even consider whether or not to take on additional debt, always check out your debt condition. One common ratio that you can use to assess your business's debt position is the *gearing ratio*. This ratio compares what your business owes – *external borrowing* – to what your business's owners have invested in the business – *internal funds*.

Calculating your debt to capital ratio is a two-step process:

1. **Calculate your total debt.**

   Current liabilities + Long-term liabilities = Total debt

2. **Calculate your gearing ratio.**

   Total debt ÷ Capital = Gearing ratio

The following is an example of a debt to capital ratio calculation:

£2,200 + £29,150 = £31,350 (total debt)

£31,350 ÷ £9,500 = 3.3 (gearing ratio)

Lenders like to see a gearing ratio close to 1 because it indicates that the amount of debt is equal to the amount of capital. Most banks probably wouldn't lend any more money to a business with a debt to capital ratio of 3.3 until its debt levels were lowered or the owners put more money into the business. The reason for this lack of confidence may be one of two:

✔ They don't want to have more money invested in the business than the owner.

✔ They're concerned about the business's ability to service the debt.

# Have a Go

The next section invites you to have a go at putting together a few Balance Sheets, so that you become more familiar with the component parts.

1. **In which part of the Balance Sheet do you find the Furniture account?**

2. **In which part of the Balance Sheet do you find the Trade Creditors (Accounts Payable) account?**

3. **Describe the Owner's Capital account.**

4. **Where do you find the Land and Buildings Account?**

5. **Whereabouts in the Balance Sheet do you find the Credit Cards Payable account?**

6. **Where do you find the Retained Earnings account?**

7. **To practise preparing a Balance Sheet in the Horizontal format, use this list of accounts to prepare a Balance Sheet for the Abba Company as of the end of May 2012:**

   | | |
   |---|---|
   | Cash | $5,000 |
   | Debtors | $2,000 |
   | Stock | $10,500 |
   | Equipment | $12,000 |
   | Furniture | $7,800 |
   | Building | $300,000 |
   | Creditors | $5,200 |
   | Loans Payable | $250,000 |
   | Owners Capital | $52,000 |
   | Retained Earnings | $30,100 |

8. **To practise preparing a Balance Sheet in the Vertical format, use this list of accounts to prepare a Balance Sheet for the Abba Company as of the end of May 2012:**

   | | |
   |---|---|
   | Cash | $5,000 |
   | Debtors | $2,000 |
   | Stock | $10,500 |
   | Equipment | $12,000 |
   | Furniture | $7,800 |
   | Building | $300,000 |
   | Creditors | $5,200 |
   | Loans Payable | $250,000 |
   | Owners Capital | $52,000 |
   | Retained Earnings | $30,100 |

9. **Your Balance Sheet shows that your current assets equal $22,000 and your current liabilities equal $52,000. What is your current ratio? Is that a good or bad sign to lenders?**

10. **Suppose that your Balance Sheet shows that your current assets equal $32,000 and your current liabilities equal $34,000. What would your current ratio be? Is that a good or bad sign to lenders?**

11. **Your Balance Sheet shows that your current assets equal $45,000 and your current liabilities are $37,000. What is your current ratio? Is that a good or bad sign to lenders?**

12. Your Balance Sheet shows that your Cash account equals £10,000, your Debtors account equals £25,000 and your current liabilities equals £52,000. What would your acid test ratio be? Is that a good or bad sign to lenders?

13. Suppose that your Balance Sheet shows that your Cash account equals £15,000, your Debtors equals £17,000 and your current liabilities equals £34,000. What would your acid test ratio be? Is that a good or bad sign to lenders?

14. Suppose that your Balance Sheet shows that your Cash account equals £19,000, your Debtors equals £21,000 and your current liabilities equals £37,000. What would your acid test ratio be? Is that a good or bad sign to lenders?

15. A business's current liabilities are £2,200 and its long-term liabilities are £35,000. The owner's equity in the company totals £12,500. What is the debt to equity ratio? Is this a good or bad sign?

16. Suppose that a business's current liabilities are £5,700 and its long-term liabilities are £35,000. The owner's equity in the company totals £42,000. What is the debt to equity ratio? Is this ratio a good or bad sign?

17. Suppose that a business's current liabilities are £6,500 and its long-term liabilities are £150,000. The owner's equity in the company totals £175,000. What is debt to equity ratio? Is this ratio a good or bad sign?

# Answers to Have a Go Questions

1. **The Furniture account is regarded as a fixed asset as furniture is kept in the business for more than 12 months.**

2. **Trade Creditors (Accounts Payable) are suppliers that the business owes money to.** This account is classified as a current liability.

3. **Owners capital can be described as the money invested in the business by the owners.** When owners put money into the business, this act can be described as capital introduced. When money is taken out, it can be taken as drawings (if the business is a sole trader or partnership), or dividends if the business is a limited company.

4. **The Land and Buildings account is part of fixed assets as land and buildings are kept in the business for a long period of time.**

5. **The Credit Cards payable account is money owed by the business to credit cards.** This account is therefore a liability. As the debt is due to be repaid within 12 months, the account is considered a Current Liability account.

6. **The Retained Earnings account tracks the earnings that the owner reinvests in the business each year, and are part of the owner's equity in the company.**

7. **The Horizontal format would look like this:**

*Abba Company Balance Sheet; as of 31 May 2012*

| Fixed Assets | | Capital | |
|---|---|---|---|
| Building | £300,000 | Opening balance | £52,000 |
| Equipment | £12,000 | Net Profit for the year | £30,100 |
| Furniture | £7,800 | | £82,100 |
| | £319,800 | | |

| Current Assets | | Current Liabilities | |
|---|---|---|---|
| Stock | £10,500 | Creditors | £5,200 |
| Debtors | £2,000 | Long Term Liabilities | |
| Cash | £5,000 | Loans Payable | £250,000 |
| Total Current Assets | £17,500 | | |
| Total Assets | £337,300 | Total Liabilities and Equity | £337,300 |

8. **Here's what the Vertical format would look like:**

*Abba Company Balance Sheet; as of 31 May 2012*

| Fixed Assets | | |
|---|---|---|
| Building | £300,000 | |
| Equipment | £12,000 | |
| Furniture | £7,800 | |
| | | £319,800 |
| Current Assets | | |
| Stock | £10,500 | |
| Debtors | £2,000 | |
| Cash | £5,000 | |
| | £17,500 | |
| Less: Current Liabilities | | |
| Creditors | £5,200 | |
| Net Current Assets | | £12,300 |
| Total Assets less Current Liabilities | | £332,100 |
| Long Term Liabilities | | |
| Loans Payable | | £250,000 |
| | | £82,100 |
| Capital | | |
| Opening Balance | | £52,000 |
| Retained Earnings | | £30,100 |
| Total Equity | | £82,100 |

9. **Calculate the current ratio:**

   £22,000 ÷ £52,000 = 0.42

   This ratio is considerably below 1.2, so it would be considered a really bad sign. A ratio this low would indicate that a company may have trouble paying its bills because its current liabilities are considerably higher than the money the company has on hand in current assets.

10. **Calculate the current ratio:**

    £32,000 ÷ £34,000 = 0.94

    The current ratio is slightly below the preferred minimum of 1.2, which would be considered a bad sign. A financial institution may loan money to this company, but consider it a higher risk. A company with this current ratio would pay higher interest rates than one in the 1.2 to 2 current ratio preferred range.

11. **Calculate the current ratio:**

    £45,000 ÷ £37,000 = 1.22

    The current ratio is at 1.22, so it would be considered a good sign and the company probably wouldn't have difficulty borrowing money.

12. **First you calculate your quick assets:**

    £10,000 + £25,000 = £35,000

    Then you calculate your acid test ratio:

    £35,000 ÷ £52,000 = 0.67

    An acid test ratio of less than 1 would be considered a bad sign. A company with this ratio would have a difficult time getting loans from a financial institution.

13. **First you calculate your quick assets:**

    £15,000 + £17,000 = £32,000

    Then you calculate your acid test ratio:

    £32,000 ÷ £34,000 = 0.94

    An acid test ratio of less than 1 would be considered a bad sign. Since this company's acid test ratio is close to one it could probably get a loan, but would have to pay a higher interest rate because it would be considered a higher risk.

14. **First you calculate your quick assets:**

   $19,000 + $21,000 = $40,000

   Then you calculate your acid test ratio:

   $40,000 ÷ $37,000 = 1.08

   An acid test ratio of over 1 would be considered a good sign. A company with this ratio would probably be able to get loans from a financial institution without difficulty.

15. **First, you calculate your total debt:**

   $2,200 + $35,000 = $37,200

   Then you calculate your debt-to-equity ratio:

   $37,200 ÷ $12,500 = 2.98

   A debt-to-equity ratio of over 1 would be considered a bad sign. A company with this ratio probably wouldn't be able to get loans from a financial institution until the owners put more money into the business from other sources, such as family and friends or a private investor.

16. **First, you calculate your total debt:**

   $5,700 + $35,000 = $40,700

   Then you calculate your debt-to-equity ratio:

   $40,700 ÷ $42,000 = 0.97

   A debt-to-equity ratio near 1 is considered a good sign. A company with this ratio is probably able to get loans from a financial institution, but the institution may require additional funds from the owner or investors as well if the company is applying for a large unsecured loan. A loan secured with assets, such as a mortgage, wouldn't be a problem.

17. **First, you calculate your total debt:**

   $6,500 + $150,000 = $156,500

   Then you calculate your debt to equity ratio:

   $156,500 ÷ $175,000 = 0.89

   A debt-to-equity ratio of less than 1 would be considered a good sign. A company with this ratio would probably be able to get loans from a financial institution.

# Chapter 15

# Reporting for Not-For-Profit Organisations

*U*nderstanding what motivates a business owner is easy – profit and business growth. Consequently, these owners need a bookkeeping system that enables them to manage that process. But what if your organisation isn't motivated by profit, but drawn together by a common interest? What if you aren't driven by growing sales and forcing up margins? Up and down the UK thousands of clubs, associations and other not-for-profit organisations exist, for which trading and making a profit isn't the main purpose. The reality is that these organisations don't need to focus on sales, margins and profit. They really need to focus on good stewardship of the organisation's funds and reporting back to the members in a simple format that those members can understand. Therefore, preparing a conventional Profit and Loss account is overkill for their needs.

In this chapter, we cover the key types of financial statements that a not-for-profit organisation may need. The bookkeeping principles are exactly the same as covered in other chapters, but the financial statements are far more basic.

# *Keeping Only Receipts and Payments Accounts*

The simplest not-for-profit organisations require only a simple annual summary of the Cashbook. If a group operates entirely on a cash basis – that is, doesn't take credit for anything it buys and receives cash for any club subscriptions and other fund-raising activities – simple receipts and payment accounts meet their needs. This type of organisation can operate just with the Cashbook, using that for both receipts and payments.

The only asset that this type of organisation has is a cash or bank balance. The books for this type of organisation are kept on a cash-basis, which is covered in Chapter 2.

Figure 15-1 shows what a typical Receipts and Payments account looks like for an imaginary club.

### The Cirencester Running Club
Receipts and Payments account for the year ended 30 June 2012

| Receipts | | Payments | |
|---|---|---|---|
| Bank balance as at 1.7.12 | £ 236 | Printing and stationery | £ 150 |
| Subscriptions received during the year | £ 650 | Coach to London Marathon | £ 300 |
| Annual fundraising event | £ 116 | Village Hall rent | £ 500 |
| Bank interest received | £ 11 | Bank balance as at 30.6.12 | £ 63 |
| | £ 1,013 | | £ 1,013 |

**Figure 15-1:** A simple Receipts and Payments account.

The low volume of transactions doesn't warrant being computerised. No trading activity exists to report on. The only sources of income are the members' subs and an annual fund-raising event. Because these two income sources account for less than £1,000 in the year, no further analysis is really required.

The bookkeeping skills required to run this organisation and prepare this type of financial statement are minimal. The only ongoing monitoring is of the bank balance.

# Tallying Income and Expenditure Accounts

Some types of not-for-profit organisations own assets and have liabilities. A sports club, for example, may own the grounds on which it plays and the clubhouse in which it socialises, or at least is responsible for paying to keep the grounds in good condition. An organisation may boost cash reserves with ongoing or frequent fund-generating activity. For example, it may have a club bar, which involves buying in and selling drink, snacks and maybe food.

## Realising that you need more accounts

Even very simple business activity is likely to have accounting issues such as stock, purchases of supplies on credit and unpaid wages. If your organisation has any assets or liabilities, the Receipts and Payments account isn't a good way of preparing final accounts because it shows only the cash balances and not the other assets and liabilities. Instead, you need the following:

- A Balance Sheet (explained in Chapter 14)
- An Income and Expenditure account that shows changes in the organisation's capital

Instead of a Capital account, which is an element in a Balance Sheet for a sole trader or partnership, the Balance Sheet for a not-for-profit organisation has an Accumulated Fund.

A sole trader or partnership uses the formula:

Capital + Liabilities = Assets

In a not-for-profit organisation, you substitute:

Accumulated Fund + Liabilities = Assets

As far as accounting rules are concerned, an Income and Expenditure account follows the same principles as the Profit and Loss statement (covered in Chapter 13), which means that you keep these books on an accrual accounting basis. The only real difference is in the terminology used, which is highlighted in Table 15-1.

| Table 15-1 | Accounts Terminology Translation |
|---|---|
| **Profit-making business** | **Not-for-profit organisation** |
| Profit and Loss statement | Income and Expenditure account |
| Net profit | Surplus of income over expenditure |
| Net loss | Excess of expenditure over income |
| Capital account | Accumulated Fund |

This type of organisation has many characteristics similar to those of a business enterprise – the use of assets, trading activity and liabilities. The only real difference is the scale of operations and the motive for being in business. Any trading or fund-raising activities are on a much smaller scale and the motivation is to swell the organisation's funds so that it can prosper as a group.

A not-for-profit organisation may have reason to prepare a Profit and Loss statement: for example, where the organisation ran an event, say a disco, with the purpose of making a profit to provide funds for the repair of the clubhouse. For this type of activity, a Profit and Loss statement needs to be prepared and any profit made transferred into the main Income and Expenditure account.

## Preparing Income and Expenditure accounts

Preparing an Income and Expenditure account is similar to preparing a Profit and Loss statement – just with different terminology, depth of information and format. The only new concept is that a not-for-profit organisation doesn't have shareholders or a proprietor. The members own the organisation, and they usually pay annual subscriptions to enjoy the facilities of the club.

It follows therefore that in preparing Income and Expenditure accounts for a not-for-profit organisation, you need to maintain the full range of journals and ledgers that you do for a profit-based business. The information in Chapter 13 can guide you in preparing financial reports.

The treasurer of the Ashcroft Gardens Football Club prepared an Income and Expenditure account and a Balance Sheet for the club, as well as a separate Profit and Loss statement for the bar run to make a profit for the club.

The first step in preparing Income and Expenditure accounts is readying a Receipts and Payments account (see the preceding 'Keeping Only Receipts and Payments Accounts' section). A sample account is shown in Figure 15-2.

### The Ashcroft Gardens Football Club
Receipts and Payments account for the year ended 31 December 2012

| Receipts | | Payments | |
|---|---|---|---|
| Bank balance as at 1.1.12 | £ 500 | Payment for bar supplies | £ 4,000 |
| Subscriptions received | | Wages: | |
| during the year: | | Ground keeper | £ 1,000 |
| 2009 (arrears) | £ 70 | Barman | £ 500 |
| 2010 | £ 1,500 | Bar expenses | £ 300 |
| 2011 (in advance) | £ 50 | Club house repairs | £ 150 |
| Bar sales | £ 6,000 | Pitch maintenance | £ 200 |
| Donations received | £ 150 | Treasurer's expenses | £ 150 |
| | | Club travel | £ 300 |
| | | Bank balance as at 31.12.12 | £ 1,670 |
| | £ 8,270 | | £ 8,270 |

**Figure 15-2:** A sample Income and Expenditure account.

The members who saw this statement agreed that it was inadequate because it didn't give a clear picture of how well the bar had performed. Also, it treated overdue and prepaid subscriptions as part of the current year's receipts, which was clearly wrong. And to add insult to injury, no provision was made for depreciation of the clubhouse (£200 per annum), the club equipment (£110 per annum) and bar stocks of £600 (last year this figure had been £500). Also, unknown to the members, the club had several creditors, a schedule of which is shown in Table 15-2.

| Table 15-2 | Ashcroft Gardens Football Club Creditors | | |
|---|---|---|---|
| **Creditor** | | **31.12.11** | **31.12.12** |
| Bar supply creditor | | £300 | £340 |
| Bar expenses owing | | £30 | £36 |
| Club travel costs owing | | £0 | £65 |

Based on this information, the treasurer, with a little help from the accountant, prepared the following accounts:

- ✔ A Statement of Affairs, which is a type of cash-based Balance Sheet, as at 31 December 2011, shown in Figure 15-3. A *Statement of Affairs* is a simplified Balance Sheet for any organisation that does not have a formal bookkeeping system and few transactions within the accounting year. Quite often, the accountant who prepares these statements does so from inadequate records – often referred to as *incomplete records*.

- ✔ A Profit and Loss statement for the bar for the year ending 31 December 2012, shown in Figure 15-4. This is prepared, as for a profit organisation, when you need to show the results for activity run to make a profit.

- ✔ The final accounts – Income and Expenditure for the year ended 31 December 2012 and Balance Sheet as at 31 December 2012, shown in Figures 15-7 and 15-8.

These accounts clearly show that the bar made a profit of £1,254, which was transferred into the Income and Expenditure account, as well as the healthy state of the club's Balance Sheet with net assets of £16,649.

### The Ashcroft Gardens Football Club
Statement of Affairs as at 31 December 2011

|  | £ | £ | £ |
|---|---|---|---|
| *Fixed Assets* |  |  |  |
| Land |  |  | 10,000 |
| Clubhouse |  |  | 4,000 |
| Club equipment |  |  | 1,100 |
|  |  |  | 15,100 |
|  |  |  |  |
| *Current Assets* |  |  |  |
| Bar stock |  | 500 |  |
| Subscription debtors |  | 70 |  |
| Cash at bank |  | 500 |  |
|  |  | 1,070 |  |
|  |  |  |  |
| *Less Current Liabilities* |  |  |  |
| Creditors | 300 |  |  |
| Bar expenses owing | 30 | 330 |  |
| Net current assets |  |  | 740 |
|  |  |  | 15,840 |
|  |  |  |  |
| *Financed by:* |  |  |  |
| Accumulated fund (difference) |  |  | 15,840 |

**Figure 15-3:** Statement of Affairs as at 31 December 2011.

**The Ashcroft Gardens Football Club**

Bar profit and loss statement for the year ended 31 December 2012

|  | £ | £ |
|---|---|---|
| Sales |  | 6,000 |
| Less Cost of Goods sold: |  |  |
| Opening stock | 500 |  |
| Add Purchases | 4,040 |  |
|  | 4,540 |  |
| Less closing stock | 600 | 3,940 |
| Gross Profit |  | 2,060 |
| Less bar expenses | 306 |  |
| Bar wages | 500 | 806 |
| Net profit (transferred to Income and Expenditure account) |  | 1,254 |

**Figure 15-4:** Bar Profit and Loss statement for the year ended 31 December 2012.

Figure 15-5 shows how the purchases and bar expenses figures are calculated for the Profit and Loss statement in Figure 15-4.

**Purchases Account**

| | | | £ |
|---|---|---|---|
| Cash | £ 4,000 | Balance brought forward | £ 300 |
| Balance carried down | £ 340 | Profit & Loss | £ 4,040 |
|  | £ 4,340 |  | £ 4,340 |

**Bar Expenses**

| | | | |
|---|---|---|---|
| Cash | £ 300 | Balance brought forward | £ 30 |
| Balance carried down | £ 36 | Profit & Loss | £ 306 |
|  | £ 336 |  | £ 336 |

**Figure 15-5:** Purchase and Expense accounts for the bar.

The workings in Figure 15-6 show how the numbers for the transport costs and subscriptions received were calculated for the Income and Expenditure account shown in Figure 15-7.

Transport Costs account

| | | | |
|---|---|---|---|
| Cash | £300 | Balance b/fwd | £0 |
| Balance c/down | £65 | Profit & Loss | £365 |
| | £365 | | £365 |

**Figure 15-6:**
Working for
Transport
Costs and
Subscription
Income.

Subscription Income

| | | | |
|---|---|---|---|
| Balance b/fwd | £0 | Cash | £1500 |
| Profit & Loss | £1580 | Balance c/dwn | £80 |
| | £1580 | | £1580 |

## The Ashcroft Gardens Football Club
Income and Expenditure account for the year ended 31 December 2012

| | £ | £ | £ |
|---|---|---|---|
| Income | | | |
| Subscriptions for 2012 | | | £ 1,580 |
| Profit from the bar | | | £ 1,254 |
| Donations received | | | £ 150 |
| | | | £ 2,984 |
| Less expenditure | | | |
| Wages — ground keeper | | £ 1,000 | |
| Repairs | | £ 150 | |
| Pitch maintenance | | £ 200 | |
| Treasurer's expenses | | £ 150 | |
| Club travel | | £ 365 | |
| Depreciation | | | |
| Clubhouse | £ 200 | | |
| Club equipment | £ 110 | £ 310 | £ 2,175 |
| Surplus of income over expenditure | | | £ 809 |

**Figure 15-7:**
Income and
Expenditure
Account
for year
ended 31
December
2012.

## The Ashcroft Gardens Football Club
### Balance sheet as at 31 December 2012

|  | £ | £ | £ |
|---|---|---|---|
| *Fixed Assets* | | | |
| Land | | | £ 10,000 |
| Clubhouse | | £ 4,000 | |
| Less depreciation | | £ 200 | £ 3,800 |
| | | | |
| Club equipment | | £ 1,100 | |
| Less depreciation | | £ 110 | £ 990 |
| | | | £ 14,790 |
| | | | |
| *Current Assets* | | | |
| | | | |
| Bar stocks | | £ 600 | |
| Debtors (subscriptions) | | £ 80 | |
| Cash at bank | | £ 1,670 | |
| | | £ 2,350 | |
| | | | |
| *Current Liabilities* | | | |
| | | | |
| Creditors — bar supplies | £ 340 | | |
| Bar expenses owing | £ 36 | | |
| Travel costs owing | £ 65 | | |
| Prepaid subscriptions | £ 50 | £ 491 | |
| | | | |
| Net current assets | | | £ 1,859 |
| | | | £ 16,649 |
| | | | |
| *Financed by:* | | | |
| | | | |
| Accumulated fund | | | |
| Balance as at 1.1.12 | | | £ 15,840 |
| Add surplus of income over expenditure | | | £ 809 |
| | | | £ 16,649 |

**Figure 15-8:**
Balance Sheet for the football club as at 31 December 2012.

In the example in Figure 15-7, the treasurer treats subscriptions owing as an asset. However, most subscriptions that have been overdue for a long time are never paid. Many clubs don't bring in unpaid subscriptions as an asset in the Balance Sheet. This obviously prudent approach ensures that the Balance Sheet assets aren't overstated. Good practice when preparing club accounts, or any other organisation that relies on subscription income, needs to exclude all outstanding subscriptions from the final accounts.

You must treat donations as income during the year in which they're received. Also, new members at some clubs (such as golf clubs) have to pay an entrance fee when they join in addition to their annual membership fee. Entrance fees are usually included as income in the year of receipt.

# *Have a Go*

This next section allows you to have a practice with some of the principles you've discovered in this chapter.

1. **Using the figures shown in the following list, prepare a Receipts and Payments account for the Ashwood Stamp Collectors Club.**

   The opening bank balance at 1 January is £500.

   Closing bank balance at 31 December is £752.

   Subscriptions received in the year are £1,570.

   Annual fund raising raises £370.

   Bank interest received is £23.

   Meeting room costs are £850.

   Coach trips to stamp collecting fairs cost £750.

   Printing and stationery costs total £111.

2. **You've received the Receipts and Payments account for the year ended 31 December 2012 and the Statement of Affairs for the Year ended 31 December 2011 for Tall Trees Tennis Club. With this information, please supply to the members of the club a Profit and Loss statement for the bar for the period to 31 December 2012, an Income and Expenditure Statement and a Balance Sheet as at 31 December 2012. Use the blank statements below and include all workings where necessary.**

The information you have is as follows:

## Tall Trees Tennis Club Receipts and Payments Account for the Year ended 31 December 2012

| Receipts | | Payments | |
|---|---|---|---|
| Bank balance as at 1 January 2011 | £732 | Payment for bar supplies | £3,000 |
| **Subscriptions received during year:** | | **Wages:** | |
| 2012 | £3,200 | Groundkeeper | £1,000 |
| 2013 (In advance) | £100 | Barman | £700 |
| **Other income** | | **Other expenditure** | |
| Bar Sales | £4,000 | Bar expenses | £200 |
| | | Club house repairs | £150 |
| | | Pitch maintenance | £200 |
| | | Treasurers expenses | £100 |
| | | Club travel | £300 |
| | | Bank balance as at 31.12.12 | £2,382 |
| | £8,032 | | £8,032 |

No provision has been made for depreciation of the clubhouse at £200 per annum, or the club equipment at £150 per annum.

Bar stocks were £400 at 31 December (previous year £300)

There were also several creditors:

| | 2011 | 2012 |
|---|---|---|
| Bar supply creditor | £200 | £300 |
| Bar expenses owing | £42 | £49 |
| Club travel expenses | £12 | £36 |

A Statement of Affairs has been produced, which shows the opening position at 1st January 2012 as follows:

## Tall Trees Tennis Club: Statement of Affairs as at 31 December 2011

| **Fixed Assets** | | | |
|---|---|---|---|
| Land | | £12,000 | |
| Clubhouse | | £3,000 | |
| Club Equipment | | £1,500 | |
| | | | £16,500 |
| **Current Assets** | | | |
| Bar Stock | £300 | | |
| Cash at Bank | £732 | | |
| | | £1,032 | |
| **Less Current Liabilities** | | | |
| Creditors – Bar Supply | £200 | | |
| Bar Expenses Owing | £42 | | |
| Travel Expenses Owing | £12 | | |
| | | £254 | |
| **Net Current Assets** | | | **£778** |
| | | | £17,278 |
| Financed by | | | |
| Accumulated Fund (difference) | | | £17,278 |

## Tall Trees Tennis Club: Bar Profit and Loss Statement
## for the year ended 31 December 2012

| *Sales* | | **£** |
|---|---|---|
| Less Cost of Goods Sold: | | |
| | | |
| Opening Stock | | £ |
| Add Purchases | | £ |
| | | £ |
| Less Closing Stock | | £ |
| Gross Profit | | £ |
| Less Bar Expenses | £ | £ |
| Bar Wages | £ | £ |
| Net Profit (transferred to Income and Expenditure A/C) | | £ |

Include your workings here for the Purchase and expense accounts for the bar

*Purchases Account*

*Bar Expenses Account*

| Tall Trees Tennis Club: Income and Expenditure Account for the year ended 31 December 2012 | | |
|---|---|---|
| **Income** | | |
| Subscriptions for 2012 | | £ |
| Profit from the Bar | | £ |
| | | £ |
| | | |
| **Less Expenditure** | | |
| Wages – Groundkeeper | | £ |
| Repairs | | £ |
| Pitch Maintenance | | £ |
| Treasurer's Expenses | | £ |
| Club Travel | | £ |
| | | £ |
| | | |
| **Depreciation:** | | |
| Clubhouse | £ | £ |
| Club Equipment | £ | £ |
| Surplus of Income over Expenditure | | £ |

Add your workings for travel expenses:

*Travel Expenses Account*

---

### Tall Trees Tennis Club: Balance Sheet as at 31 December 2012

*Fixed Assets*

| | | |
|---|---|---|
| Land | | £ |
| Clubhouse | | £ |
| Less Depreciation | £ | £ |
| Club Equipment | | |
| Less Depreciation | £ | £ |
| | | £ |
| **Current Assets** | | |
| Bar Stocks | | £ |
| Cash at Bank | | £ |
| | | £ |
| **Current Liabilities** | | |
| Creditors – Bar Supplies | | £ |
| Bar Expenses Owing | | £ |
| Travel Costs Owing | | £ |
| Prepaid Subscriptions | £ | £ |
| Net Current Assets | | £ |
| | | £ |
| Financed by | | |
| Accumulated Fund | | |
| Balance as at 1.1.12 | | |
| Add Surplus of Income over Expenditure | | £ |
| | | £ |

# *Answering the Have a Go Questions*

1. Here's the Receipts and Payments account for the Ashwood Stamp Collectors Club:

### Ashwood Stamp Collectors Club: Receipts and Payments for the year ended 31 December 2012

| Receipts | | Payments | |
|---|---|---|---|
| Bank Balance, 1 January 2011 | £500 | Printing and Stationery | £111 |
| Subscriptions Received in Year | £1570 | Coach to Stamp Collector Fairs | £750 |
| Annual Fundraising | £370 | Village Hall Rent | £850 |
| Bank Interest Received | £23 | Bank Balance, 31 December 2011 | £752 |
| | £2,463 | | £2,463 |

2. Here are the figures we hope you ended up with:

### Tall Trees Tennis Club: Bar Profit and Loss Statement for the year ended 31 December 2012

| *Sales* | | *£4,000* |
|---|---|---|
| Less Cost of Goods Sold: | | |
| Opening Stock | £300 | |
| Add Purchases | £3,100 | |
| | £3,400 | |
| Less Closing Stock | £400 | £3,000 |
| Gross Profit | | £1,000 |
| Less Bar Expenses | £207 | |
| Bar wages | £700 | £907 |
| Net Profit (transferred to Income and Expenditure A/C) | | £93 |

### Workings for Purchase Account

| Cash | £3000 | Balance b/fwd | £200 |
|------|-------|---------------|------|
| Balance c/fwd | £300 | Profit & Loss | £3100 |
| | £3,300 | | £3,300 |

### Workings for Bar Expenses Account

| Cash | £200 | Balance b/fwd | £42 |
|------|------|---------------|-----|
| Balance c/fwd | £49 | Profit & Loss | £207 |
| | £249 | | £249 |

Note: The above calculations use the opening and closing creditors figures shown earlier in the example.

## Tall Trees Tennis Club: Income and Expenditure Account for the year ended 31 December 2012

| Income | | |
|--------|--|--|
| Subscriptions for 2012 | | £3,200 |
| Profit from the Bar | | £93 |
| | | £3,293 |
| **Less Expenditure** | | |
| Wages – Groundkeeper | £1,000 | |
| Repairs | £150 | |
| Pitch Maintenance | £200 | |
| Treasurers Expenses | £100 | |
| Club Travel | £324 | |
| | | **£1774** |
| **Depreciation:** | | |
| Clubhouse | £200 | |
| Club Equipment | £150 | £350 |
| Surplus of Income over Expenditure | | £1,169 |

The workings for travel expenses are:

*Travel Expenses*
*Account*

| | | | |
|---|---|---|---|
| Cash | £300 | Balance brought forward | £12 |
| Balance carried forward | £36 | Profit and Loss Account | £324 |
| | £336 | | £336 |

## Tall Trees Tennis Club Balance Sheet as at 31 December 2012

### Fixed Assets

| | | | |
|---|---|---|---|
| Land | | | £12,000 |
| Clubhouse | | £3,000 | |
| Less Depreciation | | £200 | £2,800 |
| Club Equipment | | £1,500 | |
| Less Depreciation | | £150 | £1,350 |
| | | | £16,150 |

### Current Assets

| | | | |
|---|---|---|---|
| Bar Stocks | £400 | | |
| Cash at Bank | £2,382 | | |
| | | £2,782 | |

### Current Liabilities

| | | | |
|---|---|---|---|
| Creditors – Bar Supplies | £300 | | |
| Bar Expenses Owing | £49 | | |
| Travel Costs Owing | £36 | | |
| Prepaid Subscriptions | £100 | £485 | |
| Net Current Assets | | | £2,297 |
| | | | £18,447 |

| | | | |
|---|---|---|---|
| Financed by | | | |
| Accumulated Fund | | | |
| Balance as at 1.1.12 | | | £17,278 |
| Add Surplus of Income over Expenditure | | | £1,169 |
| | | | £18,447 |

# Chapter 16

# Preparing Your Year End Accounts

● ● ● ● ● ● ● ● ● ● ● ● ● ● ● ● ● ● ● ● ● ● ● ● ● ● ● ● ● ● ● ● ● ● ● ● ● ● ● ● ● ● ● ● ● ● ● ●

## *In This Chapter*

▶ Wrapping up Nominal Ledger accounts

▶ Looking back through customer accounts

▶ Checking for unpaid supplier bills

▶ Clearing out unnecessary accounts

▶ Moving into a new accounting cycle

● ● ● ● ● ● ● ● ● ● ● ● ● ● ● ● ● ● ● ● ● ● ● ● ● ● ● ● ● ● ● ● ● ● ● ● ● ● ● ● ● ● ● ● ● ● ● ●

*I*n bookkeeping, an accounting period, or cycle, can be a month, a quarter or a year (or any other division of time that makes business sense). All these periods occur within the accounting year. At the end of every accounting year, known as the *year end*, certain accounts need to be closed while others remain open.

Just as the best method is to add accounts to your bookkeeping system at the beginning of an accounting year (so you don't have to move information from one account to another), you also need to wait until the end of the accounting year to delete any accounts that you no longer require. With this approach, you start each year fresh with only the accounts you need to best manage your business's financial activities.

In this chapter, we explain the accounts that must be closed and start with a zero balance in the next accounting cycle (see Chapter 2 for more detail about the accounting cycle).

We also review the accounts that continue from one accounting cycle to the next, such as Assets and Liabilities accounts. In addition, we discuss the process of closing the books at year-end and how to begin a new accounting cycle for the next year.

# Finalising the Nominal Ledger

After you complete your accounting work for the accounting cycle in which your business operates, you need to re-examine your Nominal Ledger. Some accounts in the Nominal Ledger need to be zeroed out so that they start the new accounting cycle with no detail from the previous cycle, whereas other accounts continue to accumulate detail from one cycle to the next.

When you break down the Nominal Ledger, the Balance Sheet accounts carry forward into the next accounting cycle, and the Profit and Loss statement accounts start with a zero balance.

## Zeroing out Profit and Loss statement accounts

When you're sure that you've made all necessary corrections and adjustments to your accounts and you have your year-end numbers, you can zero out all Nominal Ledger accounts listed on the Profit and Loss statement – that's Revenues, Cost of Goods Sold and Expense accounts. Because the Profit and Loss statement reflects the activities of an accounting period, these accounts always start with a zero balance at the beginning of an accounting cycle.

If you use a computerised accounting system, you may not actually have to zero out the Profit and Loss statement accounts. For example, Sage 50 Accounts zeroes out your Income and Expenses accounts at year-end (by transferring them to retained earnings), so you start with a zero net profit, but the program also maintains the data in an archive so you're always able to access it.

Sage 50 Accounts makes the year-end process reasonably straightforward. Click the 'Company' tab, select 'Manage Year End' from the Tasks list, and you're presented with the Sage Year End Procedure screen shown in Figure 16-1.

The main purpose of this screen is to remind you of all the tasks you need to do prior to the year-end. Click through buttons 1 to 5 in sequence and Sage guides you through the year-end process. When you click to run your year-end process, the screen shown in Figure 16-2 appears. This screen confirms that the program now transfers all the Profit and Loss figures to Retained Earnings and carries forward the remaining Balance Sheet figures.

Click OK and complete the year-end process.

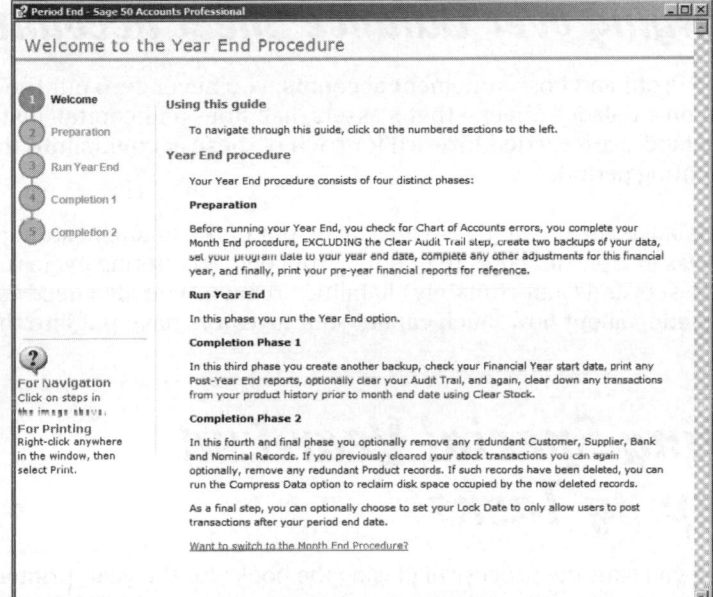

**Figure 16-1:**
Starting the year-end process in Sage 50 Accounts.

**Figure 16-2:**
Zeroing out the Profit and Loss figures at year-end in Sage 50 Accounts.

## *Carrying over Balance Sheet accounts*

Unlike Profit and Loss statement accounts, you never zero out the accounts listed on a Balance Sheet – that's assets, liabilities and capital. Instead, the balances are carried forward for each of these accounts into the next accounting period.

The Balance Sheet just gives you a snapshot of the financial state of your business at a particular date in time. From one accounting cycle to the next, your assets and (unfortunately) liabilities remain. You also need to maintain information about how much capital your investors have put into the business.

# *Conducting Special Year-End Bookkeeping Tasks*

Before you start the process of closing the books for the year, print a summary of your account information from your computerised accounting system. If you make an error while closing the books, you can always use this printout to backtrack and fix any problems. (There's no manual equivalent of this process.)

Sage 50 Accounts provides a Year End Guide Checklist as you go through the Year End Procedure screens to help you keep track of all the necessary year-end activities. In Sage 50 Accounts, follow these steps to complete the year-end processing:

1. **Before running the year-end, make sure that you take two back-ups of your data, in case things go wrong or you discover that you weren't quite ready for the year-end.**

2. **Set your program date to your year-end date.**

3. **Print any pre-year-end reports, such as audit trails and nominal activity reports.**

4. **After running the Year-End option, check that your starting date for the new financial year is correct.**

5. **Clear your audit trail and clear down any product history using 'Clear Stock', if required.**

6. **Finally, you can clear any redundant bank accounts, supplier accounts, customer accounts or product records.**

## *Checking customer accounts*

As you prepare your books for the end of an accounting year, review your customer accounts (Trade Debtors). Unless you're at the end of the year, don't close the Trade Debtors accounts you don't need any more. When you start a new accounting year, you certainly want to carry over any balance still due from customers.

Before closing your books at the end of the accounting cycle, review the customer accounts for possible bad-debt expenses. (We talk about bad debt in greater detail in Chapter 7.) Now is the time to be more critical of past-due accounts. You can use any bad debt to reduce your tax bill, so if you believe that a customer isn't likely to make good on a past-due account, write off the loss.

## *Assessing supplier accounts*

The end of an accounting period is the perfect time to review your supplier accounts to make sure that they're all paid in full and ready for the new cycle.

Also, ensure that you enter any bills into your supplier accounts that reflect business activity for the period being closed; otherwise, expenses from the period may not show up in the appropriate year-end financial statements.

Review any outstanding purchase orders to make sure that your supplier accounts aren't missing orders that have been completed but not yet billed by the supplier. For example, if you receive stock on 23 December but the supplier isn't going to bill for that stock until January, accrue for the bill in December to reflect the receipt of that stock during that accounting year (accruals are covered in Chapter 10).

## *Deleting accounts*

The closing process at the end of an accounting year is a good time to assess all your open accounts and verify that you still need them. If an account contains no transactions, you're free to delete it at any time. However, wait until the end of the year to delete any accounts you don't think you're going to need in the next year.

If you're assessing accounts at the end of an accounting period that isn't also the end of the year, just make a list of the accounts to be deleted and wait for the year-end.

Sage doesn't allow you to delete an account with transactions on that account. An account can only be deleted if it has no transactions and the balance is zero.

# Starting the Cycle Anew

You certainly don't want to close the doors of your business while preparing all your year-end reports, such as the financial statements and HM Revenue & Customs reports – after all, that process can take two to three months. So you need to continue making entries for the new year as you close the books for the previous year.

If you do the books manually, you probably need easy access to two sets of books: the current year and the previous year. In a manual bookkeeping system, you just start new journal pages for each of the active accounts. If you have some accounts that aren't very active, rather than start a new page, you can leave space for adjustments or corrections, draw a line and start the transactions for the new year on the same page.

If you keep your books using a computerised accounting system such as Sage 50 Accounts, you can continue posting transactions past the year-end date, while you wait for all the final invoices and bank statements to come through. The year-end can be run at a later date.

Part of closing your books is starting new files for each of your accounts. Most businesses keep two years of data – the current year and the previous year – in the on-site office files and put older files into storage. As you start a new year, box up your two-year-old files for storage and use the newly empty drawers for the new year's new files. For example, suppose that you're creating files for 2012. Keep the 2011 files easily accessible in filing cabinet drawers in your office, but box up the 2010 files for storage. Then keep your 2012 files in the drawers where the 2010 files were.

No hard and fast rule exists about file storage. You may find that you need to access certain files regularly and therefore don't want to put them in storage. No problem. Pull out any files related to ongoing activity and keep them in the office so you don't have to run to the storage area every time you need the files.

For example, if you have an ongoing legal case, keep any files related to that matter out of storage and easily accessible. Also remember that you have a legal obligation to keep your account records for six tax years.

# Part V
# Payroll Preparation

'Good heavens – this tax investigation must be _really_ serious – You're the _third_ tax inspector to visit my little taxidermist business this month.'

## In this part . . .

You discover how you can easily process the monthly payroll for your staff. We guide you through the basics of setting up and managing your employee payroll, and discuss what paperwork you need to complete on a monthly basis in order to comply with Her Majesty's Revenue and Customs (HMRC) regarding the PAYE scheme. We also look at the year-end payroll procedure, and show you which reports need to be submitted to HMRC.

# Chapter 17

# Employee Payroll and Benefits

. . . . . . . . . . . . . . . . . . . . . . . . . . . . . . . . . . . . . . . . . . . . . . . . . . . . . . . . .

## In This Chapter

▶ Preparing to pay your employees

▶ Calculating taxes

▶ Dealing with benefits

▶ Posting payroll

▶ Paying HM Revenue & Customs

. . . . . . . . . . . . . . . . . . . . . . . . . . . . . . . . . . . . . . . . . . . . . . . . . . . . . . . . .

*U*nless your business employs just one person (you, the owner), you probably need to hire employees, and that means that you have to pay them, offer benefits and manage a payroll.

Human resources staff and bookkeeping staff usually share responsibilities for hiring and paying employees. As the bookkeeper, you must make sure that all HM Revenue & Customs tax-related forms are completed, and you need to manage all payroll responsibilities including paying employees, collecting and paying employee taxes, collecting and managing employee benefit contributions and paying benefit providers.

 Before you proceed any further, visit the HM Revenue & Customs website at www.hmrc.gov.uk and click on the Employers link to go to the help area for new employers. Alternatively, phone the New Employer Helpline on 0845-6070143 and let them talk you through the process. You may be surprised at how helpful the people working there are.

This chapter examines the various employee staffing issues that bookkeepers need to be able to manage.

# Staffing Your Business

After you decide that you want to hire employees for your business, you must be ready to deal with a lot of official paperwork. In addition to paperwork, you're faced with many decisions about how employees are to be paid and who's going to be responsible for maintaining the paperwork that HM Revenue & Customs requires.

Knowing what needs to be done to satisfy these officials isn't the only issue you must consider before you hire the first person; you also need to decide how frequently you're going to pay employees and what type of wage and salary scales you want to set up.

## Completing new starter forms

Even before you pay your first employee, you need to start completing the HM Revenue & Customs forms related to hiring. If you plan to hire staff, you must first make sure that they have a National Insurance number. HM Revenue & Customs uses this number to track your employees, the money you pay them, as well as any PAYE (Pay As You Earn) tax and NICs (National Insurance Contributions) collected and paid on their behalf.

Design your own new starter form, which can act as a checklist to ensure that you've all the details necessary before you input the new starter details into your payroll system. Typical information required is name, address, date of birth, start date, National Insurance number, and a check box to identify whether you have a P45 or not.

The following sections explain how to deal with each of these situations.

### Obtaining an Employer's PAYE Reference

Every business must have an Employer's PAYE Reference in order to hire employees. Without this reference, you can't legally pay staff and deduct PAYE tax and NICs.

Luckily, HM Revenue & Customs makes it straightforward to obtain an Employer's PAYE Reference, which is typically a three-digit number (to identify the tax office) followed by four alpha characters (to identify the employer). The fastest way is to call HM Revenue & Customs' New Employer Helpline on 0845-6070143 and complete the form by telephone. Be prepared to provide the following information:

✔ **General business information:** Business name, trading address, name and address of employer, National Insurance number and Unique Taxpayer Reference of employer, contact telephone number, contact email address if registering using email, nature of business.

✔ **Employee information:** The date you took on (or intend to take on) your first employee(s), how many employees you intend to have, the date you intend to pay them for the first time, how often you intend to pay them.

If your business is a partnership or a limited company, you need to give additional information:

✔ **Partnership:** Names and addresses of any business partners, National Insurance numbers and Unique Taxpayer References of any business partners and your LLP number if you're a Limited Liability Partnership (LLP).

✔ **Limited company:** The company's registered address, company registration number and date of incorporation, the names, addresses, private telephone numbers, National Insurance numbers and Unique Taxpayer References of the company directors.

*Note:* You can now register as a new employer online. There are a few exceptions, so check the website and follow the online instructions. Click on the Employers tab on the HMRC website, followed by the 'I want to register as an Employer' link at www.hmrc.gov.uk.

Once you register, you receive an Employers Registration letter, which includes your Accounts Office reference and your PAYE reference. This is a particularly important document so keep it safe! You use your Accounts Office reference when you make payments to the HMRC and your PAYE reference in all other contacts with the HMRC. The letter includes a web address giving you access to the Getting Started guide, which can help you begin your payroll.

## Collecting P45s

Every person you hire should bring a P45 from his previous employer. The *P45* is a record of the employee's taxable earnings, PAYE deducted and tax code for the current tax year.

This form gives you the information you need as the new employer to make sure that you can deduct the correct amount of PAYE and National Insurance from the new employee.

Ask a new employee right from the start if he or she has a P45 from a previous employer. If an employee doesn't have a P45, you must deduct income tax out of his or her wage as if it is all taxable. We talk more about deducting taxes in the section 'Collecting Employee Taxes', later in this chapter.

The recently updated P45 is now an A4-sized four-part carbon form:

✔ **Part 1** shows details of the employee leaving work. The previous employer sends Part 1 to its tax office. This process keeps HM Revenue & Customs informed that the employee has left his old job.

✔ **Part 1A** is an exact copy of Part 1 that the employee keeps for his records.

✔ **Part 2** contains the information that you (as the new employer) need to have to ensure that you deduct the correct amount for PAYE tax and National Insurance. Keep this part in your records system. The information you need to answer the seven questions here is already filled in as a result of Part 1 being completed, so you've nothing to complete, just keep it.

✔ **Part 3** is filled in by you as the new employer. Again, questions 1 to 7 are already completed for you as a result of Part 1 being completed. You complete the bottom half of the P45 – boxes 8 to 17 – sign the declaration in box 18 and send it on to your local HM Revenue & Customs office. Fortunately, this process is straightforward. The questions you need to answer are:

• Q8: Enter your PAYE Reference.

• Q9: Enter the date the new employee started working for you.

• Q10: Enter details of the new employee's works/payroll number, branch or depot, and tick if you want these details shown on any tax code notifications.

• Q11: Enter P if the employee will not be paid by you between the employment start date and the next 5 April.

• Q12: Enter the tax code in use if different to code at Q6.

• Q13: If the tax figure you're entering on form P11 differs from item shown in Q7, enter your figure.

• Q14: Enter the employee's job title or description.

• Q15: Enter the employee's private address.

• Q16: Enter the employee's gender.

• Q17: Enter the employee's date of birth.

• Q18: Declaration and current employer's name and address.

### *Starting fresh with employees without a P45*

If a worker is new to the job market, he or she must have a National Insurance number. In some cases, however, a new employee may not have a National Insurance number or a P45.

Many new employees don't have P45s, perhaps because they've lost the form, or this is their first job, or maybe they're keeping another job as well as working for you. In these cases, your new employee must complete a P46. Essentially, the P46 is a substitute for the P45. The new employee must complete Section 1, and the new employer (that's you) completes Section 2. You then send the completed form to your local tax office on the employee's first pay day.

The end result of using a P46 is that the new employee initially pays too much tax and National Insurance until the local HM Revenue & Customs office sends you the correct tax code and cumulative taxable pay and tax paid information. In effect, the HM Revenue & Customs office provides you with what would have been on the P45.

### *Completing forms for foreign workers*

As an employer in the UK, you've a responsibility to verify that any person you hire is a UK citizen or has the right to work in the UK – you can't just accept his word. Ask to see his passport and Home Office Work Permit. If you have any doubts, contact your local HM Revenue & Customs office: EEA members are subject to change and special rules apply to some of the newer signatories.

Check the business link website (www.businesslink.gov.uk) and click the link 'Ensuring Candidates are eligible to work in the UK'. This contains detailed information about employing foreign workers.

## Picking pay periods

Deciding how frequently to pay your employees is an important point to work out before hiring staff. Most businesses choose one of these two pay periods:

- ✔ **Weekly:** You pay employees every week, which means you must do payroll 52 times a year.

- ✔ **Monthly:** You pay employees once a month, which means you must do payroll 12 times a year.

You can choose to use either pay period, and you may even decide to use more than one type. For example, some businesses pay hourly employees (employees paid by the hour) weekly and pay salaried employees (employees paid by a set salary regardless of how many hours they work) monthly.

## Determining wage and salary scales

You have a lot of leeway regarding the level of wages and salary that you pay your employees, but you still have to follow some rules laid out by the government. Under the National Minimum Wage Regulations, employers must pay workers a minimum amount as defined by law. These rules apply to businesses of all sizes and in all industries.

The three levels of minimum wage rates from 1 October 2011 are:

- ✔ £6.08 per hour for workers aged 21 years and older.
- ✔ £4.98 per hour for workers aged 18 to 20 years old.
- ✔ £3.68 per hour for workers aged between 16 and 17 years old.

The government has accepted a recommendation from the Low Pay Commission (LPC) to introduce a new apprentice rate of £2.60 per hour. This rate applies to apprentices under the age of 19 and also apprentices aged 19 and over in their first year.

Don't assume that the minimum wage isn't going to change though, and check the HM Revenue & Customs website periodically to get the current wage rates. You can get advice on the minimum wage by contacting the Pay and Work Rights Helpline on 0800-9172368.

## Making statutory payments

As well as guaranteeing minimum wage payments for workers, government statutes provide other benefits:

- ✔ **Sick pay:** Employees who are off sick for more than four consecutive work days, known as a period of incapacity for work (PIW) are entitled to receive Statutory Sick Pay (SSP). Of course, a sick employee must inform you as soon as possible and supply you with evidence of his or her sickness.

In many cases, the business continues to pay employees for short periods of sickness as part of good employment practice. However, if you don't pay employees when they're off sick for more than four days, they can claim SSP, which is based on their average earnings. As an employer, you may be able to recover some of the SSP you've paid against your NIC amounts.

The first three days that the employee is away from work are called *waiting days* and don't qualify for SSP.

✔ **Parental pay:** If employees qualify for Statutory Maternity Pay (SMP), they're paid for a maximum of 39 weeks. For the first six weeks, an employee is entitled to 90 per cent of her average wage. For the other weeks, she is entitled to £135.45 per week or 90 per cent of average earnings if this amount is less than £135.45.

New dads are entitled to Statutory Paternity Pay (SPP) for two weeks, calculated in much the same way as SMP.

Most employees who adopt children are entitled to Statutory Adoption Pay (SAP), which is payable for up to 39 weeks at the lower rate of £135.45 per week or 90 per cent of average weekly wages if this amount is less.

If your class 1 NICs are no more than £45,000 in a tax year, then you can recover 100% of your SMP payments plus an additional amount as compensation for the employers class 1 NICs that you'll have paid on SMP. Similar rules apply to SAP. See the HMRC website for details.

## Dealing with the payroll administration

Before you start to take on and pay any employees, you need to be up to speed on all the forms you need. Day-to-day payroll involves forms and more forms. The following list gives you an idea of the typical range of HM Revenue & Customs forms you have to deal with during the tax year:

✔ **P45:** You complete this form for each employee who leaves at any time during the tax year and for all new employees starting work for your business. The P45 gives details of earnings, Pay As You Earn (PAYE), National Insurance Contributions (NICs) and the tax code for the tax year.

✔ **P46:** You complete this form for any new-start employees who don't have a P45.

✔ **P46 (Car):** You use this form to notify HM Revenue & Customs when you first provide an employee with a company car or any change occurs to this benefit.

✔ **P6:** Notification from HM Revenue & Customs of a new tax code for an employee. This form is your authority to change an employee's tax code.

✔ **P11 (Deductions Working Sheet):** This form is the record of each individual employee's NICs, earnings, statutory payments, PAYE deductions and student loans.

✔ **P32 (Employer's Payment Record):** Use this form to record details of the total deductions for all employees including PAYE, student loans, NICs, Statutory Sick Pay (SSP), Statutory Maternity Pay (SMP), Statutory Paternity Pay (SPP), Statutory Adoption Pay (SAP) and the reclaims you've received for SSP, SMP, SPP and SAP.

✔ **CA6855:** Use this form to trace a National Insurance number (NINO) if a new employee can't provide one.

You can get a whole range of guides from HM Revenue & Customs (www.hmrc.gov.uk) to help you. Here are just a few:

✔ **New Employer Getting Started:** This is an online guide that is a must for any new employer. It guides you through the basics of finding payroll software including the free HMRC PAYE Tools, which includes the P11 calculator. See section below about the benefits of the HMRC P11 Calculator.

✔ **P49 (Paying someone for the first time):** The current guide on how to get your payroll started.

✔ **E13 (Day-to-day payroll):** Similar to P49, but with additional useful information and easier to understand.

You can download most forms, with the exception of the P45 and the P60 in PDF format. Type 'find a form' into the search box on the HMRC website, and a new page appears where you can enter the form title or a relevant keyword to help you find the correct form.

# Collecting Employee Taxes

As the bookkeeper, you must be familiar with how to calculate the Pay As You Earn (PAYE) tax and National Insurance Contributions (NICs) that you must deduct from each employee's wage or salary.

Although you can run a manual payroll, the calculation of PAYE and NICs is a monumental nightmare, demanding the most accurate and methodical approach to using the tables that HM Revenue & Customs provides each tax year. As well as getting the calculations correct, you have to record this information on a Deductions Working Sheet for each employee, which is very time consuming.

Save yourself a lot of grief and use a payroll bureau to run your weekly and monthly payroll and end-of-tax-year returns. If you employ more than 30 employees, this method saves you a lot of time and the cost isn't all that high. If you employ fewer than 30 employees and have the time to spare, use the P11 Calculator that HM Revenue & Customs provides online as part of the Basic PAYE tool kit, or buy an off-the-shelf payroll package.

# Sorting out National Insurance Contributions

The easiest and quickest way to work out the National Insurance Contributions (NICs) is to use HMRC's Basic PAYE Tools. This is free software that you can download from the HMRC website. It includes a P11 Calculator, which helps you work out an employee's tax, national insurance and student loan deductions. It completes an electronic format of the P11 Deductions Working Sheet for you.

### Benefits of using the P11 Calculator

Using the P11 Calculator has several benefits:

- A P11 Deduction Working Sheet is automatically created and updated each month, as you enter the pay details for each employee.

- The toolkit checks any P45s that you enter, to work out whether the tax figure on the P45 is correct.

- You can change tax codes midway through the payroll year.

- You can produce P11 summaries and also P32 summaries, which show the amount of tax and NICs payable for each pay period.

- You can complete your year-end payroll and submit the P14s and P35 (mentioned in Chapter 18) directly to the HMRC as long as you have an Internet connection.

✔ Once a year-end is performed, the P11 Calculator automatically transfers the employee details to the new tax year and you can carry on paying your staff without having to re-enter employee details for the new tax year.

### Limitations of the P11 Calculator

While this software is great at calculating your tax and NICs contributions, you can't treat it as a payroll system, sadly! Bear in mind that you can't:

✔ Print payslips

✔ Record pension contributions

✔ Record any other deductions that are unrelated to PAYE

The 'Getting Started' guide produced by HMRC and available online, provides lists of all payroll providers (both free and chargeable). Take time to read through these lists before making your decision.

If you feel completely masochistic, you can use manual Tax and NI tables, available on the website. For the purposes of this book, we want to keep the process as simple as possible so that mistakes are less likely.

We encourage you to use a simple payroll package, but if you're on a tight budget then consider using the HMRC PAYE Tools kit and the P11 calculator.

## Calculating NICs

NICs are made up of two elements:

✔ Employee contributions, which you deduct from your employees' pay.

✔ Employer contributions, which your business must pay.

Several different categories of NICs exist depending on the employee's age and sex. For most men aged 16 or over and under the male state pension age and most women aged 16 or over and under the female state pension age, you use Category A, which is referred to later as Table A. If you're unsure about which category your employee falls under, contact your local HM Revenue & Customs or go to the website at www.hmrc.gov.uk.

To calculate Category A NICs manually, you need booklet *CA38 National Insurance Contributions Tables A & J* from HM Revenue & Customs. Make sure that the tables you have are for the correct year. The tables can be downloaded from the HMRC website as a PDF file.

If your employee earns more than £107 per week or £464 per month, you must keep a record of his or her earnings even if no NICs are due.

Each year HM Revenue & Customs sets new Lower Earnings Limits (LEL) below which no NICs are payable by an employee. It also sets an Upper Earnings Limit (UEL) above which no more NICs are payable.

The employer pays NICs when the employee's earnings exceed the Secondary Threshold (ST – currently £144 weekly or £624 monthly). The employee pays NICs when their earnings exceed the Primary Threshold (PT – currently £146 weekly or £634 monthly).

Employers and their employees who are members of a contracted out state pension scheme pay a reduced NIC contracted out rate up to the Upper Accrual Point (UAP) – which is currently £770 weekly or £3,337 monthly. They then pay NIC's at a higher standard rate on employee earnings between the UAP and the UEL.

For the latest information about NIC's check the HMRC website www.hmrc.gov.uk

## Figuring out PAYE tax

Deducting Pay As You Earn (PAYE) tax is a much more complex task for bookkeepers than deducting NICs. You have to worry about an employee's tax code (of which numerous permutations exist) as well as using Table A to calculate the final tax figure to deduct.

### Considering the tax codes

A tax code is usually made up of one or more numbers followed by a letter. The number indicates the amount of pay an employee is allowed to earn in a tax year before tax becomes payable. For example, an employee with a tax code of 810L can earn £8,105 in the current tax year before becoming liable to pay any tax at all.

A letter follows the number part of the tax code: L, P, T, V or Y. The letters show how the tax code is adjusted to take account of any budget changes.

If the tax code is followed by week 1/month 1 or an X, instead of keeping a running total of the pay to date, you treat each pay day for that employee as if it is the first week or month of the tax year. For regular employees, you work on a running total basis of 'total pay to date' at each pay day.

Tax codes work on an annual cumulative tax allowance. For example, a tax code of 810L means an employee can earn £8,105 tax free in a complete tax year (52 weeks or 12 months). If the employee is paid weekly, this tax-free sum adds up as the weeks go by. In this example, in week 1 the employee can earn £155.86 total pay without paying any tax (£8,105 ÷ 52). By week 8, that employee could have earned £1246.92 total pay to date that year without paying any tax. Assuming that they have been paid in each of the intervening weeks (1 to 7), these sums earned are deducted from the total year-to-date tax-free-earnings figure to calculate how much is taxable. All this information is provided in the tax tables that you can obtain from HM Revenue & Customs. The tax tables, however, suggest that you ought to try the Basic PAYE Tools for calculating tax, as it makes the whole process so much easier and less prone to mistakes.

Finally, as if all this wasn't confusing enough, an employee may have a totally different BR tax code, which stands for Basic Rate. For an employee with a BR tax code, you must deduct tax from all the pay at the basic rate – currently 20 per cent. The BR code can also be followed by a week 1/month 1 or X, which indicates that you operate the code on a non-cumulative basis. Of course, if week 1/month 1 or X aren't indicated, you work on a running-total basis of total-pay-to-date at each pay day.

If you don't want to use manual tax tables, and you aren't using payroll software, then the easiest and quickest way to work out the tax deduction is to use the HMRC Basic PAYE Tools. See `www.hmrc.gov.uk/paye/tools/basic-paye-tools.htm`

### *Calculating the PAYE deduction for a weekly paid employee*

We run through an example of a weekly paid employee who earned £205.42 in his new employment for tax week 4, and show you how easy it is to calculate the PAYE tax that needs to be deducted, using the P11 calculator. The information from the employee's P45 states:

- ✔ Tax code is 810L
- ✔ Total pay to date is £615
- ✔ Total tax to date is £29.40

Figure 17-1 shows the entries on the form P11 (Deduction Working Sheet).

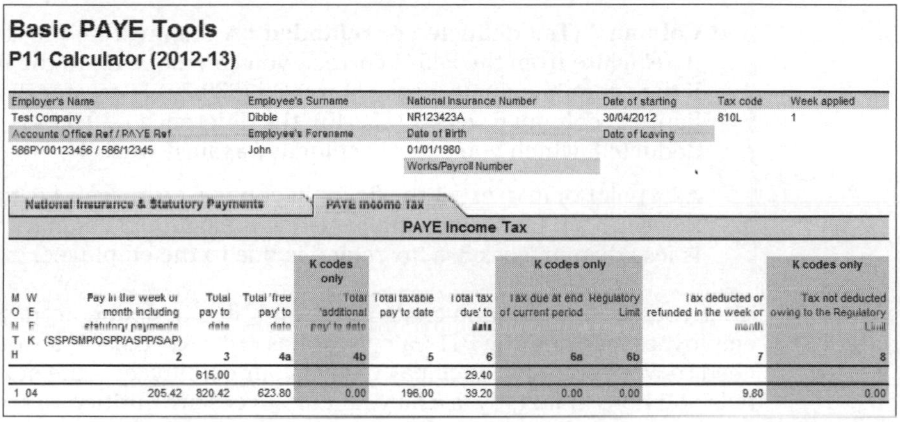

**Basic PAYE Tools**

**P11 Calculator (2012-13)**

| Employer's Name | Employee's Surname | National Insurance Number | Date of starting | Tax code | Week applied |
|---|---|---|---|---|---|
| Test Company | Dibble | NR123423A | 30/04/2012 | 810L | 1 |
| Accounts Office Ref / PAYE Ref | Employee's Forename | Date of Birth | Date of leaving | | |
| 586PY00123456 / 586/12345 | John | 01/01/1980 | | | |
| | | Works/Payroll Number | | | |

National Insurance & Statutory Payments | PAYE Income Tax

**PAYE Income Tax**

| MONTH | WEEK | Pay in the week or month including statutory payments (SSP/SMP/OSPP/ASPP/SAP) | Total pay to date | Total 'free pay' to date | K codes only: Total 'additional pay' to date | Total taxable pay to date | Total tax due' to date | K codes only: Tax due at end of current period | K codes only: Regulatory Limit | Tax deducted or refunded in the week or month | K codes only: Tax not deducted owing to the Regulatory Limit |
|---|---|---|---|---|---|---|---|---|---|---|---|
| | | 2 | 3 | 4a | 4b | 5 | 6 | 6a | 6b | 7 | 8 |
| | | | 615.00 | | | | 29.40 | | | | |
| 1 | 04 | 205.42 | 820.42 | 623.80 | 0.00 | 196.00 | 39.20 | 0.00 | 0.00 | 9.80 | 0.00 |

**Figure 17-1:** PAYE entries on form P11 for a weekly paid employee.



The following list explains how the numbers in Figure 17-1 are calculated:

- **Column 2 (Pay in the week or month):** This column shows the pay that the employee earned in the current week, which is week 4.
- **Column 3 (Total pay to date):** This column includes pay from any previous employment during the current tax year. The employee's P45 indicates that this amount is £615 for week 3 – the week before the current pay week.

  As PAYE works on a cumulative basis, you then add the current week's pay – £205.42 – to this figure to get the cumulative or 'Total pay to date' figure, which is £820.42. This is the figure shown on the line for week 4, just below the previous 'Total pay to date' figure.
- **Column 4a (Total 'free pay' to date):** The P11 Calculator has automatically worked out the tax free pay to date. No struggling with the tax tables!
- **Column 5 (Total taxable pay to date):** This column features a straightforward calculation in which the column 4a figure is deducted from the column 3 figure to see how much pay is taxable. In this example, column 3 is £820.42 for week 4 and deducting the column 4a figure of £623.80 for the same week gives you a taxable pay figure of £196 for the year to date.

✔ **Column 6 (Total 'tax due' to date):** Instead of having to use your Taxable Pay Tables, Calculator Method (the manual method), the system automatically calculates your tax due to date for you.

✔ **Column 7 (Tax deducted or refunded):** Assuming that the 'Total tax to date' figure from the P45 is correct, you can move on to the final stage. If the figure in column 6 against week 4 (£39.20) is greater than the figure in column 6 week 7 (£29.40), the difference – £9.80 – is tax to be deducted, which you enter in column 7 against week 4.

As a point of interest, if the figure in column 7 for week 4 is the same as in week 3, no tax is deductible. Also, if the figure in column 7 for week 4 is less than in week 3, a tax refund is due to the employee.

After you discover how much PAYE tax and NICs to deduct from your employees' pay and the P11 Calculator has created your P11s, you then need to work out how much pay to give your employees – the next section tells you how. In fact, by law all your employees are entitled to receive a statement (usually a payslip), which shows the deductions you've made from their pay. The statement must show: gross pay, NICs deducted and tax deducted. At the end of the year you must give all your employees a record showing the details for the whole year. (This record, the P60, is covered in Chapter 18.)

# Determining Net Pay

*Net pay* is the amount a person is paid after subtracting all tax and benefit deductions from gross pay.

After you figure out all the necessary PAYE and NICs to be taken from an employee's wage or salary (see the preceding sections), you can calculate the pay amount, which is shown on the payslip. The equation you use is pretty straightforward:

Gross pay – (PAYE + NICs) = Net pay

For a sample employee, this formula may look like this:

Gross pay = £205.42

Less: PAYE tax deducted – £9.80

Less: Employee NICs – £7.13

Net pay = £188.49

This net pay calculation doesn't include any deductions for benefits. Many businesses offer their employees health insurance, pensions, company cars and other benefits but expect the employees to share a portion of some of those costs. Most benefits are liable to PAYE tax and NICs, whereas employee contributions to pensions and some other benefits are tax deductible. To get full details on which benefits are taxable and which are not, visit the HM Revenue & Customs website (www.hmrc.gov.uk) or ask your tax advisor.

# Taxing Benefits

Many businesses offer their employees a range of benefits as well as their wage or salary. These benefits may include perks like a company car, all fuel paid for, health insurance and a business pension scheme. However, most benefits are taxable, so the employee has to pay tax on the money on the value of the benefits received. Very few benefits are non-taxable.

Fortunately the process of collecting this tax on benefits is very straightforward. Your business informs HM Revenue & Customs what benefits each employee receives each tax year, and it adjusts the employee tax code to ensure that you collect the tax due through the payroll.

However, two benefits – company cars and fuel benefits – involve some additional work for you if you're involved in the payroll.

The quickest and simplest way to calculate the value of these benefits is to use the Car and Car Fuel Benefit Calculator, which can be found on the HMRC website. Click the 'Calculators and Tools' link on the 'Quick Link' menu on the left side of the homepage. The calculator guides you through the whole process. Also, all the monthly car magazines include the taxable benefit figures in their rating for each car reviewed.

You're responsible for working out the value of the company car benefit and telling HM Revenue & Customs. In simple terms, the car benefit charge is obtained by multiplying the list price of the car plus accessories less any capital contribution by the employee by the appropriate percentage. The *appropriate percentage* is based on the car's approved $CO_2$ emissions figure. The maximum appropriate percentage is 35 per cent, but you can adjust this amount depending on the type of fuel used and whether the car is electric or hybrid.

The HMRC provide a useful *Helpsheet number 203* entitled 'Car benefits and car fuel benefits', which enables you to complete your tax returns correctly using the worksheets provided.

If an employer pays for all the fuel for company car users, they can claim an additional taxable benefit called a fuel benefit charge for the non-business fuel used. Fortunately, this benefit is even simpler to calculate. The fuel benefit charge is calculated by multiplying the fixed sum of £18,800 (2011/2012 tax year) to the appropriate percentage used to calculate the car benefit. So if your car had an appropriate percentage (based on $CO_2$ emissions) of 24 per cent, for example, then your taxable fuel benefit charge would be £4,512 (£18,800 × 24 per cent).

When you've calculated the taxable value of the company car and fuel benefit for an employee, you must inform HM Revenue & Customs so that it can issue you with a revised tax code for that employee to collect the extra PAYE and NICs due each month. You use form P46 (Car) to notify HM Revenue & Customs of any new company cars and fuel benefits, or any changes to these benefits.

# Preparing and Posting Payroll

After you deal with deductions and taxes, you have to figure out your employee's gross and net pay and post all the amounts in your journals.

## Calculating payroll for hourly employees

When you're ready to prepare payroll for your hourly paid employees, the first thing you need to do is collect time records from each person being paid hourly. Some businesses use time clocks and some use timesheets to produce the required time records, but whatever the method used, usually the manager of each department reviews the time records for each employee that he or she supervises and then sends those time records to you, the bookkeeper.

With time records in hand, you have to calculate gross pay for each employee. For example, if an employee worked 45 hours and is paid £12 an hour, you calculate gross pay as follows:

40 standard hours × £12 per hour = £480

5 overtime hours × £12 per hour × 1.5 overtime rate = £90

£480 + £90 = £570

# Doling out funds to salaried employees

You also must prepare payroll for salaried employees. You can calculate payments for salaried employees relatively easily – all you need to know are their base salaries and pay period calculations. For example, if a salaried employee is paid £15,000 per year and is paid monthly (totalling 12 pay periods), that employee's gross pay is £1,250 for each pay period (£15,000 ÷ 12).

# Totalling up for commission payments

Running payroll for employees who are paid based on commission can involve complex calculations. To show you a number of variables, in this section we calculate a commission payment based on a salesperson who sells £60,000 worth of products during one month.

For a salesperson on a straight commission of 10 per cent, you calculate pay using this formula:

Total amount sold × Commission percentage = Gross pay

£60,000 × 0.10 = £6,000

For a salesperson with a guaranteed base salary of £2,000, plus an additional 5 per cent commission on all products sold, you calculate pay using this formula:

Base salary + (Total amount sold × Commission percentage) = Gross pay

£2,000 + (£60,000 × 0.05) = £5,000

Although this salesperson may be happier with a base salary that he can count on each month, in this scenario he actually makes less with a base salary because the commission rate is so much lower. The salesperson makes only £3,000 in commission at 5 per cent if he sells £60,000 worth of products. Without the base pay, he would have made 10 per cent on the £60,000, or £6,000. Therefore, taking into account his base salary of £2,000, he actually receives £1,000 less with a base pay structure that includes a lower commission pay rate.

If a salesperson has a slow sales month of just £30,000 worth of products sold, the pay is:

£30,000 × 0.10 = £3,000 on straight commission of 10 per cent

and

£30,000 × 0.05 = £1,500 plus £2,000 base salary, or £3,500

For a slow month, the salesperson makes more money with the base salary rather than the higher commission rate.

You can calculate commissions in many other ways. One common way is to offer higher commissions on higher levels of sales. Using the figures in this example, this type of pay system encourages salespeople to keep their sales levels over a threshold amount to get the best commission rate.

With a graduated commission scale, a salesperson can make a straight commission of 5 per cent on the first £10,000 in sales, 7 per cent on the next £20,000 and 10 per cent on anything over £30,000. The following is what this salesperson's gross pay calculation looks like using this commission pay scale:

(£10,000 × 0.05) + (£20,000 × 0.07) + (£30,000 × 0.10) = £4,900 Gross pay

One other type of commission pay system involves a base salary plus tips. This method is common in restaurant settings in which servers receive a basic rate per hour plus tips.

Businesses must pay the minimum wage plus tips (minimum wage currently £6.08 for employees over 21 years of age). There is a useful guide at www.direct.gov.uk called 'Handling Tips at Work'.

As an employer, you must report an employee's gross taxable wages based on salary plus tips. Here's how you calculate gross taxable wages for an employee whose earnings are based on tips and wages:

Base wage + Tips = Gross taxable wages

(£3 × 40 hours per week) + £300 = £420

Checking this employee's gross wages, the hourly rate earned is £10.50 per hour.

Hourly wage = £10.50 (£420 ÷ 40)

PAYE and NICs are calculated on the base wage plus tips, so the net payment you prepare for the employee in this example is for the total gross wage minus any taxes due.

After calculating the take-home pay for all your employees, you prepare the payroll, make the payments and post the payroll to the books. In addition to the Cash account, payroll impacts many accounts, including:

- ✔ **Accrued PAYE Payable,** which is where you record the liability for tax payments
- ✔ **Accrued NICs Payable,** which is where you record the liability for NICs payments

When you post the payroll entry, you indicate the withdrawal of money from the Cash account and record liabilities for future cash payments that are due for PAYE and NICs payments. To give you an example of the proper set-up for a payroll journal entry, we assume the total payroll is £10,000 with £1,000 each set aside for PAYE and NICs payable. In reality, your numbers are sure to be different, and your payments are likely to never all be the same. Table 17-1 shows what your journal entry for posting payroll looks like.

| Table 17-1 | Payroll Journal Entry for 26 May 2012 | |
|---|---|---|
| | *Debit* | *Credit* |
| Gross Salaries and Wages Expense | £10,000 | |
| Accrued PAYE Payable | | £1,000 |
| Accrued NICs Payable | | £1,000 |
| Cash (Net Payment) | | £8,000 |

Table 17-1 shows only the entries that affect the take-home pay of the employees. The business must also make Employer NICs payments. Use the manual tables or the P11 Calculator from the HMRC Basic PAYE Tools to calculate this amount. The Employer NIC is a cost of employment and therefore must be treated in the books in exactly the same way as Gross Salaries and Wages. Table 17-2 shows the journal entry to record Employer NICs payments.

| Table 17-2 | Employer NICs Expenses for May | |
|---|---|---|
| | Debit | Credit |
| Employer NICs Expense | £1,100 | |
| Accrued Employer NICs Payable | | £1,100 |

In this entry, you increase the Expense account for salaries and wages as well as all the accounts in which you accrue future obligations for PAYE and employee NICs payments. You decrease the amount of the Cash account; when cash payments are made for the PAYE and NICs payments in the future, you post those payments in the books. Table 17-3 shows an example of the entry posted to the books after making the PAYE withholding tax payment.

| Table 17-3 | Recording PAYE Payments for May | |
|---|---|---|
| | Debit | Credit |
| Accrued PAYE and NICs Payable | £3,100 | |
| Current account | | £3,100 |

# Settling up with HM Revenue & Customs

Every month you need to pay over to HM Revenue & Customs all the PAYE and NIC amounts you deduct from your employees. To work out what you have to pay HM Revenue & Customs, add together:

- ✔ Employee NICs
- ✔ Employer NICs
- ✔ PAYE tax
- ✔ Student loan repayments

## Outsourcing payroll and benefits work

If you don't want to take on payroll and benefits, you can also pay for a monthly payroll service from the software company that provides your accounting software. For example, Sage provides various levels of payroll services. The Sage payroll features include calculating earnings and deductions, printing cheques or making direct deposits, providing updates to the tax tables and supplying the data needed to complete all HM Revenue & Customs forms related to payroll. The advantage of doing payroll in-house in this manner is that you can more easily integrate payroll into the business's books.

These payments must be made to HM Revenue & Customs by the 19th of the following month if paying by cheque, or on the 22nd of the following month if paying electronically. If you employ more than 250 employees, you must make monthly electronic payments. Contact Banking Operations Cumbernauld (Tel: 01236-783361) for further help on setting up this facility. A special concession exists for small businesses to pay quarterly (5 July, 5 October, 5 January and 5 April) if the average monthly payment of PAYE and NICs is less than £1,500.

To help you keep track of these payments, HM Revenue & Customs sends you a payslip booklet in which you record details of your total payments. In addition, you're sent a P32 Employment Record to work out and record your total monthly payments.

# *Have a Go*

1.  **Design a new starter form for your business. You can use a checklist format to help you, with boxes that you can fill in or tick.**

2.  **Design a payroll checklist to help you complete your monthly payroll routine.**

3. Before you enter your pay details into your chosen system, you need to have some mechanism for gathering the pay information. This might be in the form of timesheets and or simply a list of employees and their gross salary. Design a timesheet (you can use a spreadsheet for this), to calculate the gross pay for the following employee:

> Name: Deborah Donaghue
>
> Dept: Fixings
>
> Paid: Weekly
>
> Hours: 45
>
> Hourly rate: £12
>
> Overtime: 6 hours
>
> Overtime rate: £16

4. Joe Carey is a new starter at your company. He does not have a P45 and has told you that he already has another part time job. What tax code do you put him on when he starts?

5. You have a new sales director starting this month. You have been told that she is being paid an annual salary of £52,000. How much would her gross pay be each month?

# Answering the Have a Go Questions

1. Typical items to include on your New Starter form would be:

   - Full Name and address
   - Phone number
   - Email address
   - National Insurance number
   - Start date
   - Job title
   - Department
   - Salary (whether weekly or monthly)

- Payment method (BACS)

- Include a box for bank details, to include sort code, account number and account name.

- P45 (Yes or No) (if this isn't available, you need to fill out a P46 instead), attach to the new starter form

- Details of any pension scheme or pension contributions to be made

- Details of any deductions to be made such as child support or County Court payments

- Details of holiday pay and overtime rates applicable for that employee

2. **A monthly payroll checklist would include the following items.**

*Note:* You'll find it easier to design this in a checklist format, so that you can tick each completed item as you go along. This is helpful if you work in a busy office and are likely to get interrupted as you're working. This way, you can see where you've got up to and start from the appropriate point.

You may wish to have a list for both monthly and weekly payrolls.

a. Enter new starter details and set up new employees (if required).

b. Using timesheets or other input mechanism to enter the pay details for the period.

c. Check for any new tax codes to apply in the month, or any other legislation that may require a tax code change (for example changes in the national Budget).

d. Calculate the tax and NI due (if using manual system).

e. Write or print out your pay slips.

f. Print out any other payroll reports that you require for your records.

g. Ensure that you take adequate backups of your payroll data (if using a system such as Sage Payroll, we would recommend taking a backup before updating the payroll and also after updating. This gives you an opportunity to restore the payroll, if a mistake has been made and re-run the update).

h. Update your payroll if you're operating a computerised system.

i. Complete a P32 form to record details of deductions for all employees including PAYE, student loans, NI, Statutory Sick Pay, Statutory Maternity Pay, Statutory Adoption Pay for each tax month.

j. Complete your Employer Payment booklet (otherwise known as P30BC) and send your payment voucher detailing PAYE and NI due along with a cheque to the Inland Revenue. You can also pay online, but you need to make sure that you're registered with the HMRC to do this. See www.hmrc.gov.uk for further details about registering online with them.

3. **Gross pay calculation for Deborah Donaghue:**

| Basic hours: | 45 hours @ £12 per hour | £540 |
| Overtime hours: | 6 hours @ £16 per hour | £96 |
| Total gross pay: | | **£636** |

4. **Joe Carey has not provided you with a P45, therefore in order to process the payroll and give him a tax code that is suitable, you must complete a P46 form.** The P46 has two parts and you should ask Joe to complete Part 1. You must then complete Part 2 and then send the form to HMRC.

Because Joe has told you he has another part time job, he should have ticked Box C in the 'Present Circumstances' section in Part 1. As a result, you should also tick Box C in the 'Tax Code Used' section in Part 2 of the form. This means that you should use the tax code BR (Basic Rate) for the first payroll until you're advised of a different Tax Code by the Inland Revenue. This means that the employee pays Basic Rate tax on all the gross pay that you've calculated. This probably means that the employee is paying more tax than perhaps he should be, but this problem will be corrected when you receive the correct code for the employee from the Inland Revenue. At this point a refund of tax (if applicable) is generated in the following month's payroll, as long as you apply the new tax code.

5. **The monthly gross pay for your new sales director is:**

| Annual pay: | £52,000 |
| Monthly pay: | £52,000 ÷ 12 = £4,333.33 |

You apply the tax codes given to you from the P45 that you should have received.

# Chapter 18

# Completing Year-End Payroll and Reports

*E*ven when you keep diligently up to date with everything concerning your employee payroll and benefits, you still have paperwork to complete at the end of the year. You need to submit forms for each of your employees as well as some summary reports.

Yes, you guessed it. End-of-the-year HM Revenue & Customs paperwork takes time. To help make the process as painless as possible, this chapter reviews the forms you need to complete, the information you need for each form and the process for filing your business's payroll information with HM Revenue & Customs. We deal with some of the payroll basics in Chapter 17.

## Reporting on Employees

You may think that you've done a lot of paperwork relating to your payroll throughout the year, but the job isn't yet complete. Although you keep individual records for deduction of Pay As You Earn (PAYE) tax and National Insurance (NI) for each employee, and make payments to HM Revenue & Customs throughout the year, at the end of the tax year on 5 April, HM Revenue & Customs wants more information, to be sure that you haven't missed out on any PAYE tax and National Insurance Contributions (NICs).

We cover the forms you need to submit in some detail in the following sections in the order in which they need to be submitted – so you know when to panic!

HM Revenue & Customs publishes an *Employer Helpbook E10* each year that covers finishing the tax year. You can obtain this book from their website, www.hmrc.gov.uk.

## Form P14

As far as forms go, the P14, shown in Figure 18-1, is pretty straightforward. In essence the P14 is a summary of each employee's P11 that you've been working with all tax year, and you don't need any more information than what you already have on the employee's P11. We cover the P11 in Chapter 17. Please remember that if you do not send a P14 to HM Revenue & Customs for every employee each tax year, they won't have a record of that person's PAYE, NICs and other deductions record. Also, if you've more than one employee please ensure that you send these forms to HM Revenue & Customs in alphabetical order. Table 18-1 tells you what to put in each section.

**Figure 18-1:** Sample P14 End of Year Summary for 2011/12.

*Crown Copyright*

The P14 is due mid-May; check with HM Revenue & Customs for the exact date for the current year.

If you're manually completing this form, and all the end-of-the-year employee-related forms, the key word is accuracy – take care and complete the form slowly. Make sure that you pick up the correct tax year details.

Most payroll software systems automatically complete these forms for you and electronically send them to HMRC when you submit your year-end forms along with the P35 mentioned later in this chapter.

| Table 18-1 | Sections of Form P14 |
|---|---|
| *Section* | *What to Do (Manual Completion)* |
| Employer's name and address | Shows your full address, including the postcode. |
| Inland Revenue office name and Employer's PAYE reference | Enter your Inland Revenue office name and Employer's PAYE reference from the front of form P35. You can also find this information on your payslip booklet. |
| Tax year to 5 April 2012 | Usually pre-printed on the form. If submitting manually, take care to submit the correct year's figures! |
| **Employee's details**<br><br>National Insurance number | Copy this number from the front of form P11. |
| Date of birth | Enter the day and month as well as all four numbers of the year. |
| Surname and first two forenames | If you don't know all the employee's forenames, put initials. Don't put titles (Mr, Mrs, Miss and so on). |
| **National Insurance contributions in this employment**<br><br>NIC (National Insurance Contribution) Table letter | Copy from the End of Year Summary section on the back of form P11. |

*(continued)*

**Table 18-1** *(continued)*

| Section | What to Do (Manual Completion) |
| --- | --- |
| Columns 1a to 1c | Copy from the End of Year Summary of form P11. Make entries in whole pounds and right justify the figures. |
| | If an entry exists in column 1a, you must still send in form P14 even though no NICs may be payable. |
| Columns 1d to 1f | Copy from the End of Year Summary of form P11. Make entries in pounds and pence. |
| | Where you operate a contracted-out pension scheme and the column 1d total to be carried forward from the P11 is a minus figure, enter 'R' in the corresponding box immediately to the right of the column of the column 1d total boxes on the P14. |
| **Statutory payments in this employment**<br><br>Box 1g | This reflects the total amount of Statutory Sick Pay (SSP) paid in those months for which an amount has been recovered under the Percentage Threshold Scheme. |
| Boxes 1h to 1j | Copy from the corresponding columns on form P11. |
| Scheme Contracted-Out number | Complete only if the employee is a member of a Contracted-Out Money Purchase (COMP) scheme, COMP Stakeholder Pension (COMPSHP) scheme, or the COMP part of the Contracted-Out Mixed Benefit (COMB) scheme you operate. |
| | Members of these schemes only receive their Age Related Rebate (ARR) if this part is entered correctly. |
| Student loan deductions | Copy from the totals box at the bottom of column 1k on form P11. |
| | Enter whole pounds only. |

| Section | What to Do (Manual Completion) |
|---|---|
| Date of starting and date of leaving | Make entries only if an employee starts and/or leaves your employment during the tax year (2011/12 in this example). |
| | Enter date as figures: 09 05 2011, for example. |
| **Pay and income tax details** In previous employment(s) | Copy from the End of Year Summary of form P11. |
| In this employment | Copy from the End of Year Summary of form P11. |
| Total for year | Copy from the End of Year Summary of form P11. |
| | Fill in these boxes only if the employee was still working for you at 5 April. |
| Employee's Widows and Orphans/ Life Assurance contributions in this employment | Applies where an employee is legally obliged to pay contributions that qualify for tax relief but are not authorised under 'net pay arrangements' for tax relief. See *CWG2 Employers Further Guide to PAYE and NICs* for more information. |
| Final tax code | Fill in boxes from the left-hand side. |
| | Always show the last tax code you were using at the 5 April date. |
| Payment in week 53 | Use only if Week 53 is included in the Pay and Tax totals, and then put one of the following in this box: |
| | '53' if 53 weekly pay days were in the year |
| | '54' if 27 fortnightly pay days were in the year |
| | '56' if 14 four-weekly pay days were in the year. |

HM Revenue & Customs ask that you submit your P14 forms in alphabetical order.

Traditionally, the last part of form P14 is the P60. You don't send the P60 to HM Revenue & Customs. Instead, you give each employee his or her own copy, which summarises pay, tax, NICs deductions and so on made during the year.

Don't give a P60 to employees who were no longer with the business at the end of the tax year.

*Note:* You can easily print off P60s if you used the HMRC PAYE Tools to complete your payroll year-end.

## Detailing benefits on forms P9D, P11D and P11D (b)

Fortunately, you don't need these forms for the majority of your employees in the typical small business. Basically, these forms are used to report back to HM Revenue & Customs the various benefits in kind that employees received during the year.

The forms and the circumstances they address are as follows:

✔ Use the fairly simple form P9D if the employee in question earned at the rate of £8,500 per annum or less. Earnings include all bonuses, tips and benefits.

✔ Use the significantly more complicated form P11D for employees who earned at the rate of £8,500 or more and for all directors, regardless of earnings.

✔ Use form P11D(b) to:

• Confirm that by 6 July all forms P11D have been completed and sent to your HM Revenue & Customs office.

• Declare the total amount of Class 1A NICs you're due to pay. *Class 1A* contributions are the extra NICs that may be due on taxable benefits that you provide to your employees.

HM Revenue & Customs produces a series of guides to help you get this area of reporting right. Look for the publication for the current tax year:

✔ *480 Expenses and Benefits – A Tax Guide:* This guide runs to some 100 pages and is the definitive guide.

✔ *CWG2 Employers' Further Guide to PAYE and NICs.*

✔ *CWG5 Class 1A NICs on benefits in kind.*

✔ *P11D Guide*: This guide is a four-page overview, which makes reference to the *480* guide for more detail.

Within the confines of this book, we can't possibly hope to do justice to the whole detail of benefit-in-kind reporting. However, the following list gives you a brief outline of the kind of things that are deemed to be benefits in kind and need to be included on the P9D or P11D:

✔ Assets transferred (cars, property, goods or other assets)

✔ Payments made on behalf of the employee

✔ Vouchers and credit cards

✔ Living accommodation

✔ Mileage allowance payments/passenger miles

✔ Cars, vans and fuel

✔ Interest-free, low interest and notional loans

✔ Private medical treatment or insurance

✔ Qualifying relocation expenses payments and benefits

✔ Services supplied

✔ Assets placed at employees' disposal

✔ Other items – subscriptions, educational assistance, non-qualifying relocation benefits and expenses payments, incidental overnight expenses

✔ Employer-provided childcare

✔ Expenses payments made to, or on behalf of, the director or employee – general expenses for business travel, travel and subsistence not included in general expenses allowances, entertainment, trading organisations, tonnage tax companies, home telephone, other non-qualifying relocation expenses

The list seems to go on and on.

# Reporting PAYE-free earnings on forms P38, P38A and P38 (S)

Forms P38 and P38A ask you to report payments made to employees from whom you haven't deducted PAYE – such as part-time casual staff. Form P38 (S) applies to students. The following subsections show the type of payments that you need to include or omit on forms P38 or P38A.

## P38A

This is a two-page form called the Employer Supplementary Return. This form asks for details of people whom you paid this tax year, but didn't complete a form P14 for.

### Section A

In this section, you:

✔ Include payments above the PAYE threshold.

✔ Include payments to employees who have not produced a P45 and were engaged for more than one week, if both of the following conditions are met:

- The rate of pay was above £102 per week or £442 per month.

- The employee failed to complete certificate A or B on form P46.

✔ Exclude payments included on form P14.

### Section B

In this section, you:

✔ Include payments that total over £100 made to any employee, including casuals, during this tax year.

✔ Exclude those included on forms P14, those in section A (above), those payments to employees with completed P46 certificates A and B, and payments returned on forms P38(S).

## P38 (S)

P38(S) is the appropriate return for students who work for you solely during a holiday. You don't need to deduct tax from a student as long as:

✔ They fill in the student's declaration, *and*

✔ The student's pay in your employment doesn't exceed £8,105 during the tax year.

If a student's pay in your employment exceeds this figure, you must deduct tax using code 'OT week 1/month 1' in accordance with paragraphs 110 and 111 of the booklet *CWG2 Employers' Further Guide to PAYE and NICs.*

# Submitting Summary Information on Form P35

Form P35 is part of the Employers' Annual Return. In essence it lists every employee, including directors (who must be shown first with an asterisk by their name), the NIC amounts and income tax you deducted from their pay. If you've more than ten employees, you need one or more continuation sheets (form P35CS).

Also, as per the P14, you need to list employees in alphabetical order.

- ✔ Page 1 tells you what your obligations are and where to get further help: nothing to complete here.

- ✔ Pages 2 and 3 require you to list the details of your employees and summarise your payments of NICs, PAYE tax, SSP, SMP and SAP for the year.

- ✔ Page 4 contains several tick-box questions for you to complete before signing and dating the form.

## Boxing out Parts 1 and 2

If you use a computerised payroll system, the information for the P35 is imported directly from the P11 information that you entered and the system has calculated throughout the year.

If you're completing the P35 manually, have a quick read below, to see what you need to do.

You can get much of the information you need to complete Parts 1 and 2 of form P35 from the P11 forms you have for each person to whom you pay money:

- ✔ The total of each employee's and the employer's NICs are in column 1e of the P14 End of Year Summary.

✔ The total tax deducted or refunded is in the 'In this employment' box in the Pay and Income Tax section towards the bottom of the page.

Completing Parts 1 and 2 makes you check that your payments to the accounts office are correct. If this form shows that you should have paid over more to HM Revenue & Customs during the year, you need to make an additional payment.

## Ticking off the Part 3 checklist

Page 4 of the form has three sections – Parts 3, 4, and 5. Part 3 has no numbers, just a checklist of questions to answer:

✔ **Question 1:** If you had any employees for whom you didn't complete a form P14 or P38(S), tick 'No'.

These employees are likely to be part-time or casual staff. If you tick 'No', you must complete a *P38A Employer's Supplementary Return*.

✔ **Question 2:** Did you make any 'free-of-tax' payments to an employee? A free-of-tax payment is one where the employer bears any tax due.

✔ **Question 3:** Has anyone other than the employer paid expenses or provided benefits to any of your employees during the year as part of their employment with you?

✔ **Question 4:** This question is in two parts. If the answer to the first part is 'Yes', you have to complete a form P14 for each employee concerned.

✔ **Question 5:** This question asks whether you've paid any part of an employee's pay direct to anyone else, for example, paying school fees direct to a school. If you did, you need to report whether the payment was included in the employee's pay for tax and NICs purposes and in the pay shown on form P14.

This question doesn't include attachment of earnings orders or payments to the Child Support Agency.

✔ **Question 6:** This question covers IR35 under which HM Revenue & Customs has restricted workers' ability to form service companies or partnerships through which they sell their services. Your best bet is to find out more about IR35 at www.hmrc.gov.uk/ir35, to make sure that you comply. If, for example, you don't deduct tax and NICs when you need to, you may become liable for any non-payment of tax and NICs by the person employed.

If you included PAYE and NICs from workers who you deemed to be employees, tick the second box 'Yes'. If you tick the second box 'Yes' but the amount of the deemed payment is provisional, confirm on a separate sheet and send it with the form P35.

### Pensioning out Part 4

If you've a company pension scheme that was contracted-out of the State Second pension, enter your employer's contracted-out number here (you can find this number on your contracting-out certificate).

### Certifying your employer status in Part 5

This part is the check-up part, where you make sure that you've included all the necessary forms and then sign on the dotted line:

1. **Tick to confirm that you enclose all forms P14, P38A, P11D and P11D(b).**

2. **Confirm that P38A (see question 1 in the checklist of Part 3) is enclosed or not due.**

3. **Sign and print the name and capacity of the person signing and the date.**

Phew! Everything's done at last!

# Part VI
# The Part of Tens

'You say my bookkeeping predecessor
was incompetent. What happened to him?'

## In this part . . .

We join the *For Dummies* series tradition by providing you with some lists of tens. In this case, the lists contain key factors to maintaining your books and using the information collected. We highlight the top ten accounts that all bookkeepers must know in order to manage the books and give you the ten best ways to use your books to manage your business's cash.

# Chapter 19

# Top Ten Ways to Manage Your Business Cash with Your Books

## In This Chapter

▶ Keeping a handle on internal bookkeeping tools

▶ Monitoring profits and expenses

▶ Dealing smartly with suppliers, contractors and customers

**M**any business owners think of bookkeeping as a necessary evil, but in reality, if you make effective use of the data you collect, bookkeeping can be your best ally when it comes to managing your cash. The key to taking advantage of what bookkeeping offers is to understand the value of basic bookkeeping principles and how to use the information you collect efficiently and effectively. This chapter reviews the top ten ways to use your books to help you manage your business cash.

## Charting the Way

You may not think that a list of accounts, called the Chart of Accounts, is worth much attention, but this chart dictates how you collect your financial data and where in the books you put your business's transactions. In order for you to be able to use the information effectively, your Chart of Accounts must define each account precisely and determine exactly what types of transactions go where. (We talk about the Chart of Accounts and how to set one up in Chapter 3.)

# Balancing Your Entries

Balanced books are the only way to know how your business is doing. Without them, you can never know whether your profit numbers are accurate. In bookkeeping, you use a process called *double-entry bookkeeping* to keep the books balanced. We talk more about this basic principle and how to keep the books balanced in Chapter 2.

# Posting Your Transactions

In order to be able to use the information you collect regarding your business transactions, you must post the transactions accurately to your accounts. If you forget to post a transaction to your books, your reports don't reflect that financial activity, and you have a serious problem. Or, if you post an incorrect transaction to your books, any reports that draw on that information are going to be wrong – again, a problem. Find out more about the posting process in Chapter 4.

# Keeping on Top of Credit Control

If your business sells to customers on credit, you certainly want to make sure that your customers pay for their purchases in the future. (You gather customer account information in the Trade Debtors account as well as in individual records for each customer.) Review the reports based on customer payment history, called *Aged Debtor reports,* on a monthly basis to make sure that customers pay on time. Remember that you set the rules for credit, so you may want to cut off customers from future purchases if their accounts are overdue for 90 days or more. Discover how to manage customer accounts in Chapter 7.

# Paying Bills Accurately and on Time

If you want to continue getting supplies, products and services from your suppliers and contractors, you must pay them accurately and on time. Managing your payments through the Trade Creditors account ensures accuracy and timeliness, and also saves you from mistakenly paying bills twice. To be safe, you need to review Aged Creditor reports on your payment history, to ensure that you make timely and accurate payments. Manage your payments in Chapter 8.

# Planning Profits

Nothing is more important to a business owner than profit! Yet many business owners don't take time to plan their profit expectations at the beginning of each year, so they've no way to measure how well their businesses are doing throughout the year. Avoid this problem by taking time before the year starts to develop profit expectations and a budget that can help you meet those expectations. Then develop a series of internal financial reports from the numbers in your bookkeeping system to help determine whether or not you're meeting your sales targets and maintaining control over your product costs and operating expenses. We talk more about sales tracking in Chapter 7, costs and expense tracking in Chapter 8 and how to determine your net profit in Chapter 13.

# Comparing Budget to Actual Expenses

Keeping a careful watch on how well your budget planning reflects what's actually happening in your business can help you meet your profit goals. As with profits (see the preceding section), take time to develop a budget that sets your expectations for the year and then develop internal reports that give you the ability to track how closely your actual expenses match that budget. If you see any major problems, correct them as soon as possible to make sure that you meet your target profit at the end of the year. Find out more about internal financial reporting in Chapter 13.

# Comparing Sales Goals to Actual Sales

In addition to watching your expenses, you need to monitor your actual sales so that they match the sales goals you set at the beginning of the year. Designing an internal report that tracks sales goals versus actual sales allows you to monitor how well your business is doing. If you find that your actual sales are below expectations, take steps to correct the problem as early in the year as possible in order to improve your chances of meeting those year-end goals. To find out how to use internal financial reports to track your sales activity, check out Chapters 7 and 13.

# Monitoring Cost Trends

You need to be aware of the costs involved in purchasing the products you sell and the raw materials you use to manufacture your products because these costs can have a major impact on whether or not your business earns the net income you expect. If you find that the costs are going up, you may need to adjust the prices of the products you sell in order to meet your profit goals. Discover more about tracking cost trends in Chapters 8 and 13.

# Making Pricing Decisions

Properly pricing your product can be a critical factor in determining whether or not your product sells. If the price is too high, you may not find any customers willing to buy the product; if the price is too low, you lose money.

When determining what price to charge your customers, you must consider a number of different factors, including how much you pay to buy or manufacture the products you sell, the market research about what customers are willing to pay for a product, what you pay your employees and the advertising and administrative expenses you incur in order to set a price. All these items are factors in what you're going to spend to sell that product. You can find out more about tracking costs and expenses in Chapters 8 and 13.

# Chapter 20

# Top Ten Most Important Accounts for Any Bookkeeper

*E*ach and every account has its purpose in bookkeeping, but all accounts certainly aren't created equal. For most businesses, some accounts are more essential than others, so in case you're having trouble knowing where to start your account set-up and what's necessary, this chapter looks at the top must-have accounts for bookkeepers.

# Cash

All your business transactions pass through the Cash account, which is so important that if you run a manual system you actually need two books, Cash Receipts and Cash Payments, to track the activity. Computerised systems tend to use one Cash account, otherwise known as the Bank account. Don't confuse this account with the Petty Cash account, which usually represents the contents of a petty cash tin, used for small incidental purchases, such as stamps and milk. (We discuss these books in Chapter 9.) As the bookkeeper, your responsibility is to make sure that all cash – coming into the business or being sent out – is handled and recorded properly in the Cash account.

# Trade Debtors (Accounts Receivable)

If your business sells its products or services to customers on credit, you definitely need a Trade Debtors account, where you monitor all money due from customers. As the bookkeeper, keeping Trade Debtors up to date is critical, so make sure that you send timely and accurate bills to customers. We talk more about Trade Debtor processes in Chapter 7.

# Stock

Every business must have products to sell. You need to carefully account for and monitor all those money-making products, because this process is the only way a business knows what it has on hand to sell. As the bookkeeper, you contribute to this process by keeping accurate stock records in a Stock account. The numbers you have in your books are periodically verified by doing physical counts of the stock on hand. Discover how to manage stock and Stock accounts in Chapter 8.

# Trade Creditors (Accounts Payable)

No one likes to send money out of the business, but you can ease the pain and strain by monitoring and paying bills in your Trade Creditors (or Accrual) account. You certainly don't want to pay anyone twice, but you also want to make sure that you pay bills on time or else your business may no longer get the supplies, stock or other things needed to operate. Suppliers often penalise late-paying businesses by cutting them off or putting them on cash-with-order status. On the flipside, if you pay your bills early, you may be able to get discounts and save money with suppliers, so the early bird definitely gets the worm. For more on the Trade Creditors account, check out Chapter 8.

# Loans Payable

A time is bound to come when your business needs to purchase major items such as equipment, vehicles and furniture. Unfortunately, you may find that you don't have the money to pay for such purchases. The solution is to take on long-term loans that you can pay over more than a 12-month period. The Loans Payable account allows you to monitor the activity on these loans, in order to get and keep the best rates, and make all loan payments on time and accurately. We talk more about the Loans Payable account in Chapter 14.

# Sales

No business can operate without taking in cash, mostly through sales of the business's products or services. The Sales account is where you record all incoming revenue collected from these sales. Recording sales in a timely and accurate manner is a critical job of the bookkeeper, because otherwise you can't know how much revenue your business has collected every day. To find out more about sales and the Sales account, see Chapter 7.

# Purchases

Purchases are unavoidable. In order to have a tangible product to sell, your business has to manufacture the product, in which case you have to purchase raw materials, or purchase a finished product from a supplier. In the Purchases account, you track the purchases of any raw materials or finished goods. The Purchases account is a key component in calculating Cost of Goods Sold, which you subtract from Sales to find your business's gross profit. The Purchases account is explained further in Chapter 8.

# Payroll Expenses

You need to pay employees to get them to stay around. No matter how much you beg, few people want to work for nothing! To keep up to date with the biggest expense of many businesses, you record all money paid to employees in the Payroll Expenses account. You must accurately maintain this account because it ensures that all reports are filed and payroll taxes are paid. And if you don't take care of these responsibilities to HM Revenue & Customs, you can find yourself in serious hot water. We detail payroll obligations and the Payroll Expenses account in Chapters 17 and 18.

# Office Expenses

Key expenses that can drain a business's profits are office expenses. From paper, pens and paperclips to expenses related to office machinery, these expenses tend to creep up if not carefully monitored in the Office Expenses account. A review of the monthly Profit and Loss account, particularly the overheads section, provides a useful check on overhead spend. Head to Chapter 13 for more about monitoring expenses.

# Retained Earnings

The Retained Earnings account tracks any profits made by the business that are reinvested for growing the business and not paid out to business owners. This account is *cumulative,* which means that it shows a running total of earnings retained since the business opened its doors. Although managing this account doesn't take you a lot of time, the ongoing accuracy of the Retained Earnings account is important to investors and lenders who want to track how well the business is doing. We talk more about Retained Earnings in Chapter 14.

# Appendix A
# Glossary

**accrual accounting:** An accounting method in which transactions are recorded when they actually occur, even if cash hasn't changed hands. Income is recorded when earned (not when the business is actually paid for the products or services), and expenses are counted when goods or services are received, even if the business hasn't yet been paid for the goods or services. Most businesses use this accounting method. See also *cash-based accounting*.

**accumulated fund:** A form of capital account or retained earnings for a not-for-profit organisation. It shows all the surpluses the organisation has ever made.

**amortisation:** An accounting method used to show the using-up of an intangible asset by writing off a portion of the asset's value each year.

**assets:** Everything the business owns, such as cash, buildings, vehicles, furniture, and any other item used to run the business and help it generate money in the future.

**averaging:** An accounting method used to value stock by calculating an average cost per unit sold.

**bad debts expense:** A categorisation used to write off customer accounts with outstanding payments that the business determines can never be collected.

**balance sheet:** A snapshot of a business's financial picture at a point in time (usually the year-end) that shows all assets and liabilities. It also shows who has invested in the business and how the investments were used.

**capital:** A term used to describe the owner's equity. In the case of a limited company, it is the nominal value of the shares issued. In the case of a sole trader, it records the owner's investment in the business.

**capital accounts:** Used to track the value of assets owned by the business owners or shareholders after accounting for liabilities.

**cash-based accounting:** An accounting method based on actual cash flow. Expenses are recorded only when the business actually pays out cash for the goods or services, and income is recorded only when the business collects cash from the customer. See also *accrual accounting*.

**chart of accounts:** A list of all the Nominal accounts used by a business to analyse its income, expenses, assets, and liabilities.

**corporation tax:** A tax paid by limited companies on their earnings.

**cost of goods sold:** The full cost of those goods and services sold in any period. This usually includes stock, direct labour, and any other direct costs.

**credits:** Accounting entries that increase Liability or Income accounts and decrease Asset or Expense accounts. Credits always appear on the right-hand side of an accounting entry.

**current assets:** All items the business owns that are expected to be used in the next 12 months, including items, like cash, that can be easily liquidated. Other examples include cash equivalents, Trade debtors, stock, marketable securities, and prepaid expenses.

**current liabilities:** All financial obligations the business owes that are due in less than 12 months, such as Trade Creditors (money due to suppliers, contractors, and consultants) and Credit Cards Payable (payments due on credit cards).

**debits:** Accounting entries that increase Asset or Expense accounts and decrease Liability and Income accounts. Debits always appear on the left-hand side of an accounting entry.

**depreciation:** An accounting method used to account for the reduction of the value of an asset over time. Depreciation is taken over a set number of years to show that an asset is being used up and its value is diminishing.

**expenses:** All costs of operating a business.

**First-In, First Out (FIFO):** An accounting method used to value stock that assumes the first items put on the shelf are the first items sold.

**fixed asset:** An asset with an expected life greater than 12 months, which will in general be in permanent use by the business. Land and buildings, motor vehicles, and plant and equipment are all examples of fixed assets.

**gross profit:** The difference between sales and cost of goods sold. Often described as the key measure of business performance, it measures the margin made on each sale.

**income:** Money earned by a business from its trading activities; synonyms are sales and revenue.

**income and expenditure account:** A version of the profit and loss statement for not-for-profit organisations used to find the amount of surplus or deficit during a period.

**income tax:** A tax paid by individuals and partnerships on all their earnings, including earnings from direct employment and self-employment.

**intangible asset:** Anything the business owns that has value but can't be touched, such as licences, patents, trademarks, and brand names.

**interest:** Income earned from money invested in money markets, such as bank deposits.

**Last In, First Out (LIFO):** An accounting method used to value stock that assumes the last items put on the shelf are the first items sold.

**liabilities:** All debts the business owes, such as Trade Creditors, and Mortgages Payable.

**long-term assets:** All things a business owns that are expected to be due in more than 12 months, such as buildings, factories, vehicles, and furniture.

**long-term liabilities:** All debts a business owes that it expects to repay in more than 12 months. Examples are mortgages and long-term loans.

**Lower of Cost or Market Valuation (LCM):** An accounting method used to value stock based on whichever is lower: the actual cost of the stock or its current market value.

**net profit:** The bottom line after all costs, expenses, interest, taxes, depreciation, and amortisation are accounted for. Net profit reflects how much money the business makes.

**Nominal Journal entries:** Any entries made to correct or adjust balances in the Nominal Ledger accounts.

**Nominal Ledger:** A summary of all historical transactions that occurred since the business first opened its doors. This ledger is the summary of a business's financial information.

**operating cash flow:** The cash that a business's operations generate to produce and sell its products.

**operating expenses:** Expenses that a business incurs in order to continue its operations, such as advertising, equipment rental, premises rental, insurance, legal and accounting fees, entertainment, salaries, office expenses, repairs and maintenance, travel, utilities, vehicles, and just about anything else that goes into operating a business and isn't directly involved in selling a business's products.

**operating profit:** A measure of a business's earning power from its ongoing operations.

**periodic stock method:** Tracking stock that a business has on hand by doing a physical count of stock on a periodic basis, whether daily, monthly, yearly, or any other time period that meets a business's needs.

**perpetual stock method:** Tracking stock that a business has on hand by adjusting the stock counts after each transaction. A computerised stock control system is needed to manage stock using this method.

**petty cash:** All cash kept on hand at business locations for incidental expenses.

**point of sale:** The location where customers pay for products or services they want to buy, such as a register or service counter.

**profit:** All the earnings of a business after all business expenses.

**profit and loss statement:** A statement for-profit organisations use to find the amount of profit or loss during a period. It shows such key measures as Sales, Gross Profit and Net Profit.

**receipts and payments account:** A summary of the cash book/journals of a not-for-profit organisation.

**retained earnings account:** An account used to show net profits left in the business from accounting period to accounting period and reinvested in the business for future growth.

**short-term liabilities:** Those assets not kept permanently within the business and expected to change within 12 months. Examples are stock, debtors, and prepayments.

**specific identification:** An accounting method used to value stock based on the actual items sold and their individual costs.

**tangible assets:** Any items the business owns that can be held in one's hand or touched, such as cash, stock, or vehicles.

**Trade creditors:** An account used to record money due to suppliers, contractors, and consultants for products or services purchased by the business. Sometimes known as accounts payable.

**Trade debtors:** An account used to record income not yet received on products sold or services provided to customers that is to be collected at a later date. Sometimes known as accounts receivable.

**Value Added Tax (VAT):** A tax charged on most business transactions made in the UK and the Isle of Man. VAT is also charged on goods and some services imported from certain places outside the European Community (EC), as well as on some goods and services coming into the UK from other EC countries. VAT applies to all business types – sole traders, partnerships, limited companies, charities, and so on.

# Appendix B

# About the CD

● ● ● ● ● ● ● ● ● ● ● ● ● ● ● ● ● ● ● ● ● ● ● ● ● ● ● ● ● ● ● ● ● ● ● ● ● ● ● ● ● ● ● ● ● ● ● ● ● ●

*B*ookkeeping For Dummies, 3rd Edition, comes with several helpful files to make practical bookkeeping simpler for you.

Using the CD that accompanies this book couldn't be easier. You can pop it into pretty much any Mac or Windows computer made in the last ten years as long as that computer has an optical drive capable of playing good, old-fashioned CDs. If you're the hesitant type, check out the following system requirements.

## System Requirements

Make sure that your computer meets the minimum system requirements shown in the following list. If your computer doesn't match up to most of these requirements, you may have problems using the software and files on the CD. For the latest and greatest information, please refer to the ReadMe file located at the root of the CD-ROM.

- A PC running Microsoft Windows or Linux with kernel 2.4 or later
- A Macintosh running Apple OS X or later
- An Internet connection
- A CD-ROM drive

If you're reading this in an electronic format, please go to: `http://book support.wiley.com` for access to the additional content.

If you need more information on the basics, check out these books published by Wiley: *PCs For Dummies,* by Dan Gookin; *Macs For Dummies,* by Edward C. Baig; *iMacs For Dummies* by Mark L. Chambers; *Windows XP For Dummies* and *Windows Vista For Dummies,* both by Andy Rathbone.

# Using the CD

To access the items on the CD, follow these steps.

1. **Insert the CD into your computer's CD-ROM drive.**

   The license agreement appears.

   *Note to Windows users:* The interface won't launch if you have autorun disabled. In that case, choose Start⇨Run. (For Windows Vista, choose Start⇨All Programs⇨Accessories⇨Run.) In the dialog box that appears, type *D:\Start.exe*. (Replace *D* with the proper letter if your CD drive uses a different letter. If you don't know the letter, see how your CD drive is listed under My Computer.) Click OK.

   *Note for Mac Users:* When the CD icon appears on your desktop, double-click the icon to open the CD and double-click the 'Start' icon. Also, note that the content menus may not function as expected in newer versions of Safari and Firefox; however, the documents are available by navigating to the Contents folder.

   *Note for Linux Users:* The specifics of mounting and using CDs vary greatly between different versions of Linux. Please see the manual or help information for your specific system if you experience trouble using this CD.

2. **Read through the license agreement and then click the Accept button if you want to use the CD.**

   The CD interface appears. The interface allows you to browse the contents and/or install them on your computer with just a click of a button (or two).

# What You'll Find on the CD

The following sections provide a summary of the files and software you'll find on the CD. If you need help with accessing the items provided on the CD, refer to the instructions in the preceding section.

## Software

You'll find OpenOffice.org software on your CD. OpenOffice.org is a free multi-platform office productivity suite. It is similar to Microsoft Office or Lotus SmartSuite, but OpenOffice.org is absolutely free. It includes word processing, spreadsheet, presentation, and drawing applications that enable you to create professional documents, newsletters, reports, and presentations. It supports most file formats of other office software. You should be able to edit and view any files created with other office solutions.

## *Author-created material*

The following list summarises all the files on the CD:

- ✔ Cashflow template
- ✔ Completing a Cashflow
- ✔ Income and Expenditure Statement template
- ✔ Month or Year End Accounts Checklist
- ✔ Payroll Checklist
- ✔ Year End Payroll Checklist

## *Other software*

The software programs on the CD fall into one of the following categories:

- ✔ *Freeware programs* are free, copyrighted games, applications, and utilities. You can copy them to as many computers as you like – for free – but they offer no technical support.

- ✔ *Shareware programs* are fully functional, free, trial versions of copyrighted programs. If you like particular programs, register with their authors for a nominal fee and receive licenses, enhanced versions, and technical support.

- ✔ *GNU software* is governed by its own license, which is included inside the folder of the GNU software. There are no restrictions on distribution of GNU software. See the GNU license at the root of the CD for more details.

- ✔ *Trial, demo, or evaluation* versions of software are usually limited either by time or functionality (such as not letting you save a project after you create it).

# Troubleshooting

Hopefully, you won't encounter any problems using the CD. In the unlikely event that you do, two possible problems are that you don't have enough memory (RAM) or you have other programmes running that are affecting installation or running of a programme.

If you get an error message such as Not enough memory or Setup cannot continue, try one or more of the following suggestions and then try using the software again:

- ✔ **Turn off any antivirus software running on your computer.** Installation programs sometimes mimic virus activity and may make your computer incorrectly believe that it's being infected by a virus.

- ✔ **Close all running programs.** The more programs you have running, the less memory is available to other programs. Installation programs typically update files and programs; so if you keep other programs running, installation may not work properly.

- ✔ **Ask your local computer shop to add more RAM to your computer.** This is, admittedly, a drastic and somewhat expensive step. However, adding more memory can really help the speed of your computer and allow more programs to run at the same time.

# Customer Care

If you have trouble with the CD-ROM, please call Wiley Product Technical Support at 877-762-2974. Outside the United States, call 317-572-3993. You can also contact Wiley Product Technical Support at http://support.wiley. com. John Wiley & Sons, Inc. will provide technical support only for installation and other general quality control items. For technical support on the applications themselves, consult the program's vendor or author.

To place additional orders or to request information about other Wiley products, please call 877-762-2974.

# Index

# About the Authors

**Jane Kelly** is a qualified Chartered Management Accountant currently living and working in the Peak District. She has used Sage software for a number of years and has taught bookkeeping to further education students, as well as co-authoring this latest edition of the bestselling *Bookkeeping For Dummies*. Her first book *Sage 50 Accounts For Dummies* is currently selling well and is now into its second edition. You can contact Jane via her blog, www.sagemadesimple.co.uk, which offers hints and tips for Sage 50 users. Jane is also the author of *Sage One For Dummies*.

**Paul Barrow** trained and qualified as a Chartered Accountant with Deloitte & Touche before obtaining his MBA at Bradford University. As a senior consultant with Ernst & Young he was responsible for managing and delivering quality consulting assignments.

Paul is a Visiting Fellow at Cranfield University where he teaches on the Business Growth Programme. This programme is designed specifically for owner managers who want to grow and improve their businesses. He also teaches at Warwick University and Oxford Brookes on similar programmes.

Paul has written several other business books aimed at owner managers trying to grow and improve their businesses: *The Business Plan Workbook* and *Raising Finance* (both Kogan Page/Sunday Times); *The Best Laid Business Plans* and *The Bottom Line* (both Virgin Books).

**Lita Epstein**, who earned her MBA from Emory University's Goizueta Business School, enjoys helping people develop good financial, investing, and tax planning skills.

She designs and teaches online courses on topics such as investing for retirement, getting ready for tax time, and finance and investing for women. She's written more than ten books, including *Streetwise Retirement Planning* and *Trading For Dummies*.

# Dedication

I would like to dedicate this book to my daughter Megan. At ten years old, she is already a great creative writer, and I'd like to think that my writing inspires her.

**– Jane Kelly**

To my late father, Colin Barrow who, out of kind desperation many years ago (when I couldn't decide how to make a living), introduced me to a partner in a Leeds firm of chartered accountants. I took up articles, which was akin to being a lowly paid slave, and suffered some years of financial hardship before surprising everyone (including myself) by qualifying as a chartered accountant.

The supreme irony has been that I left the profession the day I qualified, but that over the subsequent 30 years I've drifted in and out of the world of accountancy and bookkeeping. Having these skills and the immensely valuable chartered accountant's qualification after my name has enabled me to earn very well over the years. Thank you Dad.

**– Paul Barrow**

To my father, Jerome Kirschbrown, who taught me the importance of accounting, bookkeeping, and watching every detail.

**– Lita Epstein**

# Author's Acknowledgments

I hope that this book helps the many small businesses who may be struggling with their accounting systems, whether computerised or manual. I can't emphasise enough the need to put proper accounting systems in place. A well-organised system ensures the smooth running of any business, and produces accurate and timely reports for the business managers.

I would like to thank everyone at Wiley for all their support throughout the process of updating this book, in particular to Rachael Chilvers who helped me pull together all the chapters. I would also like to extend my thanks to Claire Ruston, who has worked with me on several projects with Wiley.

Thanks also to Sage UK Ltd, who have kindly allowed us to use their software for illustration purposes throughout the book.

Finally, I would like to say thank you to my husband Malcolm, and my daughter Megan, for their never-ending understanding and support when book deadlines loom!

**– Jane Kelly**

## Publisher's Acknowledgments

We're proud of this book; please send us your comments at http://dummies.custhelp.com. For other comments, please contact our Customer Care Department within the U.S. at 877-762-2974, outside the U.S. at (001) 317-572-3993, or fax 317-572-4002.

Some of the people who helped bring this book to market include the following:

### Acquisitions, Editorial, and Vertical Websites

**Project Editor:** Rachael Chilvers
 (Previous Edition: Jo Jones)

**Commissioning Editor:** Claire Ruston

**Assistant Editor:** Ben Kemble

**Proofreader:** Kim Vernon

**Production Manager:** Daniel Mersey

**Publisher:** David Palmer

**Vertical Websites:** Laura Moss-Hollister,
 Josh Frank

**Cover Photos:** © iStock / Pgiam

**Cartoons:** Ed McLachlan

### Composition Services

**Project Coordinator:** Kristie Rees

**Layout and Graphics:** Christin Swinford

**Proofreaders:** Lindsay Amones

**Indexer:** Valerie Haynes Perry

**Special Help:** Manuela Radauer, Sony DADC

# FOR DUMMIES®

## Making Everything Easier!™

# UK editions

## BUSINESS

**978-0-470-97626-5**

**978-0-470-74737-7**

**978-1-119-97527-4**

## REFERENCE

**978-0-470-68637-9**

**978-0-470-97450-6**

**978-1-119-97660-8**

## HOBBIES

**978-0-470-69960-7**

**978-1-119-99417-6**

**978-1-119-97250-1**

**Asperger's Syndrome For Dummies**
978-0-470-66087-4

**Basic Maths For Dummies**
978-1-119-97452-9

**Body Language For Dummies, 2nd Edition**
978-1-119-95351-7

**Boosting Self-Esteem For Dummies**
978-0-470-74193-1

**British Sign Language For Dummies**
978-0-470-69477-0

**Cricket For Dummies**
978-0-470-03454-5

**Diabetes For Dummies, 3rd Edition**
978-0-470-97711-8

**Electronics For Dummies**
978-0-470-68178-7

**English Grammar For Dummies**
978-0-470-05752-0

**Flirting For Dummies**
978-0-470-74259-4

**IBS For Dummies**
978-0-470-51737-6

**Improving Your Relationship For Dummies**
978-0-470-68472-6

**ITIL For Dummies**
978-1-119-95013-4

**Management For Dummies, 2nd Edition**
978-0-470-97769-9

**Neuro-linguistic Programming For Dummies, 2nd Edition**
978-0-470-66543-5

**Nutrition For Dummies, 2nd Edition**
978-0-470-97276-2

**Organic Gardening For Dummies**
978-1-119-97706-3

# FOR DUMMIES®

## Making Everything Easier!™

## UK editions

## SELF-HELP

Cognitive Behavioural Therapy For Dummies
978-0-470-66541-1

Creative Visualization For Dummies
978-1-119-99264-6

Mindfulness For Dummies
978-0-470-66086-7

## STUDENTS

Philosophy For Dummies
978-0-470-68820-5

Student Cookbook For Dummies
978-0-470-974711-7

Sociology For Dummies
978-1-119-99134-2

## HISTORY

The Tudors For Dummies
978-0-470-68792-5

Medieval History For Dummies
978-0-470-74783-4

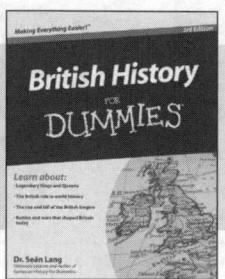

British History For Dummies
978-0-470-97819-1

Origami Kit For Dummies
978-0-470-75857-1

Overcoming Depression For Dummies
978-0-470-69430-5

Positive Psychology For Dummies
978-0-470-72136-0

PRINCE2 For Dummies, 2009 Edition
978-0-470-71025-8

Project Management For Dummies
978-0-470-71119-4

Psychometric Tests For Dummies
978-0-470-75366-8

Renting Out Your Property For Dummies, 3rd Edition
978-1-119-97640-0

Rugby Union For Dummies, 3rd Edition
978-1-119-99092-5

Sage One For Dummies
978-1-119-95236-7

Self-Hypnosis For Dummies
978-0-470-66073-7

Storing and Preserving Garden Produce For Dummies
978-1-119-95156-8

Study Skills For Dummies
978-0-470-74047-7

Teaching English as a Foreign Language For Dummies
978-0-470-74576-2

Time Management For Dummies
978-0-470-77765-7

Training Your Brain For Dummies
978-0-470-97449-0

Work-Life Balance For Dummies
978-0-470-71380-8

# FOR DUMMIES®

## Making Everything Easier!™

# FOR DUMMIES®

## Making Everything Easier!™

## COMPUTER BASICS

978-0-470-57829-2

978-0-470-61454-9

978-0-470-49743-2

## DIGITAL PHOTOGRAPHY

978-0-470-25074-7

978-0-470-76878-5

978-1-118-00472-2

## MICROSOFT OFFICE 2010

978-0-470-48998-7

978-0-470-58302-9

978-0-470-48953-6

Access 2010 For Dummies
978-0-470-49747-0

Android Application Development
For Dummies
978-0-470-77018-4

AutoCAD 2011 For Dummies
978-0-470-59539-8

C++ For Dummies, 6th Edition
978-0-470-31726-6

Computers For Seniors For Dummies,
2nd Edition
978-0-470-53483-0

Dreamweaver CS5 For Dummies
978-0-470-61076-3

iPad 2 For Dummies, 3rd Edition
978-1-118-17679-5

Macs For Dummies, 11th Edition
978-0-470-87868-2

Mac OS X Snow Leopard For
Dummies
978-0-470-43543-4

Photoshop CS5 For Dummies
978-0-470-61078-7

Photoshop Elements 10
For Dummies
978-1-118-10742-3

Search Engine Optimization
For Dummies, 4th Edition
978-0-470-88104-0

The Internet For Dummies,
13th Edition
978-1-118-09614-7

Visual Studio 2010 All-In-One
For Dummies
978-0-470-53943-9

Web Analytics For Dummies
978-0-470-09824-0

Word 2010 For Dummies
978-0-470-48772-3

WordPress For Dummies, 4th Edition
978-1-118-07342-1